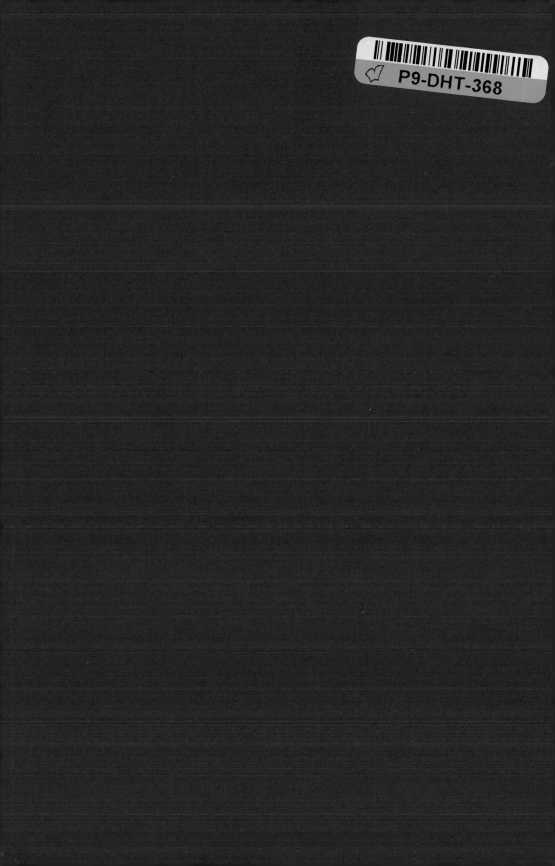

Wondrous Times on the Frontier

Also by Dee Brown

NONFICTION

Fighting Indians of the West (with Martin F. Schmitt)

Trail Driving Days (with Martin F. Schmitt)

Grierson's Raid

The Settlers' West (with Martin F. Schmitt)

The Gentle Tamers: Women of the Old Wild West

The Bold Cavaliers: Morgan's Second Kentucky Cavalry Raiders

Fort Phil Kearny: An American Saga
(republished as *The Fetterman Massacre*)

The Galvanized Yankees

Showdown at Little Big Horn

The Year of the Century: 1876

Bury My Heart at Wounded Knee:
An Indian History of the American West

Andrew Jackson and the Battle of New Orleans

Tales of the Warrior Ants

The Westerners

Hear That Lonesome Whistle Blow

FICTION

Wave High the Banner

Yellowhorse

Cavalry Scout

They Went Thataway (republished as *Pardon My Pandemonium*)

The Girl from Fort Wicked

Action at Beecher Island

Teepee Tales of the American Indians

Creek Mary's Blood

Killdeer Mountain

A Conspiracy of Knaves

Wondrous Times on the Frontier

Dee Brown

August House Publishers, Inc.
LITTLE ROCK

Published by August House, Inc.,
P.O. Box 3223, Little Rock, Arkansas, 72203,
501–372–5450.

Printed in the United States of America

10 9 8 7 6 5 4 3 2 1

LIBRARY OF CONGRESS CATALOGING-IN-PUBLICATION DATA

Brown, Dee Alexander
Wondrous Times on the Frontier / Dee Brown.
p.   cm.
Includes bibliographical references and index.
ISBN 0–87483–137–7 (alk. paper) : $23.95 hb
ISBN 0–87483–181–4 (lim. ed.: alk. paper) : $48.50 hb
1. Frontier and pioneer life—West (U.S.)
2. West (U.S.)—Social life and customs. I. Title.
F596.B864   1991
978—dc20   91-24937

First Edition, 1991

Executive editor: Liz Parkhurst
Editorial assistants: Tonya Holley & Ed Gray
Design director: Ted Parkhurst
Cover design: Harvill Ross Studios, Ltd.
Typography: Lettergraphics, Little Rock

This book is printed on archival-quality paper which meets the
guidelines for performance and durability of the Committee on
Production Guidelines for Book Longevity of the
Council on Library Resources.

AUGUST HOUSE, INC.   PUBLISHERS   LITTLE ROCK

For my friends and former colleagues—
librarians everywhere

Contents

What This Book is About

LIFE ON AMERICA'S WESTERN FRONTIER was hard, unpleasant most of the time, definitely lacking in almost all amenities or creature comforts. It was dangerous too, not so much from other human beings committing violent acts, but from infectious diseases spread by other human beings. Death by drowning was a common event at unbridged river crossings. And because so many venturers into the frontier equipped themselves with an arsenal of small arms, and handled them carelessly, fatal accidents from these weapons multiplied with each rising wave of immigration. Wagon mishaps, including falls under the wheels and kicks from draft animals, added to the casualties. Hailstorms, tornadoes, blizzards, heat waves, floods, prairie fires, and insect pestilence contributed to the frontier experience.

This grim environment was surely a basic determinant of the humor of America's westward marching pioneers. The first venturers were often alone in the wilderness, spending much of their time attempting to survive. Some of them knew how to read, but they usually had nothing to read. Probably as an antidote to the harshness and boredom of their lives, they invented the tall tale. Whenever they encountered fellow frontiersmen on the trail or at a fur traders' rendezvous, or in a military post or burgeoning settlement, they strove to outdo each other with tall tales, exaggerating real or imaginary incidents into humorous fiction.

Among the practitioners still remembered are Davy Crockett, Jim Bridger, and a collection of fanciful blowhards from the Rockies and Great Plains. They invented big lies that entered the oral tradition of the frontier, eventually being appropriated by the likes of Mark Twain and other creative persons belonging to what we now call the print media. These imaginative writers built on the stories until they became quite elaborate, the best ones eventually entering the literary repository of America.

The lore of the frontier is filled with contradictions that liken it to those great epics of the distant past populated by characters like Eric the Red and El Cid, who were uncertain of the differences between good and evil. For instance, western hospitality and kindness to strangers, especially to those in distress, is one of the most solid of American traditions. Yet at the same time a common stereotype is the frontiersman's demonstrated contempt for a tenderfoot, or newcomer. Let a tenderfoot fall into the hands of a western miner, cowboy, gambler, soldier, or whomever, and he is certain to be tricked and harassed, cheated of his money at cards, fired upon and made to dance, put into the saddle of the wildest bronco, and otherwise physically endangered or harmed.

Elaborate practical jokes and deceptions, frequently aimed at tenderfeet, served to beguile the general public as well. Newspapers and their scribes were among the leading perpetrators, but they also included such salty characters as lawyer Roy Bean, salesman Soapy Smith, boatman Mike Fink, outlaw Black Bart and similar fabricators.

Through the ages, love and romance have always been subjects for satire and bawdy humor. On the frontier—a world that within walls of cramped cabins lacked all privacy—men and women poked more ribald fun at the difficulties of pairing than any folk since the days of Chaucer or Casanova. Until settlement began, there was always a shortage of white females, thus creating an atmosphere of earthy humor around the white males' relations with Indian women.

Many of the comic frontier stories that survive were set in saloons and dance halls—crude situation comedies involving bartenders, cowboys, outlaws, lawmen, gunfighters, entertainers, and prostitutes. The dance hall girls were know by euphemisms such as soiled doves, prairie flowers, scarlet ladies, *filles de joie*, calico queens, Cyprians, painted beauties, frail sisters, giddy ladies, come-on girls, hurdy girls, and calico cats.

Names of prostitutes were colorful indeed, as court records and newspaper accounts reveal: Little Dot, Hop Fiend Nell, Emporia Belle, Scar-faced Lillie, Miss One Fin, Squirrel Tooth Alice, Ogallala

Shorty, Jack-Rabbit Sue, Four-Ace Dora, Kansas Cow, Razorback Jennie, Society Annie, Sallie Purple.

If we may judge by written and printed records, weather on the frontier most of the time seemed like pure hell to the newcomers. At any rate it was a subject of constant comment in letters, diaries, and newspaper columns. Mirages, seldom seen in the East, were quite common in the West before modern-day smog blurred the atmosphere. There is scarcely a diary of a western crossing that does not contain some humorous or wonderstricken reference to incredible visions of wagons rolling upside down in the sky, of silent running buffalo herds, or colorful castles and lakes glittering on the horizon. The pure and transparent atmosphere itself was conducive to awe and hallucinations, one young woman noting that she was so overwhelmed by her first luminous view of the Great Salt Lake Valley that she and her husband temporarily lost their identities until after they came down from the heights.

Almost always on the surface, or just below, frontier humor carried an element of violence. While there were not nearly as many shootouts between bad men and lawmen as our popular culture would have us believe, constant challenges did occur, resulting in black comedy that often involved hangmen and undertakers. Indians and blacks were frequent dupes in these conflicts. If the fracas resulted in bloodshed followed by a hanging, and the person to be hanged was of a minority race or a foreigner, large crowds gathered to observe the proceedings, which usually generated some true gallows humor.

Difficult as frontier travel was, those journeyers lucky enough to possess keen senses of humor managed to endure the experience with considerable élan. Lodgings for stagecoach passengers were so wretched, however, that only the humorous-minded could have borne the overcrowded sleeping places, the grubbiness, the insect pests, and the abominable food and drink. Because of the popularity of published travel accounts in the nineteenth century, a considerable amount of witty literature still survives on these subjects by such famed scribblers as Oscar Wilde, Rudyard Kipling, Henry Morton Stanley, Robert Louis Stevenson, Horace Greeley, and numerous others. A troupe of female correspondents—from Europe as well as eastern America—outdid their male rivals in recording wry comments about life in the hostelries along the trails and byways of the American West. Although several members of European nobility (including young remittance men) contributed accounts of their travels, they more often than not were also the butts of practical jokes and acerbic quips from chauvinistic American observers of these foreigners' outlandish ways.

Methods of travel changed rapidly—from Conestoga wagons to stagecoaches and army ambulances, to steamboats and railroads—forcing tellers of funny stories to advance from one mode to the other with successive variations of context. Railroad travel provoked considerably more attempts at caustic humor than did other means of transport, possibly because the early accidents were so horrendous and the discomforts so acute.

For centuries the professional and privileged classes of mankind have inspired satirical assaults from the commonality who are offended or harmed by, or are envious of, those who seem unrestrained by morality—those who cheat, lie, steal, misinform, poison, and prey upon their inferiors behind screens of professionalism. Lawyers probably stand at the head of these offenders; almost every frontier story about members of this profession is interlaced with barbs and aspersions. And because most politicians are of the lawyer class, they also were popular subjects for derisive jokes. Abraham Lincoln belonged to that minority of lawyers who recognized the rascalities of the profession, and he enjoyed jesting about his peers as well as himself. Yet in the annals of frontier humor there appear to be no lawyers remembered as "beloved," a term occasionally bestowed upon members of the medical profession. Physicians in general, however, were feared and avoided except when a gunfight or a fall from a horse created a dire need for medical attention. Doctors of that day had few remedies for any of the numerous contagious diseases then plaguing mankind, and not many frontiersmen lived long enough to suffer from the various degenerative ailments so prevalent today.

Schoolteachers were viewed in that unlettered world as unavoidable necessities, the populace's esteem placing them scarcely a notch above hangmen and undertakers. Perhaps that was because the first teachers were school*masters*. Many tricks were played upon them by students who were sometimes older and bigger than their instructors, and except for those tyrants who lorded over their classrooms like iron suzerains, schoolteachers were treated mostly with a kind of gentle humor, rarely black. Late in the nineteenth century, when schoolmarms began to replace the schoolmasters, those earnest females were regarded by male members of frontier communities less as educators than as objects for matrimony, and the humor they inspired was generally of the homely pattern set by Owen Wister in *The Virginian.*

As for the journalists and editors—who formed a much higher percentage of the professional class on the frontier than they do in our electronic age—they were occasionally horsewhipped or run out of town by offended readers. Vituperative and mendacious though many newspapers were, readers of those times recognized that most papers were mouthpieces for political parties or factions, or some other special interests, and they paid little attention to editors' fabrications unless they were personal attacks virulent enough to warrant retaliation. The editors quarreled among themselves more than they did with the public, reserving their supreme insults for their rivals in the crowded field of print.

The servants of God—parsons and preachers, priests and rabbis—became early victims of the stereotype in frontier humor. In actuality few churchmen were either the wimpy or officious characters so often portrayed in timeworn images. Instead they were a tough breed, appreciative of the value of comic parables. To further their own causes they boldly formed alliances with gamblers and prostitutes, thus creating situations out of which developed a considerable amount of pithy merriment.

Chief rivals of God's preachers in that almost Godless land were traveling entertainers who came first to the frontier on boats—graduating from flatboats and keelboats to steamboats and finally to elaborate showboats. As soon as roads and railways penetrated the wilderness, small circuses followed—a few exotic animals, an acrobat or two—and eventually troupes of dramatic actors. During the heyday of the Old West, the great names of theater from New

York and abroad were performing in towns and cities everywhere beyond the Mississippi.

To accommodate the growing numbers of entertainers, theaters were quickly built, varying from canvas flimsies to expansive halls usually called "opera houses." Frontier audiences were mostly masculine. They admired actresses who danced in pink tights, and were highly critical of posturing male performers. Somewhat in the manner of spectators in Elizabethan theaters, they made themselves a part of the show, shouting compliments or insults, tossing bags of gold dust and other gifts upon the stage, or seizing disliked performers and bouncing them in blankets. A goodly lot of mirth came out of confrontations between audiences and actors in frontier theaters.

Cowboys and Indian-fighting soldiers specialized in prankish humor, their favorite victims being tenderfeet and rookies. If there were no neophytes nearby to bedevil, they bedeviled each other. Cowboy comedy worked both ways, however; even the most experienced trail drivers could become victims themselves when they met the sharpies and harpies who awaited them in the cattle shipping towns along the railroads.

If we may believe Bret Harte and others who recorded incidents of life in the goldfields of the West, the miners were the most sentimental of all frontiersmen. They lived strenuously, they fought each other over the most trivial matters, and drank and swore hard. Yet many droll stories about miners include treacly scenes involving orphans, lost or dying children, and loose ladies with hearts of gold. Incidentally, that hoary-headed cliché about prostitutes may very well have originated in the mining towns of the Old West where gold was in everybody's heart.

Perhaps the miners' sentimentality was but a part of the Victorian age which was then in full flower, and may explain the shortage of bawdy Rabelaisian stories from that most open and free-spirited time and place in America's nineteenth century. We know there was an underground literature of erotica and pornography during those years, yet only in the most private of frontier writings is one likely to find very much humor concerning physical relations between the sexes. The attitudes, styles, and tastes of

Victorianism affected all the English-speaking world. Avoidance of "delicate" subjects was the rule; prudish euphemisms suffused the exterior planes of life.

The North American Indians who lived in western Canada, or those from the United States who occasionally crossed the border, knew there was a Queen Victoria. They called her "the Grandmother," and Canada was "the Grandmother's Land." But that was about the extent of the Queen's influence upon the native Americans. The humorous stories of the Indians were completely free of the constraints of Victorianism and were very bawdy indeed.

When young Francis Parkman, a proper Bostonian sort of Victorian, journeyed westward to gather material for his great literary classic, *The Oregon Trail,* he and his half-blood interpreter lived for several weeks with a band of Sioux Indians. Parkman could not help being squeamish over their frankness about sex in their merry tales. "As the pipe passed the circle around the fire in the evening," Parkman noted in his journal on July 29, 1846, "there was plenty of that obscene conversation that seems to make up the sum of Indian wit, and which very much amuses the squaws. The Indians are a very licentious set."

That opinion depends upon one's viewpoint, of course. The folktales of the American Indians were the spice of the frontier's son-of-a-gun stew of good humor, but some readers may like their stew bland, some may like it hot, and some may like it not at all.

Print, illustrations, and motion-picture films have had a powerful influence upon the universal image of the American frontier and its inhabitants. With rare exceptions, popular fiction of the nineteenth century and movies of the twentieth created a frontier that never was. Let the name of almost any walk of life be mentioned and a stereotype leaps involuntarily to mind—the timid parson and the noble gambler, the humorless Indian and the singing cowboy, the dance-hall girl and the sunbonneted woman, the stagecoach driver and the railroad laborer, the bumbling doctor and the politician, the miner, settler, newspaper editor, and schoolteacher. Almost all are engraved illusions.

Ethnic, religious, and racial variations formed such a mosaic of peoples that generalizations about frontier Americans are meaning-less. The whole truth about the past can never be arrived at, of course, and there is no point in berating myths and their makers. Some myths are useful and not far from the truth; others are hurtful and so false they need to be demolished. In some cases, the factual frontier is far more fascinating than the fictitious.

Each generation revises its history to suit its attitudes, but the sources can never be revised. To know what the frontier past was like, one needs only to turn to the words of those who lived then. They left millions of words that tell why they were there, what they believed in, how they endured, and how they used humor—both light and dark—to contend with the burdens of their world. Some of these words can be found among the accounts that follow.

CHAPTER ONE

The Chaucerian Way West

ANYONE TRAVELING WESTWARD by wagon, stagecoach, steamboat, horseback, or on foot was not likely to enjoy a painless journey. Yet there were times of pleasure in which the wayfarers defied the daily miseries with merrymaking and a sincere wonder for the awesome land through which they were passing. Most of those traveling overland formed companies for mutual security against the unknown. The rate of movement was not much speedier than that of Geoffrey Chaucer's pilgrims to Canterbury, and there were Chaucerian attitudes among the journeyers who represented the trades and professions of that time—millers, cooks, clerks, merchants, wheelwrights, saddlers, wagonmakers, lawyers, blacksmiths, typesetters, preachers, daguerreotypists, and physicians. Most of the men and women feared God and prayed regularly, but they enjoyed bawdy comedy and could break into sudden laughter if so moved. During the weeks required to reach their destinations, few secrets were concealed from one another. Over campfire in the long evenings they told each other amusing tales of roguery and romance in which the narrators played leading or supporting roles.

A surprising number were unprepared for an overland crossing and were forced to learn the routines for survival by hard experience on the trails. John Davies, a young Mormon bound for Utah, was handed a whip and told to drive the oxen, using the voice commands "woo ah" and "gee." It was all new to Davies. "When the cattle went gee too much, we would run to the off side, and yelling at them woo ah, and bunting. And we was puffing and sweating...this was a great experience for us and indeed a tuff one, but by the time we got half way across the Plains, we could drive the ox teams as well as you can enny day."[1]

Marian Russell, who traveled to Santa Fe at the impressionable age of eight, held a high opinion of oxen. "Mules draw a wagon a bit more gentle than horses," she recalled, "but oxen are best of all. 'Tis true they walk slowly but there is a rhythm in their walking that sways the great wagons gently."[2]

Bad weather was the great spoiler of the pleasures of wagon travel. Wind blasts and driving rain and hail on the Plains ripped canvas off the beds of vehicles, and harried animals and human beings alike. The early trails tracked across naked earth that turned to muck after steady downpours. In the few places where ruts of the old trails are still preserved today, one can see how deep the wheels sank. A traveler across Kansas in 1877 was not amused when he recorded how often he had to stop to clean the wagons wheels, "the mud so sticky that it fills the wheels up solid from the fellows to the hub."[3]

Many pilgrims also made darkly humorous observations of the jumpoff towns where steamboats loaded and wagon trains assembled for westward journeys. "St. Joe [Missouri] is the muddiest nastiest border ruffian town on the earth," one man noted in June 1859. "It offends the eye, ear and nose; with foul sights, sounds and smells, and in fact every sense made to minister to enjoyment, is here only an avenue to pain, and is the object of foul outrage." Upriver a few days later at Omaha, he was less acerbic, and was surprised to find the Indian women wearing petticoats and leggings. "They are very accommodating and smile when they meet you and pat you on the back."[4]

Night encampments were enjoyed by the wagon passengers except for the most fearful, who interpreted every strange sound as an Indian signal for attack. Gradually they came to recognize the eerie cries of coyotes and the serenades of wolves. After supper, groups usually gathered around their cooking fires to dance to a fiddler's renditions or to sing the popular songs of the time— "Turkey in the Straw," "Betsy from Pike," "Soapsuds over the Fence," "Joe Bowers," and of course "O, Susanna."

Freight wagons sometimes joined the western trains of homeseekers, and the veteran bullwhackers who drove the oxen offered entertainment during the evenings. Their experience made them experts at handling the long whips with which they controlled the oxen, and they used these lashes in their contest. "A favorite pastime among them," said magazine illustrator Theodore Davis, "is the cutting of a coin from the top of a stake thrust loosely into the earth. If the coin is knocked off the stake without disturbing the stake it is forfeit; if the stake is disturbed the thrower of the lash loses the value of the coin. A bullwhacker, noted for the accuracy with which he threw his lash, bet a comrade a pint of whiskey that he could cut the seat of his pantaloons without touching the skin beneath. The bet was accepted. The blow was delivered at the stooping form of the acceptor of the wager, who is said to have executed the tallest jump on record, at the sight of which the thrower of the lash remarked: 'Thunder! I've lost the whiskey!' The other party was minus a piece of skin as well as a large fragment of breeches."[5]

Sundays were generally welcomed as rest days, but the only holiday that brought wagon trains to a halt for merriment was the Fourth of July, noted in many contemporary diaries as "the Day we Celebrate." The degree of jollity depended somewhat upon the location, the mood of the travelers, and the ingenuity of the commemorators.

The wagon train in which Lemuel McKeeby was traveling in 1850 spent a considerable part of the Fourth trying to find a suitable stopping place for a celebration. When at last they halted and camped, it seemed that almost everyone was too weary for diversion. Finally one man organized a little parade and led the way to the front of a large wagon where he mounted the doubletree and waited until a crowd of about two hundred gathered around. "Then he commenced and gave a pantomime of a speech," McKeeby wrote, "putting in all the gestures and making all kinds of faces and contortions of body that would be assumed by an extravagant 4th of July orator, without uttering a word. For the first three minutes of his efforts the crowd looked on with wonder, then they comprehended and such shouting and laughter went up that it could be heard in every camp within a half mile. This wound up the speechmaking and all hands went to their tents laughing."[6]

When possible, travelers camped near a fort where the Fourth was celebrated with the booming of cannon, flag raisings, drills, and other military exercises. "Evidently they had up their best flag today," George Hardesty wrote in his diary while in southern Colorado. "It was a new one and very large. It looked very pretty floating there with the grand old mountains in the background. I felt somewhat enthused and began singing Star Spangled Banner long may it wave much to the disgust of the balance of the party I suppose probably not because of the nature of the song as the execution of it."[7]

No Fourth of July in those times was complete without a plenitude of toasts accompanied by suitable beverages. The first toast was drunk to the day itself, then to the Constitution and Declaration of Independence, and on to George Washington, and whatever western territory the pilgrims might be crossing, to the President, to women, to families left behind, and whatever or whomever might come to the minds of the happy celebrants.

Travel across the West by stagecoach was more rapid than by wagon, although the cramped seat space made it less comfortable. And they were probably more dangerous because the "knights of the reins" who drove them were determined to maintain schedules regardless of the hazards.

A Frenchman visiting Colorado in 1867 was reminded of the Louis XIV coaches of his native land, and noted that the vehicles had changed very little since America was first colonized. "Within are nine seats, priced alike, three in front, three behind, three in the middle. Ladies have a right to the front seats even if they come last. In the middle seats you are backed only by a leather strap, which runs across the stage from one side to the other, and takes you in the middle of the back—not exactly comfortable."[8]

Although ladies may have had the privilege of riding in the front seats, this did not guarantee a joyride for them or anyone else. In May 1883, a passenger wrote an account for the *Cheyenne Daily Leader* of a typical stage journey across Wyoming. On getting aboard he found the two front seats piled roof-high with express packages and valises. Two Texas cowboys occupied the back seats. "Room was made for me by the driver removing some goods to the top of the coach and placing the valises on the passengers' knees.

Once inside, the curtains were pinned down, and we passengers not being able to get out, glared in the dim light at each other...

"Beside me was piled on the seat, a sack of flour and several boxes, the topmost being a twelve by sixteen wooden packing case, that appeared to be almost empty from the ease with which it tumbled on my head at every second jolt of the stage. A score of times I was tempted to hurl it out in the mud, but the thought of the possible value restrained me. I saw that box opened here at the Chug. It contained nothing more than a lamp shade packed in hay."[9]

Runaway teams afforded passengers considerable excitement especially in mountainous areas. In 1881, Mrs. M.B. Hall and her young daughter were traveling by stage to Leadville, Colorado. On one of the sharp declines, the hand brake failed and the heavy coach lunged against the horses and frightened them into a downhill run. "Talk about the ride of Paul Revere," Mrs. Hall said afterward. "That was an easy canter compared to our wild ride. At the first plunge we went to the floor, but we did not stay there."

The driver managed to keep a tight hold on the reins but he could not slow the horses. "There were people on the road who depended on the stage for their mail. I remember glimpses of them staring at us, with letters in their hands for the outgoing mail, but even Uncle Sam's mail could not stop us...We finally reached the station, the horses having run every step of the way."[10]

The stage driver was generally a romantic figure, but he was harassed by weather, a multitude of dangerous emergencies, and by weariness of muscle and bone. If he drove without an armed guard on the high seat beside him—and most of them did—loneliness enveloped him. Against all these vexations the western coachman often resorted to strong spirits from a flask, with results sometimes highly amusing or disastrous to his passengers.

The driver of a stagecoach bound for the Black Hills once became so intoxicated that he fell off his seat to the ground. None of the passengers inside observed the incident, and horses continued for some miles along the crooked road. Eventually one of the women aboard began complaining about the unusual jolting of the wheels, and then one of the men noticed the coach was running perilously close to the edge of a deep canyon. Suddenly the horses halted. Two passengers stepped out, calling to the driver, but when they looked up they saw an empty seat with reins dangling. After a lengthy consultation, a volunteer climbed up to take the reins, and drove the coach and its perturbed passengers to Deadwood.

A similar but more tragic incident occurred in the Indian Territory during the great blizzard of 1886. Horses coated with frost and ice brought a stagecoach into Camp Supply with the driver sitting on the box frozen to death. None of the passengers bundled inside with robes and blankets was aware of the fatality until they alighted at the station.

Heavy drinking inside the coaches was fairly common also, and pilgrims unused to western ways frequently protested the constant imbibing by fellow passengers, especially those "armed to the teeth" with pistols, rifles, and shotguns. Celebrated humorist Artemus Ward (Charles F. Browne) made no protest while experiencing a terrifying ride from California into Nevada, but at the first stop he did ask the driver what he would do about casualties in the event of a serious accident. "Them as is dead," the coachman replied, "I shall let alone, but them as is mutilated I shall finish with the king-bolt! Dead folks don't sue. They ain't on it."

In the months immediately following the Civil War, when it seemed that every one in the eastern United States was westbound, obtaining a seat on a stagecoach became extremely difficult unless one was flush with money. A stranded traveler in Fort Kearney noted somewhat enviously in his journal on July 12, 1866: "Today there came up a chartered coach occupied by two New York City gents bound for Calif. They were young fellows not more than 25 years and paid 4,000 for the exclusive rights of the coach from Atchison to Va. City Nev. They had beds so arranged as to spread them down or take them up at pleasure. They had a full armament of guns, pistols, and knives to say nothing of the cigars and liquors *absolutely* necessary for such a pleasure excursion."[11]

For those who could not obtain seats on a coach, there were horses in plenty, but buyers and hirers had to keep sharp eyes out for deceivers. No consumers' agency existed to protect them from misrepresentation by dealers in horseflesh. A schoolteacher on the Arkansas frontier wanted to hire a horse to take him to a town several miles distant, about a half day's ride. "I was shown a specimen of the equine species," he said, "standing in a corner of the fence, with head down and bones almost exposed to the light, apparently contemplating the uncertainties of life, or ruminating upon his younger days, when fodder stacks stood more ready to relieve his temporal wants. He was, in fact, a subject that a buzzard would gaze upon with delight. The landlord, however, informed me that he was, like a singed cat, better than he looked...By dint of a great deal of persuasion and hickory, I succeeded in reaching my destination late in the afternoon well convinced that my horse would not carry me back that day."

Irate because the animal's condition forced a night's stopover, the schoolteacher refused to pay an added day's charge when he returned the horse to its owner. "I objected on the ground that the animal was unable to make the journey in less time. Mine host was indignant, and said that I should pay that or nothing and even proposed to give me the horse, if I were dissatisfied. This last threat was sufficient. I payed the sum demanded and left the village."[12]

Even before the Civil War, inventive Americans sought to relieve the shortage of transport for travelers, and to offer more speedy crossing, by utilizing the constant winds of the Great Plains for propelling vehicles westward. In various staging towns along the frontier the talk of "wind wagons" created numerous jokes, although hopeful inventors sent off drawings of various models to the U. S. Patent Office. Gail Borden, who later won fame and fortune by devising methods for preserving meat and milk, actually built a "land schooner" in Texas, but apparently none was put into service before the railroads made them obsolete. After all, the prevailing winds blew from west to east.

In the spring of 1859, two letters sent to the *Missouri Republican* in St. Louis told of a visit to see a "prairie ship" or wind wagon near Westport. "The inventor is named Thomas," said one,"...and he takes advantage of these windy days to sail his ship a short distance over the prairie...It is a queer looking affair, and I was forcibly struck with the picture it presented...and thought at once of Don Quixote and the windmill. The affair is on wheels which are mammoth concerns, some twenty feet in circumference, and the arrangement for passengers is built somewhat after the style of an omnibus-body. It is to be propelled by the wind, through the means of sails. As to the wheels, it looks like an overgrown omnibus, and as to the spars and sails, it looks like a diminutive schooner. It will seat about twenty-four passengers."[13]

For elegant traveling, the steamboat surpassed all other means, but unless the wayfarers were going up the Missouri they were not likely to get very far into the West. The Arkansas, the Red, and the Rio Grande were not navigable to the Great Plains, and during years of low rainfall even the Missouri offered a challenge to steamboat captains and pilots.

Joseph Hanson, a veteran riverman, liked to tell a story about a Missouri steamer struggling upstream over a sandbar. The boat's engines were straining, paddlewheels were churning madly, and every member of the crew was holding his breath as the vessel crept inch by inch over the bar. A woodchoper living in a cabin on the river bank chose this moment to come down to the stream's edge for a pail of water. As he turned away with a brimming pail, his action caught the captain's eye. "Hey! you!" shouted the exasperated captain. "Put that water back!"[14]

Even the comparative luxury of a steamboat cabin could become tedious from delays and extended passages. After more than a month of travel on the Missouri in 1866, a passenger went happily ashore at Sioux City "feeling very much like a caged bird set free. The boys all felt like indulging in a little recreation, after being so long shut out from civilized community, and they all partook—some largely—of the invigorating beverages which make us all think we are boys again."[15]

The confirmed landsmen of the frontier were inclined to look somewhat askance at pilgrims arriving in the West on steamboats. In the spring of 1860, a reporter for a Kansas City newspaper took aim at a traveling dandy: "With what a defiant air does he pace the upper deck of the steamer that is fortunate enough to secure his passage, or strike an attitude when the boat touches at a landing, to be admired by the natives who congregate on the shore. They behold with amazement this formidable looking individual, as he stands there in his majesty, with a heroic quid of solace on the concave side of the cheek, and occasionally ejecting his saliva with a lordly grace...We warrant he will be crying for his mother in less than a week."[16]

It was common practice for new arrivals in the West to write letters home, or jot entries into their diaries, criticizing the condition of the towns, the lodgings, the food that they encountered along the way. Typical is a letter of August 1, 1869, from Plattsmouth, Nebraska: "Dear Charley: There is but one tavern here worth running, and there you will find no comfort. I am boarding there, but pray for deliverance. This is a little one horse town where no white man should come for pleasure."[17]

During the boom in westward travel immediately preceding the Civil War, the optimists of Kansas City built too many hotels, and consequently the managers sent runners to meet arriving Missouri River steamboats in search of prospective paying guests. Rivalry among the runners must have entertained, or possibly dismayed, pilgrims fresh from the East, as was observed by a correspondent for the *Missouri Republican*. A little fat man with a peculiarly amusing accent was crying the superiorities of the Eldridge House. The bedbugs were scaled thrice each week; the building was four stories high, the top floor being secure against sudden river rises. A runner for the Union House thundered that his hotel was the best in the city, and that the Eldridge was a hole in the ground with only six little rooms. "Gentlemen!" the fat man from the Eldridge House retaliated. "If I had a wife, or a sister, or a daughter who would enter the Union House, I would forever disown her!"[18]

In other frontier towns there was usually a shortage of hotel rooms. A visitor to one of Mark Twain's favorite river landings—Napoleon, Arkansas—described lodging there in 1851: "I will state that the best hotel in the place is an old dismantled Steam Boat...In one of the staterooms of this old Boat I have my chamber about six feet by four..."[19]

After gaining admittance to a hotel, guests often found the sitting room so crowded on cold winter evenings that it was difficult for late arrivals to get close enough to the fireplace to warm themselves. A Wyoming wagon driver, half-frozen after a long day on the road, solved the problem by tossing a handful of cartridges over the heads of the other guests into the fire. A few moments later there was plenty of room.

Guests awaiting bedtime in the sitting rooms of frontier taverns were always grateful for any kind of entertainment, be it a tall story or rough horseplay. In 1860 a newspaper editor in the Ozarks witnessed a practical joker at work on a visiting stranger who had fallen asleep beside the fireplace. The stranger had removed his shoes, and his big toe was showing through a hole in his sock. After heating a poker red hot, the practical joker held it closer and closer to the sleeper's bare toe.

"One by one the other guests as they caught the joke began to open their eyes, and being awakened, their mouths expanded into grins, and the grins into suppressed giggles…Closer and closer the red-hot poker neared the naked toe. The heat caused the sleeper restlessly to move his hands. Practical Joker was just about to apply the poker, when the sound of click! click! arrested the situation. He looked at the stranger, who with one eye had been watching the proceedings, and silently brought a pistol to bear upon Practical Joker. In a voice just audible he muttered in a tone of great determination: 'Jist burn it! Burn it! and I'll be damned if I don't stir you up with ten thousand hot pokers in two seconds.' Practical Joker laid down the poker and remarked: 'Stranger, let's *take a drink,* in fact, gentlemen, all of you!'"[20]

Pilgrims who spent their nights in taverns along the way West soon learned to size up a place by its outward appearance, and occasionally preferred to sit all night by the fire rather than endure the miseries of the establishment's beds. "I have slept in beds active with snakes, lizards, scorpions, centipedes, bugs and fleas," said J. Ross Browne, a traveler in the Apache country of the Southwest, "beds in which men stricken with plagues had died horrible deaths— beds that might reasonably be suspected of smallpox, measles and cholera. Standing, sitting, lying down, doubled up, and hanging over; twisted, punched, jammed and elbowed by drunken men, snored at, sat upon and smothered by the nightmare; burnt by fires, rained upon, snowed upon, and bitten by frost—in all these positions and subjected to all these discomforts, I have slept with comparative satisfaction. There are pleasanter ways of sleeping to be sure, but there are times when any way is a blessing."[21]

Albert D. Richardson, a newspaper correspondent who traveled the West during this same postwar period, took shelter one night in the cabin of a Kansas squatter who offered a couch for sleeping. "The couch was in the possession of insectile inhabitants, who resented our invasion of their premises in the most aggressive and bloodthirsty manner. The reader shall be spared the bristling terror of that memorable night. It combined the horrors of a prize-fight with being buried alive."[22]

Richardson's account was corroborated by numerous other lodgers, many of whom wrote humorously on the subject. "I was awakened early this morning by bed-bugs gnawing on my delicate frame," Joseph Camp recorded after a night at Fort Kearney in 1859, "to say nothing about the myriad of fleas that were cantering over me in their playful manner the whole night."[23]

Body lice evidently were so common on the frontier that veteran travelers came to expect them. In her book, *The Cheyenne and Black Hills Stage and Express Route*, Agnes Wright Spring quoted a bullwhacker who said that during a period of about six years he was lousy with but an intermission of only twenty-four hours. "I once went into Cheyenne," he said, "with a roll of several hundred dollars in bank notes, and it was full of lice and nits. I spent several hours stark naked, on the banks of Crow Creek, with soap and water, had a new suit of clothes which I carried there on the end of a long stick; also I had a couple of towels and a large can of anquintum (blue ointment), which I put on my body after being thoroughly dried; also I filled the seams of my new garments with it. But in a few hours I was as lousy as ever."[24]

The editor of the *Rio Abajo Weekly Press* of Albuquerque, New Mexico, took a light view of travelers' insect problems, and offered a remedy for the annoyance: "B.P., who went from here to Fort Wingate a few days ago, passed the night at the Rito, unable to sleep for several hours on account of the chinchas which amused themselves racing over his body. About midnight he sent one of the house for a leg of mutton, paying him a dollar for his services. Putting the meat in the middle of the floor, the chinchas went to the banquet and B.P. slept very well until morning. We publish this remedy for the public good."[25]

Privacy was virtually unknown in hotel accommodations, guests sharing rooms and beds with each other. Anyone carrying large sums of money had to sleep with one eye open. "The landlord showed us to a dark room," recalled one traveler, "in which two men were...playing cards, and a third lay drunk on the floor...We sat down on the side of the bed, and began to figure in our mind upon the chances. We had several hundred dollars in our pocket. We imagined that in case they should get 'short' they might call for our 'pile.'

"After studying a while we threw down the outside blanket and quietly crawled into bed with all our clothes on except cap and boots. We had a good bowie knife in our belt and clasped a pistol in each hand, and in this way we lay until daylight; and a longer night we never wish to see. When we got up, our roommates were still playing cards."[26]

A pilgrim from Illinois stopped at a familiar hotel and asked for the best room in the house. The proprietor replied that he could have a room that had just been vacated by Senator Stephen A. Douglas, the famous Democratic politician from Illinois. The traveler was delighted, and followed the hotel keeper upstairs to a room containing four beds. Two men were asleep in each of three beds, and one man was in the fourth.

"Landlord," said the man from Illinois, "this is a fine room, and I should be honored to sleep in one so lately occupied by Senator Douglas, but I *will* not sleep with the whole Democratic party!"[27]

In their search for comfort and diversion, guests from off the Western trails could do considerable damage to hotel property. As is true today, some of the worst offenders were from what are still viewed as the elite classes—upper-crust professionals accustomed to having their own way, in the settled East or on the frontier. A writer for *Spirit of the Times* in 1846 revealed how a bumptious lawyer, identified as Mr. S——, destroyed a female innkeeper's splendid Yankee clock and then with slick lawyerly cunning made her feel guilty for his own offense.

Awakened in the night by the ticking of the clock, the lawyer, according to the *Spirit of the Times* contributor, "lambasted the timepiece with a stick of wood, exclaiming with fiendish glee, as bits of the clock clattered to the floor in all parts of the room: 'Damn you, that will stop you, if nothing else will.'"

Next morning the proprietess appeared on the scene to find her beloved clock in bits on the floor, and demanded to know who had committed the deed. The account continued:

> "Aunt Patty," said the crafty lawyer, "do you know that I came near losing my life last night by your clock?"
>
> "Losing your life," asked Aunt Patty in wild-eyed astonishment. "How so, Mr. S——?"
>
> "I will tell you, Madam," answered S——, with the utmost gravity. "I was lying on the floor before the fire as usual, when your clock bursted, and the pieces flew like lightning just over my head. It was a wonder I was not killed."
>
> "Mr. S——" said Aunt Patty, "I'm glad you ain't hurt, but I never heard tell of a clock burstin' afore."
>
> "You never did?" asked S——. "Why sometimes when they get to running too fast, or the works go out of order, they will burst just like the boiler of a steamboat, and kill everybody near them."
>
> "Well, well!" exclaimed the gullible old lady. "If I'd know'd that, I wouldn't had one of 'em in my house...that I wouldn't, thank fortune, none of you's hurt."[28]

Pilgrims from the East brought novelties that seemed outlandish to those who had lived all or most of their lives on the frontier. A young man heading west in 1846 was so surprised by the merriment created among the natives who saw him using a manufactured toothbrush that he wrote a piece about it to *Spirit of the Times:*

"After going through with my morning ablution (which was performed outdoors and in public) I took out my toothbrush and commenced brushing my teeth. While so engaged, I happened to look up, and found a whole crowd gathered in front of me, regarding the dainty operation I was performing with the most astonishment. Their mouths were wide open, and their eyes intently fixed upon me. At last, one of them, who had recovered a little from amazement, raised his hands and exclaimed:—'Well, well! I've seed a power of strange things in this world, but I never before seed a man scrubbing his teeth.' 'Stranger,' said another, 'what mout be the matter with your teeth?'

"I told him I found the meat in this country rather tough, and that the brush in my hand was a machine newly invented for the purpose of sharpening teeth.

"One of them asked permission to look at it. The brush then passed from hand to hand, each one, as he examined it, making some remark about its shape, structure, utility, etc. They all, however, concurred in pronouncing it one of the most curious things they had ever beheld."[29]

Within twenty years, the manufactured toothbrush was in common use—in community use, as it were—in some parts of the West. In 1867, at a stagecoach relay station in Colorado, Frenchman Louis Simonin was surprised to find a wash basin with soap, and a roller towel. "You will find mirrors, combs, and brushes, all fastened to a long string, so that everyone may help himself and no one carry them off. You might laugh in Paris at these democratic customs; here they are accepted by all and are even welcome, except perhaps the toothbrush, which is regarded with suspicious eye."[30]

Early in the successive waves of westward migration, pilgrims were confronted with signboards, posters, and broadsides, as the burgeoning art of advertising swept across the nation. A considerable number of crudely lettered boards dealt with food and lodging. Sir Richard Burton noted one during his trek across the West in 1860:

> TOM MITCHELL!!! Dispenses Comfort to the
> Weary (!) Feeds the Hungry (!!) and
> Cheers the Gloomy (!!!) at his Old
> Well-known Stand Thirteen Miles East of
> Fort Des Moines. DON'T PASS BY ME.[31]

Twenty years later at a hotel near the Union Pacific Railroad in Green River, Wyoming, another Briton was intrigued by a notice posted prominently on a wall near the entrance. The Proprietor, G.W. Kitchen, evidently had been affronted many times by demanding guests, and must have had the poster made up in an effort to fend off all manner of complaints and expectations before they could be uttered.

THE DESERT HOUSE

This hotel has been built and arranged for the special comfort and convenience of boarders. On arrival each guest will be asked how he likes the situation; and if he says the hotel ought to have been placed upon the knoll or further down towards the village, the location of the house will be immediately changed. Corner front rooms, up only one flight, for every guest.

Baths, gas, water-closets, hot and cold water, laundry, telegraph, restaurant, fire alarm, bar-room, billiard-table, daily papers, coupé, sewing machine, grand piano, a clergyman, and all other modern conveniences in every room. Meals every minute, if desired, and consequently no second table. English, French, and German dictionaries furnished every guest, to make up such a bill-of-fare as he may desire without regard to the bill-affair afterwards at the office. Waiters of any nationality and colour desired. Every waiter furnished with a libretto, button-hole bouquet, full-dress suits, ball-tablets, and his hair parted in the middle. Every guest will have the best seat in the dining-hall, and the best waiter in the house.

Any guest not getting his breakfast red-hot, or experiencing a delay of sixteen seconds after giving his order for dinner, will please mention the fact at the office, and the cooks and waiters will be blown from the mouth of the cannon in front of the hotel. Children will be welcomed with delight, and are requested to bring hoop-sticks and hawkeys to bang the carved rosewood furniture especially provided for that purpose, and peg-tops to spin on the velvet carpets; they will be allowed to hang on the piano at all hours, yell in the halls, slide down the banisters, fall down stairs, carry away dessert enough for a small family in their pockets at dinner, and make themselves as disagreeable as the fondest mother can desire.

The office clerk has been carefully selected to please everybody, and can lead in prayer, play draw-poker, match worsted at the village store, shake for the drinks at any hour, day or night, play billiards, is a good waltzer and can dance the German, can make a fourth at euchre, amuse children, repeat the Beecher trial from memory, is a good judge of horses, as a railway and steamboat reference is far superior to Appleton's or anybody else's guide, will flirt with any young lady and will not mind being cut dead when "pa comes down." Don't mind being damned any more than a Connecticut river. Can room forty people in the best room in the house when the hotel is full, attend to the annunciator, and answer questions in Hebrew, Greek, Choctaw, Irish, or any other polite language at the same moment, without turning a hair...

The proprietor will take it as a personal affront if any guest on leaving should fail to dispute the bill, tell him he is a swindler, the house a barn, the table wretched, the wines vile, and that he, the guest, "was never so imposed upon in his life, will never stop there again, and means to warn his friends."

G.W. KITCHEN[32]

Mr. Kitchen did not go into detail about the food served at the Desert House, but many a western pilgrim in other locations and situations commented upon the subject at length, using Chaucerian humor to describe the comestibles and potables encountered along the way.

Crossing Kansas en route to the Colorado mines, Albert Richardson and a companion stopped at "a neat little log-house," their appetite voracious, their hopes high for generous servings of wholesome fare: "Alas, for human hopes! The coffee was like a pool of yellow soap suds. The conglomerate substance by courtesy called butter was rank and smelled to heaven. The ham was strong enough to perform the labors of Hercules. The English language affords no vituperative epithet which can do justice to the corn bread. Despairingly, we called for sweet milk. Doubtless it *had* been sweet at some previous stage, but the period was far remote. Not a dish was palatable; the trail of the serpent was over them all.

"In utter disappointment we left the table, sat for a while in ominous silence, and went to bed, a morose and melancholy pair."[33]

While traveling from Colorado to Montana in 1867, Alexander McClure reported a similar experience at a stagecoach stop called Pleasant Valley Station. The coffee, he said, was nothing more than water made bitter by some nauseous ingredient, the bacon was stale, the eggs worse than stale. "It would have required a first-class quartz-mill to masticate the bread," McClure said, "and nothing more dainty than a buzzard could have eaten the other articles. The cook was an Irishman who was filthy enough himself to sell as real estate."

At Moose Creek, later on the journey, McClure spent a night fighting off bedbugs while lying on a straw pallet in the kitchen. He awoke to see the landlady making biscuits for breakfast. "As soon as she saw I was awake, she displayed the proverbial sociability of Western people by entering into a spirited conversation, made up mainly of interruptions on her part and monosyllables on mine. As I was lying on the floor, I had a good view of her feet, and, after mature reflection decided that she had not washed them since spring, if even then; and, if they were to be cleaned up for winter, I concluded that nothing short of a grindstone run by water-power would scour them white."[34]

The unrestrained Captain John G. Bourke obviously enjoyed himself describing a meal at a stagecoach station in Arizona. "The supper was in strict keeping with the rest of the establishment: a bare pine table, china plate, tin cups and knives and forks in various stages of decreptitude. There was tea, made from the native grasses of the territory, biscuits, with an extravagant excess of soda, bacon, putrid and sour, sugar that would have delighted the soul of an entomologist, it was so full of ants and bugs and flies; stewed dried apples, each separate slice standing out sodden and distinct from its fellows..."

Captain Bourke was also amused by an aptly named restaurant in Tucson, the Shoo Fly. "Some grumblers," he said, "used to take exception to the number of flies in the soup, forgetting that the poor little flies had appetites as well as any other form of creation and that if the soup were not good they wouldn't fly into it."[35]

Many of the rest stops offering meals and overnight accommodations were known as ranches. On his journey through the Colorado mountains in 1867, Alexander McClure stopped at three, "known by the euphonious names of the 'Red-Headed Woman's Ranch,' 'Pretty Woman's Ranch,' and the 'Dirty Woman's Ranch.' Afer a most tedious and anxious drive, we arrived at the last named, so called from the untidy person and habits of the divinity who once presided over it, and who, as the legend runs, finally died of dirt."[36]

In 1880, two railroad surveyors, looking for a place to stay the night in the Ozarks, came upon a rough board cabin at Cross Hollows. "Hitching our horses," one noted, "we entered and found two men the sole occupants, evidently the operators...who voiced no greeting, but one of them pointed to one corner of the room, otherwise vacant, in which stood a large barrel about fifty gallons, open-topped and filled with moonshine whiskey to within a foot of the barrel rim. Hanging from a nail on the wall and suspended by a string, dangled a large tin cup. A piece of paper tacked to the wall and written with pencil bore the inscription DRINK ALL YOU WANT FOR 5 CENTS. We tasted the liquor merely, and left our two hosts."[37]

Pilgrims arriving from the urbane East were usually startled by the earthy table manners of frontier folk, especially when they dined en masse and irregularly in booming settlements. "They [breakfast] in the midst of the night," said Steven Masset, "dine when they ought to be breakfasting and take supper when they should be dining, and the 'feed' is most distasteful—all noise, dirt, grease, mess, slop, confusion, and disorder, chunks of meat of all kinds and no flavor, placed in plates, and 'sot' on the table; and before you [have] time to look at your meat, a piece of very flat pie, with a doughy crust, and dried fruit inside is placed under your nose, on the same plate with your meat. Men pick their teeth with forks and jackknives, gobble down gallons of water, and 'slide.' This is the style in Oregon."[38]

Accustomed to rough manners and plain food, the frontiersmen themselves became sources of merriment when their wanderings brought them into Denver, Kansas City, or San Francisco—after a few high-toned restaurants were established in these larger centers. Cowboy folklore abounds with jokes about trail drivers' encounters with exotic food in fancy dining rooms.

Typical is the story of a Westerner visiting New Orleans on business. Entering a splendid restaurant he was handed a menu with everything listed in French, which he could not read. When the waiter came to take his order, the frontiersman pointed to several different items on the menu and said, "I'll take some of this, some of those, and some of that." After a while the waiter brought a bowl of soup, a few stalks of celery, and a crab. Later the waiter returned and stood awaiting further orders. The Westerner glared at him for a moment and said sternly: "I drank your slop, I et your bouquet, but hell dammit to God, I can't eat that big bug."[39]

By the time overlanders crossed the Great Plains and entered the passes through the Rockies, they were either short of rations or had grown weary of the dried and preserved foods they carried. Those who took the central route found friendly Indians eager to trade fresh buffalo and antelope meat for pots and pans, buttons, mirrors, needles, and various other manufactured articles. Farther into the Northwest, the tribes occasionally provided fresh roots and salmon. Along the southern trails through Utah and Nevada, however, the Indians offered foodstuffs unfamiliar to Easterners— viands that sometimes brought black humor into the diaries of those willing to experiment.

In the summer of 1846, Edwin Bryant and his companions met three Indians near Warm Springs, Utah, and with sign language asked if they had any meat to trade. The Indians had no meat, but soon afterward brought up three women of the tribe carrying baskets containing what the traveler discovered to be serviceberries crushed to a jam and mixed with grasshoppers. "This composition being dried in the sun until it becomes hard is what may be called the 'fruit-cake' of these poor children of the desert...No doubt these women regarded it as one of the most acceptable offerings they could make to us. We purchased all they brought with them, paying them in darning-needles and other small articles, with which they were much pleased. The prejudice against the grasshopper 'fruit-cake' was strong at first, but it soon wore off, and none of the delicacy was thrown away or lost."[40]

Later in the same year, Heinrich Lienhard reported a meeting with Indians along the Humboldt River. They offered small yellowish roots that tasted like parsnips. One of the Indians pressed a live grasshopper, its legs still thrashing, against a piece of root. "Then he offered me the grasshopper," Lienhard said, "together with the root, about as one would hand buttered bread to a child." Surprised that Lienhard would not accept the offering, the Indian ate it himself.

That evening Lienhard ate some of the root with his evening meal, but during the night he suffered severe diarrhea. When the Indians returned next day, bringing more roots to trade, he could not understand why Lienhard expressed disgust at the sight of them.

"Only through signs," Lienhard noted, "could I make him understand, so I bent forward, holding my belly with both hands, and groaned as though I had severe abdominal pains; then I produced with my mouth certain sounds such as at times escape entirely different human organs, at the same time making a gesture with my hands toward my rear. The Indians understood me perfectly and a veritable storm of laughter burst from their throats. My friend (the Indian) laughed if possible hardest of all, and tossed his roots on my back. We of course laughed with them and parted, for all that, as good friends."[41]

Roast dog, the most often mentioned outlandish meat dish of some western tribes, was encountered by Lewis Garrard in 1847, while he was traveling with a party of veteran traders from St. Louis on the Santa Fe Trail. Garrard, who was then only seventeen and fresh from Cincinnati, told of approaching the camp's cooking fire and asking what the Indian women were preparing for dinner:

> "Tarrapin!" promptly replied Smith.
> "Terrapins?" echoed I, in surprise, at the name. "Terrapins! how do they cook them?"
> "You know them hardshell land tarrapins?"
> "Yes."
> "*Well!* the squaws go out to the sand buttes, and bring the critters in, and cook 'em in the shell alive—those stewin' thar ar cleaned first. Howsomever, they're darned good!"
> "Yes, hos, an' that's a fact, wagh!" chimed in Greenwood.
> I listened of course with much interest to their account of the savage dish, and waited, with impatience, for a taste…When the squaw transferred the contents of the kettle to a wooden bowl and passed it to us, our butcher knives were in immediate requisition. Taking a piece…without thought as to what part of the terrapin it was, I ate it with much gusto, calling "for more." It was extremely good, and I spoke of the delicacy of the meat, and answered all their questions as to its excellency in the affirmative…After fully committing myself, Smith looked at me awhile in silence, the corners of his mouth gradually making preparations for a laugh, and asked:
> "Well, hos! how you do like dog meat?" and then such hearty guffaws were never heard…
> A revulsion of opinion, and dog meat, too, ensued, for I could feel the "pup" crawling up my throat, but…I broke the shackles of deep-rooted antipathy to the canine breed, and putting a choice morceau on top of that already swallowed, ever after remained a stanch defender and admirer of dog meat.[42]

Male pilgrims quickly learned to prepare their own food, the favorite dish being flapjacks whenever the ingredients could be found. Albert Richardson was convinced that enough flapjacks were made while he was in the Colorado mining region to pave the road from Leavenworth to Denver. "At every camp one saw perspiring men bending anxiously over the griddle, or turning the cake by tossing it skillfully into the air. To a looker-on, such masculine feats were decidedly amusing."[43]

The same was true in the California gold mining camps. "Flapjacks were the staff of life to the miners in those days," recalled Lemuel McKeeby, "and we became quite expert in flapping them over in a frying pan; it was not difficult for me to throw them some two or three feet up in the air and land them safely, batterside down in the pan. I have heard some experts in this line who claimed that they could throw them up the chimney, then run around on the outside of the cabin and catch them in the pan; however, I have never seen one do it."[44]

As the present-day reader must perceive, no governmental regulatory agency then existed to oversee the quality or sanitation of foods on the frontier. Swindles, adulterations, and substitutions abounded. For example, cheese and axle grease in that time were packed in similar wooden containers, and one roadside merchant thought it a fine practical joke to sell the cheap grease at the price of the more expensive cheese to those unable to read the labels. After watching a westbound customer spread the thick yellow lubricant on crackers and eat them, he asked if it was satisfactory. "Pretty good," replied the stranger, "but a little bit randsom."

On the Missouri frontier, knavish merchants fell into the habit of mixing sand with the sugar they sold out of barrels. One victim was so exasperated by the practice that he placed a notice in the Washington County *Post* that was reprinted in the Hannibal *Daily Journal* on July 26, 1853:

> NOTICE: I purchased of a grocer in this city a quantity of sugar from which I obtained ONE POUND OF SAND. If the rascal who cheated me will send to my address seven pounds of good sugar (scripture measure of restitution), I will be satisfied; if not, I shall expose him.

According to the Hannibal newspaper, on the following day

nine seven-pound packages of sugar were left at his residence, from as many different dealers, each supposing himself the person intended.

Certainly the basic requirements of any traveler setting forth into the western frontier were to keep a sharp lookout at all times for scalawags and falsifiers, to have a tolerance for physical discomfort, to possess the patience of a stoic, to disregard disagreeable environments, and to be blessed with a strong stomach and a placid digestive system. And even with all these strengths, without laughter most of the pilgrims would have failed to reach their Canterburys.

CHAPTER TWO

Bigwig and Littlewig Sojourners

BY MID-CENTURY, VARIOUS CELEBRITIES from the nation and the world were traveling into the American frontier, not to become a part of it but to hunt its wildlife, to observe and report on its human denizens, and to entertain them, or instruct them about the finer things of life. Some notables came for all these purposes, others for only one or two. In the course of their visits, the sojourners often amused frontier folk in ways not intended.

Horace Greeley did not originate the saying "Go West, Young Man." They were words of an obscure writer for a Terre Haute, Indiana, newspaper, but Greeley adopted and popularized them in his *New York Tribune* editorials. Actually, during Greeley's early years as an editor, he strongly opposed rapid expansion of the frontier, and scolded pioneers who wanted to travel beyond the "jumping-off places," a phrase that he supposedly did originate to designate the frontier border. In 1843, when he learned that several hundred pilgrims were leaving the Missouri jumping-off places in wagons bound for Oregon, Greeley described the venture as "foolhardy," "palpable homicide," and "insanity," predicting that nine-tenths of the travelers would never reach the Columbia River alive.

Like many other Easterners of the mid-nineteenth century, Greeley viewed the Great Plains as an American desert and the Rockies as an eternal barricade to land travel to the Pacific. He feared that travelers would die of starvation or at the hands of Indians, and that children and women would suffer acutely from the strains of the long journey.

Horace Greeley was not a small-minded man with fixed ideas, however, and after he began receiving enthusiastic letters from travelers who had reached the Pacific coast with no loss of life or ill effects, he gradually changed his opinions about the westward movement and became an ardent supporter. In the 1850s, the decade in which he made the *New York Tribune* into a national newspaper, he published more material about the West than any of his rivals. Quite a number of young men later attributed their presence in the West to reports they had read in the *Tribune*. The *Tribune* was also popular on the frontier and was said to be the most used newspaper for papering the walls of settlers' cabins, providing semi-permanent reading matter for visitors and establishing the pleasant custom of "reading the walls" whenever a family moved into a previously occupied cabin.

In 1855 Greeley's advice to young men was to follow in their fathers' footsteps on farms or in workshops, with this addendum: "If you have no family or friends to aid you, and no prospect opened to you there, turn your face to the great West, and there build up a home and fortune."[1]

During the years that followed, Greeley shortened that maxim to "Go West, young man, and grow up with the country." In 1859, he decided that he should go and have a look at the West himself. His journey by stagecoach across the Plains and the Rockies provided considerable amusement for onlookers, but probably not very much for Horace, who was then forty-eight years old, a handsome, open-faced, and very dignified man.

Leavenworth, Kansas, was Greeley's "jumping-off place" for his western journey. He stopped there long enough to be amazed by the acres of wagons and herds of oxen assembled for transporting freight across the Plains. Dressed in an old white linen duster, carrying a well-worn traveling bag stamped 154 NASSAU STREET, NEW YORK, and armed with a blue cotton umbrella, he boarded a mule-drawn stagecoach bound for Denver. He was accompanied most of the way by Albert Richardson who that year was covering the frontier for a Boston newspaper.

Along the way west, the fast-moving stagecoach passed numerous wagons bearing the slogan PIKES PEAK OR BUST, and occasionally they met disillusioned gold seekers returning home with lettering beneath their faded sign: BUSTED BY THUNDER!

Whenever the coach stopped for the night at a small settlement, the famous editor was usually invited to give a speech, and he usually complied. On one occasion a settler asked Richardson if Greeley's newspaper had failed, forcing him to join the Pikes Peak gold rush to dig.

Being a veteran stagecoach traveler, Greeley was aware that all passengers, regardless of their importance, were expected to aid the driver in times of difficulty. One day they came upon an immigrant wagon so mired in a muddy creek that it blocked other vehicles, and the editor joined the driver and passengers in helping remove the obstacle. After Greeley assisted in lifting a wagon wheel, one of the immigrants (they were from Ohio) asked him what business he was in. Greeley replied that he was connected with a New York newspaper.

"What newspaper?"

"The *Tribune.*"

"Ah, that's old Greeley's paper, isn't it?"

"Yes, sir."

At this moment one of the stagecoach passengers introduced Greeley by name. The man from Ohio was astonished that so eminent an American would get down into the mud to labor over a mired wagon.

As the coach rolled farther along toward Colorado Territory, they met more and more bands of Indians—mostly Arapaho and Cheyenne—in search of buffalo herds. One day three friendly Cheyenne came racing alongside the coach, frightening the mules. The mules broke a harness line and ran down a steep embankment, overturning the coach with a tremendous crash. The fore-wheels broke loose, to be carried away by the terrified mules. The driver and all passengers except Greeley escaped without injuries. The famous editor was temporarily trapped inside.

"From a mass of cushion, carpet-sacks and blankets," said Albert Richardson, "soon emerged my companion, his head rising above the side of the vehicle like that of an advertising boy from his frame of pasteboard. Blood was flowing profusely from cuts in his cheek, arm and leg; but his face was serene and benignant as a May morning. He was soon removed from his cage, and taken to Station Seventeen, a few yards beyond, where the good woman dressed his galling wounds."[2]

Although his leg had been badly wrenched and lacerated and his face was covered with home-made plasters, Greeley continued gamely into Denver to brave the crudities of the Denver House, derisively known as "the Astor House of the Gold Fields." The roof and windows of the log building were covered with canvas, and the six bedrooms were separated by walls of cotton sheathing.

Still aching from sprains and cuts, Greeley managed to endure the Denver House with good humor, noting that "every guest is allowed as good a bed as his own blankets will make...I had the honor to be shaved by the nephew (so he assured me) of Murat, Bonaparte's king of Naples—the honor and the shave together costing me but a paltry dollar. Still, a few days of such luxury surfeited me, mainly because the drinking room was also occupied by several blacklegs as a gambling hall, and their incessant clamor...persisted in at all hours until midnight, became at length a nuisance...Then, the visitors of that drinking and gambling room had a careless way, when drunk, of firing revolvers, sometimes at each other, at other times quite miscellaneously, which struck me as inconvenient for a quiet guest."[3]

As soon as the miners and other inhabitants of Denver learned of Greeley's presence, they demanded a speech from him. He gave it in the big saloon and gambling room at the front of the hotel. Standing between a crowd of tipplers at the bar, and a host of gamblers at the tables, the famous journalist "made a strong anti-drinking and anti-gambling address, which was received with perfect good humor."[4]

Next morning, still walking with a limp and wearing "a variety of extemporized plasters," Greeley set out for Gregory Diggings, the most recent big gold strike, forty miles to the northwest. Because there was no stage road, they had to hire saddled mules for a two-day journey into the mountains.

Having heard that Greeley was coming, some of the miners "salted" a mine to impress the great editor. They loaded a shotgun with a charge of gold dust and fired it into a partly worked claim. Soon after Greeley arrived, they maneuvered him to the right location, handed him a pan, and showed him how to search for the precious ore. He was amazed at the riches he found in every pan, and most likely he never learned in his lifetime how he had been tricked. That evening he delivered an alfresco speech against the evils of gambling and intoxicating drinks.

Upon returning to Denver, Greeley sent off a glowing dispatch to the *New York Tribune*, describing the ease with which gold could be mined in Colorado Territory. Although he added a few cautionary paragraphs warning of shortages of food and shelter, the high prices of necessities, and dangers of travel, those paragraphs were often omitted by editors around the nation who reprinted the enthusiastic assurances of wealth for the digging in Colorado. Weeks later, veteran miners were blaming the journalist for bringing down upon them a swarm of novice gold seekers who only added to the crowded confusion, the conflicts, crime, and misery of the Colorado mining camps. Such was the power of Greeley's pen and the *Tribune*.

Greeley spent about two weeks in Denver, recovering from his accident and writing about the booming town of 150 log houses, five women, and hundreds of men dressed in buckskin, slouch hats, boots and moccasins, and armed with knives and revolvers suspended from their belts, a town of "more brawls, more fights, more pistol shots with criminal intent...than in any community of greater numbers on earth."[5]

After leaving Denver he journeyed to Salt Lake City to examine Brigham Young and the Mormons. Along the way, his bad luck with vehicles continued. While crossing the flooded Laramie River, the mail wagon in which he was riding overturned in midstream. Mail and baggage were retrieved and Greeley escaped with only a chilly soaking. Then again at the Sweetwater crossing, he was hurled sprawling into the river with mail bags tumbling after him. His handbag and a small trunk in which he carried his manuscripts swirled away. An immigrant helped retrieve his handbag, but the trunk sank beneath the swift current. "I would rather have sunk a thousand dollars there," Greeley declared. "On the whole my fourth of July was not a happy one."

In Salt Lake City, he found Brigham Young willing to give him a two-hour interview. The editor was critical of Young's grammar, but said the church leader had no apparent desire to conceal anything about Mormonism. "Nor did he repel any of my questions as impertinent...In appearance he is a portly, frank, good-natured, rather thick-set man of fifty-five, seeming to enjoy life, and to be in no particular hurry to get to heaven."[6]

The single event of Horace Greeley's tour of the West that created the most merriment and made the greatest imprint upon the American consciousness was a wild stagecoach ride with the celebrated California driver, Hank Monk. Greeley boarded Monk's stage at Carson City, Nevada, for the arduous journey over the Sierras to Placerville, California. So much folklore now surrounds that ride, however, that it is impossible to get at the facts.

Apparently Greeley had arranged to give a speech in Placerville, and he asked Hank Monk to try to get him there on time. The request was a challenge to the driver, who kept his horses racing at a faster than usual speed over one of the most rugged and dangerous roads in the West. As the coach swung around curves and jolted against stones and stumps, the passengers were bounced about mercilessly inside. The legend has it that Greeley protested loudly again and again, but that Hank Monk was determined to prove he could get the great man to Placerville on time.

In his own account of the ride, Greeley described how the road ran along the side of a steep mountain, "a mere shelf with a fifteen hundred foot precipice on one side, and scarcely a place where two meeting vehicles could pass." The coach, he said, was travelling as fast as four wild California horses could draw it.

At the time, Greeley probably did not even know the name or stature of the driver (he did say that he was skillful) but having endured three previous stagecoach accidents, he must have been wary of another in that reckless descent. "Had the horses seen fit to run away...I know that he could not have held them, and one might have been pitched headlong down a precipice of a thousand feet, where all of the concern that could have been picked up afterward would not have been two bits per bushel. Yet at this break-neck rate we were driven for not less than four hours or forty miles, changing horses every ten miles, and raising a cloud of dust through which it was difficult at times to see anything...I cannot conscientiously recommend the route I have traveled to summer tourists in quest of pleasure…"[7]

Most accounts state that Greeley was in a rather shaken condition when he stepped down from the coach at Placerville, his hat crushed from constantly banging his head against the top of the coach, his clothing dust-covered and in disarray. The legend began there among the miners and Placerville citizens who were witnesses, with Hank Monk himself adding embroidery. In a short time it spread around California, each tale-teller contributing nuggets of exaggeration. Very soon Artemus Ward added the ride of Horace Greeley to his repertoire of humor, and two years later Mark Twain gave the incident a classic treatment in *Roughing It*.

Twain claimed that he heard the tale on his first journey west in 1861 from a stage driver at Julesburg, Colorado, then again at Denver, Fort Bridger, and Salt Lake City. According to Twain: "The coach bounced up and down in such a terrific way that it jolted the buttons all off of Horace's coat, and finally shot his head clean through the roof of the stage, and then he yelled at Hank Monk and begged him to go easier—said he warn't in as much of a hurry as he was awhile ago. But Hank Monk said, 'Keep your seat, Horace, and I'll get you there on time'—and you bet he did, too, what was left of him." Twain did add a qualifying footnote in which he said that the oft-repeated anecdote was especially aggravating because the adventure it celebrated never occurred. Probably very few people, however, read the small print of the footnote.[8]

Local journalists and travel writers from the East quickly picked up the story, adding their embellishments. By the time Horace Greeley ran for President of the United States in 1872, practically everybody in the nation knew one version or another of the hilarious tale of his ride with Hank Monk. Greeley lost the election. Even in our own cynical times, a single ludicrous incident can derail a candidate running for public office. Who can say whether he was done in by the popularity of Ulysses Grant or by a frontier stagecoach ride with Hank Monk?

During Greeley's campaign, Hank Monk supposedly wrote the candidate to ask a favor in exchange for his vote. Greeley replied that he would rather see the stagecoach driver ten thousand fathoms in Hell than give him a crust of bread. "You are the only man who ever had the opportunity to place me in a ridiculous light, and you villainously exercised that opportunity, you damned scamp."[9]

Of all the mighty hunters who came to the American frontier from abroad, probably none excited the entire nation more than did the Grand Duke Alexis Romanov of Russia. Alexis visited the Wild West to hunt buffalo in January 1872. He was accompanied by a considerable retinue of fellow countrymen and a collection of American characters colorful enough to beguile the folk on the frontier. Among the Americans were George Armstrong Custer, Buffalo Bill Cody, General Philip Sheridan, Texas Jack Omo-hundro, Spotted Tail, and an entire camp of Brulé Sioux.

Only twenty-two years old, quite handsome, and dressed in splendid nineteenth-century operatic-style royal garb, Alexis and the American press created one of those frenzied love affairs with foreign nobility that sweep across the Republic about once in every generation. Alexis-mania reached its heights when he was escorted to the Plains of western Nebraska to hunt buffalo.

Soon after his arrival in eastern America, Alexis had met General Sheridan, commander of the Army's Military Division of the Missouri, which encompassed most of the great buffalo herds of the West. When the grand duke expressed a desire to hunt buffalo, Sheridan returned to his Chicago headquarters and began dispatching telegrams to his generals in the Plain forts, ordering them to organize a hunt for mid-January.

Sheridan demanded daily reports on locations and movements of buffalo herds. He assigned General George Forsyth to collect an abundance of fine foods and drinks. He gave General Innis Palmer authority to commandeer the fanciest Pullman and parlor cars, and to establish schedules and timetables. He ordered Omaha Barracks converted into a supply base for the hunting expedition. He telegraphed George Armstrong Custer, summoning him to join the group at Omaha.

Learning that Buffalo Bill Cody was about to leave Fort Mc-Pherson, Nebraska, to serve as chief of scouts with the Fifth Cavalry in Arizona, Sheridan canceled the assignment. Cody was then only twenty-five years old, but he had already established his reputation as a hunter and guide, and Sheridan wanted him for the duke.

Meanwhile enough reports of buffalo herds had come in for Sheridan to locate a camp somewhere about fifty miles south of North Platte, Nebraska, which was a convenient stop on the Union Pacific Railroad. Sheridan thereupon telegraphed Buffalo Bill, instructing him to assist General Forsyth in finding a suitable site. As soon as that was done, Cody was to search for Spotted Tail, chief of the Brulé Sioux, and bring him and about a hundred warriors to the camp. The grand duke wanted to see some wild Indians, and Sheridan meant to supply them.

Spotted Tail's winter camp at the Brulé agency was about 150 miles away across snow-clad plains, but Cody succeeded in his mission. All he needed to do was tell the Indians they could leave their agency, visit their forbidden hunting grounds, and hunt buffalo with a great chief from another country. In addition they would be presented with twenty wagon-loads of free food and blankets from the Army.

Christmas military furloughs were canceled for a considerable number of enlisted men of the Second Cavalry, who were marched out to Red Willow Creek from Fort McPherson to build a hunting camp that Sheridan named "Camp Alexis." The men had to remove a coating of snow, level the ground, and erect about forty tents, including a mess tent, and two large hospital tents that were to be used as quarters for Sheridan and the grand duke. The cavalrymen placed floor boards in tents assigned to high-ranking officers, and spread a thick carpet over the boards in the duke's tent. For several days they fed, watered, and curried a herd of trained hunting horses.

The Grand Duke Alexis, after spending more than a month being fêted in Eastern cities, traveled by special train to Omaha. Waiting for him there were Sheridan and several other generals, thousands of citizens, and all the schoolchildren of the city. They greeted the royal visitor "with loud and continuous cheers," according to the *Omaha Tribune*, which added that the duke was six feet, two inches in height, straight as an arrow, and thick-set. "Despite his side-whiskers and downy moustache, the ladies call him perfectly handsome. His hair is light golden, brushed straight back from his high white forehead. His hands are very large. He abominates gloves, and only resorted to them when propriety demanded it. His feet are immense, and he wore heavy, double-soled boots, more serviceable than elegant."[10]

George Custer and several newspapermen joined the assemblage on January 12, and the expedition departed in ten sumptuously appointed railroad cars behind a locomotive draped in American and Russian flags. It was called the Imperial Train.

At six o'clock the next morning, the train arrived at North Platte, its passengers suffering hangovers after spending most of the night eating and drinking. In the gray light of a wintry dawn, the few citizens of the little frontier town had lined up along the side track to view the duke. When he stepped down they removed their hats—as Russian peasants might have done. One newspaperman commented that there were no cheers or excitement, "but a sort of reverential curiosity."[11] One wonders. Frontier folk were masters at putting on acts, for the sheer merriment of the game.

Sheridan hustled Alexis and his troupe of Russians out to a line of waiting ambulance wagons. He introduced them to Buffalo Bill Cody, who was dressed in a buckskin coat trimmed with fur, and was wearing a black slouch hat over his long hair that hung in ringlets down his shoulders. Cody took the lead on horseback, and the party set off at a fast pace across the plains for Camp Alexis. An escort of cavalry rode alongside.

At lunchtime, right on schedule, a company of cavalry from the camp met them with a wagonload of sandwiches and champagne. After an hour's rest, the caravan rode on to Camp Alexis, arriving to the sound of brass from the Second Cavalry's band, which was playing "Hail to the Chief."

Next morning after a serenade of Russian music, the duke celebrated his twenty-second birthday by slaying his first buffalo. Accounts of this adventure vary considerably, although most agree that Buffalo Bill rode out before daylight to find a herd. He was back in camp by breakfast time and reported buffalo in plenty about fifteen miles distant.

Some newspapermen reported that Sheridan assigned Custer the honor of initiating Alexis into the art of hunting buffalo; others said Buffalo Bill was the royal instructor. Both versions are probably correct. Most agree that Sheridan was indisposed and unable to join the first day's hunt, but the reporters were too politic to suggest that the commanding general may have consumed more than enough champagne during the previous two nights of celebration. (Journalists who made unflattering comments about high military officers would not have fared well in the West during the years of the Indian-fighting army.)

A surviving photograph made on the spot proves that the ducal hunting costume consisted of a fancy jacket with trimmings and numerous buttons, a pair of gray trousers stuffed into shiny knee boots, and a fur turban. Custer, standing on Alexis's right, was all buckskins and boots topped by what one reporter described as "a comical sealskin hat." Cody, on the duke's left, was in fur strippings and fringes to the knees, his costume dominated by an enormous hat with brim up in front so that even now, a century later, it would fit right into a Hollywood film about the Old West.

They galloped off like a trio of adolescents, the duke practicing running and shooting at imaginary buffaloes along the way. Alexis believed it would be more sporting to use a revolver instead of a rifle, which meant that he would have to ride alongside or amidst the herd to deliver his shots.

According to one reporter, who may or may not have been a witness, when they reached the herd Custer charged in with the duke, maneuvering a big bull into position for the Russian to make an easy kill. Alexis put two shots into the buffalo and it turned down a ravine, both men in pursuit. The duke quickly caught up with the wounded animal, killing it with a third shot.

Bill Cody's version of the same incident was completely different. The duke fired six shots from his revolver, Cody said, but missed every shot. Then Cody gave Alexis his own revolver, but again the Russian failed to drop a buffalo. Seeing that the herd was about to escape, Cody rode up beside the duke, handed him a rifle, and told him to shoot. From ten feet, Alexis made his kill. Buffalo Bill, of course, knew how to turn a story to his advantage, and most of his printed ones were ghostwritten anyhow.

Another member of the hunting party arrived in time to see the duke cut off the buffalo's tail, wave it in the air, and "let go a series of howls and gurgles like the death song of all the foghorns and calliopes ever born."[12] Meanwhile the herd moved swiftly away and action was suspended while corks were popped from champagne bottles.

When the hunting party returned to camp, they found that Spotted Tail had arrived with considerably more than the hundred braves that he had been asked to bring. Most of the Indian hunters had their families with them, and numerous tepees were being erected all along the opposite side of Red Willow Creek.

The Russians were delighted to meet the Brulés. Spotted Tail had brought his wife and young daughter, Red Road, whose beauty immediately attracted the notice of Alexis and Custer. During the remaining days of hunting, the two men evidently became friendly rivals for the girl's attention.

A reporter for a Lincoln, Nebraska, newspaper gave the edge to Custer, stating that he took advantage of his knowledge of the Indian vernacular and sign language that he had acquired while serving in the West. He was also ten years older than the duke, and knew what sort of presents to give Indian maidens. On one occasion Custer requested the privilege of putting rings in Red Road's ears, and she immediately granted permission, giggling incessantly while he attempted to attach them.

"He consumed much more time in this pleasant occupation than was needed," the newspaperman reported, "and having adjusted one of them in her ear, without changing his position put his arms around her neck in order to adjust the other. As she made no objection to this proceeding, he claimed the only reward he could request for his pleasing liberty, and the scene was ended by his kissing her. It was done so graciously that old Spotted Tail has no cause to scalp him for his temerity..."[13]

Next morning the Indians joined the hunt for buffalo. Under Custer's guidance, the duke managed to slay a cow and calf. The cow's head was removed and prepared for shipment to Russia. During the afternoon, an ambulance wagon arrived with sandwiches and champagne for the royal party, after which they galloped back to camp to be entertained with dances by the Sioux. To express his thanks to the Indians, the duke presented each warrior with a silver half-dollar.

And so this was "roughing it" ducal style on the frontier of the Old West. After another day the expedition returned to the Imperial Train and journeyed to Denver, leaving the troopers of Second Cavalry to dismantle the camp and see that the Sioux returned to their agency.

After attending a grand ball in Denver, the Russians were ready for another buffalo hunt. As Custer was familiar with the hunting areas of the Colorado–Kansas plains, General Sheridan put him in charge of arrangements. In his grandiose way, Custer spared no expense. He sent numerous scouts out to find a big herd and telegraphed Fort Wallace to start seventy-five cavalry horses, four six-mule wagon teams, and four ambulances toward the town of Kit Carson, Colorado. He then requisitioned "every kind of liquor, champagne, all sorts of delicacies in the way of eatables." All this for one day of buffalo hunting.

In proper military fashion, the grand duke's special train, the horses and other equipment from Fort Wallace, and the food and drink came together at Kit Carson. Only five miles to the south an immense buffalo herd was grazing. The hunting party was soon in motion, accompanied by the ambulances and supply wagons. A low hog-back hill screened the herd, and the hunters took advantage of it, halting and forming a military line for a charge.

At the last moment, Sheridan decided to stay with the ambulances, his only companion being a scout named Chalkley Beeson. Soon after the hunters charged up the slope and disappeared, a rattle of gunfire echoed back, and the restless Sheridan decided to ascend the hill on foot to watch the action. Beeson accompanied him. Just as they reached the top, two or three wounded buffalo came running from the opposite direction. Behind them galloped the entire hunting party, shooting at the fleeing animals.

"The bullets were dropping all around us," Chalk Beeson later recalled, "and we...made tracks down the hill trying to get out of range. Sheridan was too short in the legs to run, and threw himself down on the ground with his face in the buffalo-grass to get out of range."

Beeson had some difficulty gaining the attention of the exuberant Custer and his Russian companions. "At last they stopped, and when Sheridan got to his feet I think he was the maddest man I ever saw. On horseback his short legs did not show much, and he was a fine soldierly figure, but on foot, with his long body, short legs and his waist-measure, he was far from impressive. But when he turned loose on that bunch he was impressive enough. There was only one man in the army who could equal him when it came to a certain kind of expletive, and that was Custer himself. I don't know what kind of language Pa Romanoff used to Alexis when he got mad, but that slip of royalty got a cussing from Phil Sheridan that day that I bet he will never forget. He didn't spare anybody in the bunch, not even Custer and the grand duke, and he included all their kinsfolk, direct and collateral. It was a liberal education in profanity to hear him. The grand duke didn't seem to care—he was having the time of his life."

For several hours more the hunt continued, and then they all returned to a temporary camp that Custer had ordered to be set up near Kit Carson. The soldier and civilian cooks and servants left there had evidently become bored while awaiting return of the hunters, and they had been sampling the delicacies and beverages.

"Everybody was drunk and happy," Chalk Beeson said. "Champagne bottles, liquor bottles, and every other kind of bottle littered the ground. That battlefield showed more 'dead ones' than the hunting-ground did buffaloes. Then it was Custer's turn. All that Sheridan had done that morning in the way of cussing was equated and surpassed. I cannot pay his efforts higher compliment than to say that when Custer got through with that bunch they were pretty near sober, and that is cussing some."[14]

George Custer traveled with the Russians back east across Kansas. From an open baggage car, he and Alexis fired shots at buffalo herds along the way.

After returning to Russia, the Grand Duke Alexis eventually was made commander-in-chief of the Russian Navy, a career that one contemporary historian described succinctly as "an outstanding failure." He died in 1908, ten years before his uncle, Czar Nicholas II, was executed by the Bolsheviks to end the dynasty of the Romanovs.

The man who profited most from all the merriment at Camp Alexis and in Colorado was Buffalo Bill Cody. The enormous amount of publicity in the press helped propel the young scout and hunter into show business and started him on his long career as the world's symbol for America's Wild West.

The biggest losers were the herds of buffalo that were already beginning to decline in numbers before Alexis Romanov visited the West to hunt. After his much-heralded adventure, it seemed that every sportsman in the world who possessed a rifle or a revolver decided to emulate the Russian duke. They came to join the army of professional hide-hunters in the great slaughter of the 1870s. By 1883 the buffalo herds were gone, and in 1897 the last wild buffalo in Yellowstone Park was killed, as the species approached extinction.

"To shoot buffalo seems a mania," a frontier army officer wrote six months after the departure of the celebrated royal hunting party. "Many come from London—cockneys, fops and nobles—and from all parts of the Republic to enjoy what they call sport. Sport! When no danger is incurred and no skill required. I see no more sport in shooting a buffalo than in shooting an ox, nor so much danger as there is hunting Texas cattle."[15]

Ten years after the visit of the Grand Duke Alexis, the American West was no longer entirely frontier. Cities large and small were flourishing from Kansas City and Omaha to Denver and San Francisco, but there were still vast areas of Wild West between them, and the cities themselves retained many frontier characteristics.

Most of the inhabitants had come from the East where they had access to the culture of Europe brought by visiting actors, musicians, artists, and lecturers, as well as the nascent culture of young America. Those bearers of entertainment and information who ventured into the West usually found sizable audiences eager to see and hear them.

When Oscar Wilde agreed to a tour of America in 1882, he expected to visit only major cities in the East, but as Duke Alexis had done, he created such a national commotion that he was persuaded to add twenty lectures in the West. In 1882, Wilde was twenty-eight, a taller-than-average man with long arms and large hands. His hair, parted in the middle, was so long that some

Americans thought he was wearing a wig. One observer noted something "womanly" about his mouth, the lips sometimes being painted for stage appearances. He usually wore well-cut English suits while traveling, but for lecturing he donned a costume of knee breeches, silk stockings, patent leather shoes with bright buckles, shirts with Lord Byron collars and frilly lace cuffs, and a cavalier cloak.

Being a natural showman, he added a sunflower in his lapel and often carried a lily in one hand. Americans laughed at all this frippery, but Wilde soon began seeing imitations of his style in audiences and among crowds that greeted him—especially the sunflowers and lilies.

Wilde had recently published a slight book of poems that had been pirated and sold widely in America. A few people had seen Gilbert and Sullivan's *Patience* in which he was satirized, and an occasional cartoon of him as a leader of the aesthetic, or art for art's sake, movement in Britain. Wilde's great literary works were still ahead of him; it was his personality and showmanship combined with the wide readership of newspapers filled with columns about him that created the phenomenon of Oscar Wilde in the American Wild West.

His jumping-off place was Omaha (the same as Duke Alexis's) because the transcontinental railway began there and could take him direct to San Franciso. On the journey he was bored by the Great Plains, saying they reminded him of "a piece of blotting paper." But he was surprised by the crowds that gathered to see him at almost every station stop along the way, and was astonished that in such remote places there were some who knew enough about him to wear imitations of the eccentric costume he had devised. He could not have been aware that most of the imitators were doing this not out of admiration but only for the creation of local merriment. Eventually he grew weary of making appearances on the steps of the rear parlor car, and was relieved when an actor traveling with a troupe aboard the same train offered to substitute for him.

Wilde delighted in his San Franciso reception. He liked what he saw of frontier clothing, and added corduroys and a broad-brimmed white hat to his wardrobe. Back in the East, where short hair was in fashion for men, the press and public had ridiculed his long locks. In California shoulder-length hair was admired, in the tradition of Buffalo Bill and George Custer. "The Western people are much more genial than those in the East," he told a reporter for the San Francisco *Examiner*.[16]

Some members of San Francisco's Bohemian Club invited Wilde to dinner, hoping to get him drunk so they could poke fun at him and his knee breeches, but he outtalked and outdrank the lot of them, and was still sober at dawn. The members were so impressed that they asked him to sit for a portrait to hang in the club. Another feat, undocumented, that supposedly charmed San Francisco's players was his winning a hand of dollar ante with four deuces over three aces and a full house.

From San Francisco, Wilde began his journey to Denver, stopping for one lecture at Salt Lake City where his Mormon audience greeted him with sunflowers in lapels and lilies in their hands. On the train to Denver next day he encountered for the first time copies of his pirated book of poems.

A noisy train butch came down the aisle of the car shouting his wares: "Oscar Wilde's poems for ten cents!"

Wilde supposedly said: "Great God, is it possible my poems have reached such a beastly figure as that?" He grabbed a copy of the book and scolded the boy for "a hellish infringement of the right of an English author."

"Do you suppose the feller that rit the book cares a damn?" asked the boy. "Why, he won't know it."

"I am the author of those poems," Wilde declared.

The train butch of course did not believe him, but when a passenger later informed the boy that the gentleman was indeed Oscar Wilde, he took the poet some oranges as a gift. What seemed to distress Wilde more than the piracy of his book was the wretched way in which it had been reproduced. "Vilely printed on a kind of gray blotting paper," he said.[17]

Denver had made elaborate preparations for the arrival of the great aesthete. The town's mining magnate, Horace A.W. Tabor, ordered his ornate opera house readied for Wilde's appearance, and with other leading citizens had planned a reception at the railroad station. Although the train arrived after dark in the midst of an April snowstorm, the crowd was sizable, many following Wilde's carriage through muddy streets to the opera house.

The managing editor of the *Denver Tribune* at that time was the prankish Eugene Field, lover of practical jokes and much admired for his ability to deflate the hoity-toity in his newspaper columns. Field's readers had expected him to make merry with the renowned Apostle of the Decorative Art. Field, however, commented mildly: "He may be in earnest or he may be a sham." The newspaperman would have his fun with Wilde later, when he returned to Denver for a second appearance after lecturing at Leadville and Colorado Springs.

Leadville boasted that it was the toughest and richest city in the world. The tales of violence that Wilde heard about the place made him reluctant to go there, but Horace Tabor wanted him to address the miners and visit the silver mine that had made Tabor a millionaire.

No welcoming crowd awaited Wilde's arrival in Leadville, nor were there any of the usual curious onlookers in the Clarendon Hotel lobby. This lack of enthusiasm made Wilde uneasy, but he donned his knee breeches and dared to give a lecture on the interior and exterior decorative art of houses. He was interrupted a few times with raucous comments from the miners, and there was only mild applause at the end.

After giving Wilde an opportunity to change into the corduroys and wide-brimmed hat that he had recently acquired, Horace Tabor's retinue took him off for a tour of Leadville's saloons. In one of there garish places of entertainment, he was amused by a sign over the piano: DON'T SHOOT THE PIANIST. HE'S DOING HIS DAMNEDEST. Wilde commented: "The only rational method of art criticism I have ever come across."

Around two o'clock in the morning, Wilde's hosts persuaded him to make a descent into the Matchless Mine. They dressed him in Horace Tabor's India rubber suit, loaded him into an ore bucket, and dropped him down a shaft. Undoubtedly by prearrangement a dozen miners were waiting for him at the bottom, each with a full bottle of spirits. "By invariable Western custom every bottle must make the rounds," the *Denver Tribune* reported next day. "Within a few minutes all have had twelve snorters. The miners without exception are rather dizzy, but Wilde remains cool, steady, and went away showing neither fatigue nor intoxication."[18]

Wilde's schedule now took him to Colorado Springs, from which city he was to return to Denver for another lecture before leaving the West. While on this circuit he added a cowboy neckerchief to his traveling costume, and began tucking his trousers into his boots. The poet, who had come west to teach frontiersmen the art of proper dress, had wound up adopting their style of clothing.

Somehow he missed the scheduled train from Colorado Springs to Denver, but sent a telegram to his representative there, informing him that he would arrive in time for the lecture on a later train. Aware that the delay would disappoint a reception party that was assembling at the railroad station, the representative asked Eugene Field for advice. Should the receptionists be told of the delay, or should they be allowed to wait for three or four more hours?

Field responded with a plan for an elaborate hoax. He knew that most of the nouveau rich who comprised the reception party had never seen Oscar Wilde by daylight or in close proximity, but only on the stage during his previous brief stop in Denver. Field proposed that he impersonate the Apostle of Decorative Art.

Only two or three trusted associates were involved, and although one version of the hoax states the Field merely rode around town in an open carriage, the performance evidently was more creative than that. In one account written some years later, a colleague of Field's, Joseph G. Brown, gave full details of how the hoax was accomplished.

With the aid of friends, Field collected an overcoat with a large fur collar, a broad-brimmed felt hat, a wig of long curly auburn hair, a brilliant cravat, a rose-colored handkerchief, a sunflower for his lapel, and a calla lily to carry in his hand. Driving a buggy to the nearest station south of Denver, Eugene Field, disguised as Oscar Wilde, boarded the train that Wilde had failed to board at Colorado Springs. When it rolled into the Denver station, the reception committee was waiting to greet the honored guest with obsequious cordiality.

"To the cheering crowd on the platform," recalled Joseph Brown, "Field with bared head, bowed gravely. Then followed a leisurely drive through the principal business streets where he created a sensation." Lounging on the carriage seat in a carelessly dramatic attitude, Field pretended to be reading a book, and his performance apparently fooled everybody except those in on the hoax. When the carriage stopped in front of the *Denver Tribune* building where the real Wilde was supposed to be interviewed, the identity of the false Disciple of the Beautiful was exposed.[19]

The impersonation naturally created a considerable amount of merriment in Denver, except among the city's beau monde who had been so easily deceived. Arrival of the genuine Oscar a few hours later was almost an anticlimax.

Immediately after delivering his lecture on the uses of art in houses and clothing, Wilde returned to his Pullman car and was soon on his way to Kansas, the Sunflower State. At Kansas City, he found an audience somewhat diminished because of competition from a traveling circus. One newspaper praised his lecture. Another summed it up: "Throughout the delivery, one was reminded of a college lad scanning stanzas of Vergil...There are some things so infernal bad that they are good, and Mr. Wilde's lecture is one of those things."[20]

And so the frontier West bade farewell to Oscar Wilde, who had come there to instruct its denizens in the finer things of life. Whatever the individual Westerner may have thought of the visitor, all would have agreed that his presence brought a goodly amount of jollity to their lives, whether he intended it or not.

Inquisitive travelers began visiting the American frontier before it moved westward from the Allegheny wilderness, and they grew in numbers as the line of settlement extended toward the Pacific Ocean. Some visitors were delighted by what they encountered; others grudgingly endured the experience. Still others were exceedingly critical—inclined to compare the frontier condition unfavorably with their own habitats—just as some modern Americans travel about Europe deriding everything that is not familiar.

Typical of a few of the early tourists into the Rockies were two
women from Iowa (after that state was no longer frontier). They
were passengers on a stagecoach traveling on the west side of the
range, from Sapinero to Lake City in Colorado. The driver went out
of his way to take them by a site that offered a magnificent view. "It
is beautiful, I suppose," one of the women said, "but I'd rather see
an Iowa cornfield."

The stage driver turned, spat over the wheel, and replied: "So
would a hog, ma'am, so would a hog."

Mountain climbing came into vogue as early as 1860, when
Albert Richardson joined a party of four climbers, including two
women wearing bloomers, for an ascent of Pikes Peak. On the
second day's climb, Richardson noted: "I began to comprehend the
emotions of a pack mule, and to wonder whether a man who would
carry twenty-seven pounds of blankets up Pikes Peak, did not
belong to the long-eared species himself."

Caught in a heavy downpour that afternoon, they made an
early camp under a rock outcropping. "On the third morning we
breakfasted morosely, sore and stiff in every joint. Less than half the
journey was accomplished, and we had but one day's provisions
remaining. One of the ladies had worn through the soles of her shoes
in several places, and both were wet, chilled and exhausted; but they
would not for a moment entertain the idea of turning back." Not
until the end of that day did the climbers reach the base of the peak
itself, every member of the party thoroughly exhausted.

"On the fourth morning ice was lying thick about our camp.
All the party wore a lean and hungry look; but our scanty larder
allowed to each only a little biscuit, a bit of meat as large as a silver
dollar, and ample draughts of tea."

They climbed to the summit that fourth day, under a clear blue
sky, to be awed by the distances their eyes could reach through
atmosphere then unspoiled by pollution. "It seemed impossible to
grow weary of the wonderful picture; but my companions, though
wrapped in heavy blankets, were shivering with the cold. So we iced
and drank a bottle of champagne which a Colorado friend had thrust
into one of the packs; and then, like more ambitious tourists, placed
a record in the empty bottle, which was then carefully re-corked and

buried under a pile of stones.

"We spent a few minutes in the schoolboy pastime of snow-balling. Then, after two hours upon the summit, we reluctantly commenced the descent; for living without eating was becoming a critical experiment."

Two days later, the climbers were back in Colorado Springs. "No lasting inconvenience was experienced from the uncompromising hunger, which continued at intervals for the next two weeks. If 'he is well paid who is well satisfied,' the journey was far the most remunerative any of us had taken."[21]

A large number of western tourists of those frontier days were military men and their wives. General William T. Sherman liked the Rockies and the Pacific Coast, but he thoroughly disliked the South-west and the Great Plains. His remarks about Texas were decidedly uncomplimentary. The Plains, he declared, "were fit only for Nomadic tribes of Indians, Tartars, or Buffaloes...It is impossible to conceive of a more dreary waste."

During one of Sherman's railroad tours through the Southwest in the 1880s, a delegation from the little town of Phoenix traveled to the junction at Maricopa to invite the general to visit them. Sherman wanted to know something about the place. "A paradise," he was told, "lacking only water and a larger measure of good society."[22]

"Hell," replied Sherman, "labors under precisely the same handicaps."

Most wives of ranking officers adjusted better to frontier conditions than did their husbands. Several wrote books about their experiences, and if these women did not at the time enjoy the rigors of tent and garrison life, all of them in retrospect recalled considerable merriment in their adventures. Elizabeth Custer, wife of George Armstrong Custer, was an example of a military wife who could never have endured without a sense of humor. The violent pranks of her husband and his brother, Tom, and their collections of rattlesnakes, raccoons, porcupines, wolves, wildcats, and dozens of mongrel dogs that ran free in camp would have driven a humorless woman to madness. The animals climbed into her bed, gnawed the sheets, chewed tablecloths, and devoured the rations.

"Our tents were usually a menagerie of pets," she said. "The wolf was the only one of the collection to which I objected. I was afraid of him and besides, he kept us, with his nightly howls, surrounded by his fellow vagrants of the plains."[23]

Travelers from Britain were the largest contingent of foreign visitors to the Old West. Whether they were of the nobility or not, Westerners usually referred to all the males as "English Lords." They provided jollity to observers of their outlandish ways, and frontier folk enjoyed deflating their occasional arrogant attitudes.

A visiting duke and a Texas cowboy met in a saloon in Dodge City, and the Englishman offered to buy the Texan a drink. When the duke reached in his pocket for money to pay the barkeep, he chanced to bring out an old English coin. He showed it proudly to the cowboy. "You see the head of his Majesty the King on this coin? He made my grandfather a lord."

The cowboy regarded the strange coin with interest, then reached into his pocket and brought out an Indian-head penny. "See the head of that Indian on this here penny? He made my grandpappy an angel."[24]

Another touring Briton was in a New Mexico saloon one evening when four cowboys, thirsty from all-day range chores, did not stop to dismount and hitch, but rode their horses right into the saloon and up to the bar, jostling the Briton aside. He began complaining bitterly to the barkeep, who fixed a cold eye on the stranger, and retorted: "What the hell are you doing here on foot anyhow?"[25]

Captain John G. Bourke, being the son of Irish immigrants, was naturally amused whenever he encountered a haughty Englishman adrift on the rugged frontier. He described one who dismounted from a stagecoach at an Arizona station in 1880. "In dress and manner and speech, he was the typical 'Bow Bells' Cockney, baggy plaid trousers, cloth gaiters, short sack-coat, little hat with a blue veil, umbrella and goggles—the Henglish tourist's idea of a suitable costume for traveling in the wilds of America."

Bourke went on to relate how the Englishman, after trying to cleanse alkali dust from his face and hands at the stage station wash-up basin, then turned to a dirty towel hung from a peg on the adobe wall. By closing his eyes tight, Bourke said, the Englishman managed to get through with the towel without becoming sick. "The poor fellow thought at the time that that was the dirtiest towel he had ever seen; before he had been in Arizona a week, he learned to look back upon it as one of the daintiest pieces of linen that ever lady's fair hand had embroidered."[26]

A genuine English lord, a certain Sir John, who came to Wyoming for a hunting expedition in the late 1870s, insisted upon transporting a large tin bathtub into the wild country along the North Platte. At Rawlins, where he left the railroad, Sir John employed a local inhabitant to serve as his valet. Each morning for three days the nobleman ordered the valet to fill the tub from the Platte for a bath. On the fourth morning the valet suggested that the labor of filling the tub could be saved if Sir John would take a swim in the river. When his lordship refused, the man from Rawlins retorted angrily: "You ain't quite the top-shelfer you think you is. You ain't even got a shower-bath for cooling your swelled head...but I'll make you a present of one, boss!" Pulling a large revolver from his holster, the temporary valet emptied its contents into the bottom of the tub.[27]

In 1885 a young British visitor, John Fox, got off the train at Cheyenne wearing a brown derby and English riding breeches and leggings. Fox was smart enough to realize that the hilarity he was creating along the streets was brought on by his foreign clothing. He immediately entered a dry goods store and acquired a blue flannel shirt, a pair of denims, a stiff-brimmed cavalry hat, and a pair of cowboy boots—and quickly blended into the environment.

In Carbon, Wyoming, shortly afterward, Fox witnessed an incident that convinced him that he was in the genuine Wild West. As dawn was breaking, a cowboy and a girl came riding along the street at a fast trot. Both were yelling at the tops of their voices, and the cowboy was firing his revolver. "He was evidently well 'lit up' and the noisy female rode astride her pony, her long hair streaming behind her. She had on nothing but a chemise! To a very green young man, born and raised in the sleepiest, most conservative little country town in Wessex, this was Life with a capital L."[28]

With the coming of railroads the number of tourists increased rapidly. This faster method of travel also created new versions of old yarns. Newspaper editors began writing flowery salutes to the Iron Horse. "Today the iron horse is here," announced the *Lubbock Avalanche*, "the first to blow its steam breath into the bracing atmosphere of one of the grandest countries in the world."[29]

The exotic Pullman car was the scene of many a revised version of low-comedy bedroom skits. One such story began with two gentlemen boarding a train in Kansas. Only a single lower berth was available, but they agreed to share it. After an hour of being jogged in the ribs and listening to snores, one of the travelers left the berth and sat down in the conductor's seat in the rear of the car. About midnight a woman got on, demanding Pullman accommodations. The gentleman in the conductor's seat said she could have his share of a lower berth. His little son was there, he explained, but she could lie down if she wished.

She accepted the offer, but the snoring and kicking of the other occupant resumed. "Lie still and be quiet, sonny," said the woman, patting her berth companion on the back.

"Hullo," exclaimed the wakened sleeper. "What's the matter. I'm not your sonny. I'm a member of the Kansas legislature."[30]

To add merriment to weddings, young couples began boarding westbound parlor cars on which the ceremonies were performed while the train was in motion. "Out on the Burlington & Missouri the other day," reported the *Nebraska Herald* of January 12, 1871, "a couple were married, while the cars were going at the rate of 30 miles per hour. Marital matters and things are becoming of such frequent occurrence on our railways that we suggest the keeping of train ministers and doctors to meet cases of emergency."

To gain favorable notice in the local press—stories that often were reprinted in newspapers back east—the western railroads offered editors free rides on special excursions. When dining cars were introduced in the 1870s, local newspapermen were wined and dined, and some wrote glowingly of "flying dining palaces" that served the finest dishes topped off by bourbon, champagne, port, and Havana cigars. In 1872 the *Omaha Bee* observed that "travelers would hardly think that they were taking their meals while going at the rate of 25 miles per hour."[31]

Later on, after the railroads began employing their own publicity writers, the local editors turned on those early ballyhoo artists and accused them of outrageous puffery. "The truth is," said the *Ashland* (Nebraska) *Times*, "a certain literary deadbeat, who, like the rest of his species, is barefooted on top where his brains out to be and wears sandstone goggles to keep him from seeing anything useful,—this peripatetic old sardine, one Prof. Butler, spends his time riding on the road on a free pass."[32]

After the early and somewhat inefficient refrigerator cars were introduced to ship meat and fruits across the West, swift transportation was essential. A traveling Englishman, C. Reginald Enoch, noted various legends scrawled on these cars. "'Rush this through' is a favorite message scrawled in large letters...At one station I beheld a string of refrigerator cars...and upon a board, conspicuously placed, were the words, 'Rush this through like hell—perishable!'"[33]

As the railroads grew more powerful and more arrogant, they lost a good deal of the support that was given to them in the early years by the local press and public. Jokes were made about accidents, unrealistic timetables, and slow trains. Reginald Enoch heard a story about a traveler who was forbidden by the conductor to bring his dog aboard the passenger cars. Knowing how slow the train ran, the traveler allowed his dog to amble along behind the cars. After some distance was covered, the train stopped, and the conductor came into the car and told the dog's owner "that he guessed he had better take his dog aboard, for the gol-darned beast had been running along behind the train and had *licked off all the axle grease!*"[34]

Whenever they could do so, Westerners liked to have fun with the mighty railroads, taunting and teasing, obstructing and annoying. During the time that Ben Thompson, a gambler–gunman–lawman, was marshal of Austin, Texas, the railroad refused to cooperate with him in a certain legal matter, and he resolved to square accounts. An elite daily express train was the pride of the road, keeping to exact schedules, the engineers boasting that watches could be set by their arrivals and departures. One day Ben Thompson drove his buggy upon the track right in front of the locomotive just as it was preparing to pull out. At the first emission of steam, Thompson covered the engineer with his revolver and ordered him to hold the train.

In a leisurely manner the marshal then called to acquaintances on the station platform and carried on bantering talk with them for several minutes while the engineer cursed and fumed. When Thompson was certain that the express would be late at its next station, and probably all along the line, he slowly picked up his reins, slapped his horse into motion, and rolled the buggy off the tracks with a parting shout at the engineer: "You needn't think, sir, that any corporation can hurry me!"[35]

There's a One-Eyed Man in the Game

GAMBLING AND BARROOM DRINKING added to the merriment and the dramatic local color in the dance halls of the frontier. Multitudes of ongoing comedy dramas transpired within barroom walls, and may explain why dance halls (with bars and gaming tables) have been the settings for so many scenes in western novels and films.

In his study of saloons in the Old West, Richard Erdoes catalogued the many uses of that institution. It was an eatery, a hotel, a bath and comfort station, a livery stable, gambling den, bordello, barbershop, courtroom, church, social club, political center, dueling ground, post office, sports arena, undertaker's parlor, museum, trading post, grocery, and ice cream parlor.[1]

According to a visitor to San Francisco in 1849, there were more new gambling establishments in that city "than there are catfish in the Mississippi," and he noted that they all had their own species of "bait" to lure the customers.

"In one is a very handsome Chilano girl, bejeweled like a dowager, who claps down her ounces as if they were so many brass buttons. At another...three comely-looking American girls tend bar, and are deep in the mystery of making rum punches, brandy smashers, and gin cocktails. In one is a band playing Hail Columbia; in another the Scotch Bagpipes are wheezing away Roy's Wife; in another is a man blowing his brains out through a key bugle; in another an Italian, who beats the bass drum, plays the cymbals, plays the Pandean pipes, rings a set of musical bells on his head, and plays on several other instruments, all at the same time; then there is the banjo and the violin, the harps, the hurdy gurdys, and the grinding organs and monkeys. Add to this sweet compound of sound the rattling and jingling of money and dice on the tables, the clinking of glasses, the roaring of some inebriate, the rumbling of carts, the knocking and banging of carpenters, and you have a very faint idea of life in California."[2]

Another visitor to San Francisco the following year so disapproved of entertainment of this sort that he viewed the great fire of May 1850 as an act of retribution when it destroyed a considerable number of gambling and drinking establishments. "The very best part of the city was left in ashes in four or five hours," he recorded in his diary. "Truly it was a visitation of the almighty's and a just one too, the fire it is said commenced in the United States, another gambling house next to the Empire; the Greater part of the houses in the square were those of infamy in fact they could be called nothing short of houses of the Devil. I often thought this would be the end of such places, yet no person but one going in and seeing them could believe the extent to which Gambling and profanity were carried on; they also sold spirits in those places and the walls were hung with pictures of naked women in different poses, as large as life."[3]

The recognized authority, the boss whose responsibility it was to keep the customers happy and simultaneously to maintain order, was usually the bartender, who more than likely was also the owner. As Mark Twain put it, "the cheapest and easiest way to become an influential man and be looked up to by the community at large was to stand behind a bar, wear a cluster-diamond pin, and sell whiskey."[4]

Any good bartender arriving in a new boom town could always find plenty of help in getting a saloon started. When Joe King stopped at Salida, Colorado, in 1880, he immediately saw the need for a saloon, but could not obtain any lumber to construct one. A group of miners and mule skinners came to his aid. They hijacked a train of freight wagons loaded with lumber bound for Leadville, and removed enough boards to build a shanty. Anticipating the bartender's next requirement, they secured two barrels of whiskey in a similar manner. One of the miners donated a tin cup, and Joe King stepped behind his bar and began a brisk business.[5]

The ethics and social responsibility of bartenders, however, were not always of the highest grade. Some enjoyed taking advantage of tenderfeet, especially naive cowboys from Texas and soldiers recently arrived from the East. Richard Ackley, who worked a bar near Fort Kearney, Nebraska, in 1858, said it was common practice to mix whiskey with large amounts of water and then sell it for a dollar a pint, or three dollars for filling a soldier's canteen. "After our whiskey began to get low," Ackley said, "I used to cut up a lot of tobacco and mix with it to give it strength, and then put in plenty of water. If they only wanted a drink we charged twenty-five cents and measured it out to them."[6]

On the other hand, bartenders usually had a soft spot in their hearts for ministers of the gospel, although professionally they were arch-rivals, especially on Sundays. During the boom days of the 1880s in Gunnison, Colorado, Fat Jack's Place and the Red Light Dance Hall had a standing rule that their orchestras would always observe the Sabbath by playing only sacred music on Sunday evenings for the patrons to dance by.

"It was by no means an uncommon sight to see sundry couples cavorting about on the floor of a Sabbath evening," George Root recalled, "the 'ladies' bedecked and bespangled in brief and extravagantly décolleté dresses, with their sturdy companions, garbed in miner's costume of khaki, or the smart outfit of a successful gambler, or perchance the outfit of a cowboy—buckskin breeches with wide fringes running down the legs, pants tucked in boots, spurs on their high-heeled footwear, blue flannel shirt, red bandanna tied loosely about the neck with the knot at the back, a wide-brimmed hat covering their usually unkempt hair, and a brace of sixguns strapped to their hips. These were the sort of patrons who celebrated every evening, Sunday included, at which time they tripped the 'light fantastic toe' to the strains of such good old hymns as 'Jesus, Lover of My Soul' or 'The Beautiful Gates Ajar.' Other old-time sacred standbys, written to common or four-four time, also apparently served the crowd as satisfactorily while they went through the evolutions and convolutions of the old-time square dancing. No stranger could set foot in one of these dance halls without being importuned to have at least one dance or to stand treat—the 'ladies' receiving a certain percentage on every dance or treat."[7]

In towns where the competition was fierce, operators of these centers of entertainment were among the earliest users of advertising, and they learned how to exploit everything in the public eye in order to attract customers. In Fort Scott, Kansas, which had more saloons than any other type of business, Joseph Darr (who called himself General Darr) was the leading promoter among the saloon keepers.

When the Fort Scott officials passed a law to destroy all dogs running at large after a certain date, General Darr advertised that he would serve a "Dog Lunch" to celebrate the occasion. The local newspaper, of course, carried a notice of the lunch, which consisted of highly flavored bologna sausage. "The General calls it 'Dog Lunch' and says it will be served regularly, every day at 10 A.M. All are invited."

Soon afterward Darr announced that he had acquired a splendid piano presided over by a first-class musician, and promised that a splendid violinist would soon be added. "The General also informs us," the newspaper continued, "that he has engaged the professional services of a leading prima donna of one of the eastern opera troupes, who will shortly make her *debut* in Fort Scott. These attractions together with the 'Dog Lunch,' the General thinks will 'swell the receipts enormously.'"[8]

Although they were peripatetic by nature, seldom staying long in one town, gamblers were necessary components of the saloon and dance hall setting. When customers came for recreation, they expected gambling to be a part of the program, and they preferred to lose their money to a well-dressed gentleman instead of to a crude tin-horn lout who dressed no better than they did.

Most of the elegant gamblers who came west had learned their profession on Mississippi riverboats. They considered themselves to be aristocrats, and dressed the part. They usually wore black, with long tails on the coats, and they fancied frilled shirts and silk hats. They displayed considerably more expensive jewelry than their colleagues, the bartenders.

Gamblers by the hundreds followed the building of the railroads westward. Whenever a newly created town gave some evidence of being permanent, some of these "knights of the green table" would linger a few months in the better saloons and dance halls. Many preferred not to use their real names, adopting sobriquets. In Cheyenne, Wyoming, during the 1870s the leading gamblers were known as Poker Dan, Whiffletree Jim, Coon Can Kid, Squirrel Tooth, and Timberline. Significantly, there was one called The Preacher. Because members of both professions dressed in black, at first sight a gambler was often mistaken for a preacher until his diamond rings and stickpins came into view.

The Cheyenne gamblers arrived with the Union Pacific Railroad builders, and remained for a while when they recognized the permanence of the place. Hundreds of others, however, followed the successive Hell on Wheels towns—so called because they were "gambling hells" moved on wheeled railroad cars— that sprang up as temporary tent camps at the end of track, and then would move on to the next camp.

One such town was Benton, fifty miles west of Medicine Bow. During its heyday in 1868, Benton had twenty-three saloons and five dance halls, with an accompanying army of gamblers. In two weeks Benton became a city of three thousand people, with a mayor and aldermen, a daily newspaper, and numerous land speculators.

"The streets were eight inches deep in white dust as I entered the city of canvas tents and pole-houses," said newspaper correspondent John H. Beadle. "The suburbs appeared as banks of dirty white linen, and a new arrival with black clothes looked like nothing so much as a cockroach struggling through a flour barrel."

Beadle went on to describe "the great institution of Benton, the 'Big Tent,' sometimes with equal truth but less politeness, called the 'Gamblers' Tent.' The structure was a nice frame, a hundred feet long and forty feet wide, covered with canvas and conveniently floored for dancing to which and gambling it was entirely devoted...

"As we enter, we note that the right side is lined with a splendid bar, supplied with every variety of liquors and cigars, with cut glass goblets, ice-pitchers, splendid mirrors, and pictures rivaling those of our Eastern cities. At the back a space huge enough for one cotillion is left open for dancing; on a raised platform, a full band is in attendance day and night, while all the rest of the room is filled with tables devoted to monte, faro, rondo coolo, fortune-wheels, and every other species of gambling known. I acknowledge a morbid curiosity relating to everything villainous, and though I never ventured a cent but once in my life, I am never weary of watching the game, and the various fortunes of those who 'buck against the tiger.'

"During the day the 'Big Tent' is rather quiet, but at night, after a few inspiring tunes at the door by the band, the long hall is soon crowded with a motley throng of three or four thousand miners, ranchers, clerks, 'Bullwhackers,' gamblers, and 'cappers.'* The brass instruments are laid aside, the string-music begins, the cotillions succeed each other rapidly, each ending with a drink, while those not so employed crowd around the tables and enjoy each his favorite game. Tonight is one of unusual interest, and the tent is full, while from every table is heard the musical rattle of the dice, the hum of the wheel, or the eloquent voice of the dealer. Fair women, clothed with richness and taste, in white and airy garments, mingle with the throng, watch the games with deep interest, or laugh and chat with the players. The wife of the principal gambler—a tall, spiritual and most innocent looking woman—sits by his side, while their children, two beautiful little girls of four and six years, run about the room playing and shouting with merriment, climbing upon the knees of the gamblers and embraced in their rude arms, like flowers growing on the verge of frightful precipices...

"The evening wears along, many visitors begin to leave, the games languish, and a diversion is needed. The band gives a few lively touches, and a young man with a capacious chest and a great deal of 'openness' in his face, mounts the stand and sings a variety of sentimental and popular songs, ending with a regular rouser, in the chorus of which he constantly reiterates—in other words however—that he is a bovine youth with a vitreous optic 'which nobody can deny.' As he wears a revolver and bowie-knife in plain view, nobody seems inclined to deny it. A lively dance follows, the crowd is enlivened, and gambling goes on with renewed vigor."[9]

In Virginia City, Nevada, during this period, the dance halls

---

* A capper was a gambler's confederate who was allowed to win large sums of money to decoy the suckers into making reckless bets.

were slightly more refined, with a false air of permanence about them. While the Civil War was still raging in the East, the nation's foremost humorist, Artemus Ward (Charles Farrar Browne) stopped at that turbulent mining town during a lecture tour. In company with his publicist, Edward Hingston, and Mark Twain of the *Territorial Enterprise*, Ward toured Virginia City's centers of amusement.

"As we ramble through it in the evening," Hingston reported, "we find innumerable dance-houses wherein miners in their red shirts are dancing to the music of hurdy-gurdys played by itinerant maidens. At Sutcliffe's Melodeon a ball is taking place, and at the Niagara Concert Hall there are crowds assembled round the door, while from within come forth the sounds of negro minstrelsy, with the clack of bones and the twang of banjos."[10]

The dance hall with its bar downstage was the setting for countless scenes of merriment that included spontaneous skits, one-liners, and entire situation comedies. These entertainments still survive in bastardized form in cinema and television plays about the American frontier.

For instance, during Eugene Field's days as reporter for the *Denver Tribune*, he was the leading performer in a number of extemporaneous light comedies in Perrin's Saloon. One evening when he approached the bar for a drink, the proprietor, Wesley Perrin, showed him a due bill for $31.25, and demanded that he first pay something on the arrears. Field protested that he was broke, like most newspapermen of the 1880s.

Because he admired Field, Perrin abruptly tore the bill into bits. Then he informed Field that his bill was paid. "You don't owe me a cent," Perrin said, "but don't try to run up any more bills, especially by ordering drinks for customers who would otherwise pay me in cash."

Field immediately expressed his thanks, continuing to do so while Perrin began locking up the saloon for the night. "It's time to close, Gene," Perrin said, "and time for you to get to work at the paper."

Field began strutting back and forth in front of the bar.

"Come on," Perrin called. "I could be fined for not locking up on time."

"I'm waiting for my due," Field declared.

"You've got more than your due," Perrin retorted. "What do you want now?"

"Don't you know?" Field answered. "Don't you know that it is a custom among gentlemen that when a customer's bar bill is paid, the bartender must set 'em up?"

Perrin locked the door from the inside, dimmed the lights, and set a bottle and a glass on the bar. Field took his drink leisurely, and then departed, with a cordial "good night" to the outdone Wesley Perrin.[11]

In the back country of Colorado around this same time, there were frequent alarms of Ute Indian uprisings that ingenious men turned to their advantage, sometimes unintentionally creating comic skits in barrooms. On a cold October night a man named McCann rode up to the door of Jimmie Howard's saloon in Howardsville. He dashed breathlessly to the bar. "Git up and git out of here," McCann shouted. "The Indians have massacred everybody in Animas City and are moving on Silverton. I have got dispatches for the governor for arms and troops and am going to Antelope Springs before daylight. Jimmie! Give me a drink!"

As it turned out, the entire monologue was the invention of McCann, who had no funds but was thirsting for a drink against the chill of the autumn night.[12]

In 1876 the population of Dodge City, Kansas, numbered twelve hundred, and for their recreation the inhabitants had a choice of nineteen saloons and dance halls. Most of these places depended, of course, upon transient trade. Into one of the saloons an unwashed buffalo hunter strode one day, taking a seat and propping his feet on the table. He demanded a glass of beer, a sandwich, and some Limburger cheese, all of which were served him promptly. After a minute or so, he shouted a complaint to the proprietor: "This cheese is no good. I can't smell it!"

The proprietor shouted back: "Damn it, take your feet down, and give the cheese a chance."[13]

In 1877 the *Dodge City Times* printed a news item that illuminates the contemporary difference in status between dance hall girls and gambling gunmen: "Miss Frankie Bell, who wears the belt for superiority in point of muscular ability, heaped epithets upon the unoffending head of Mr. Earp to such an extent as to provoke a slap from the ex-officer, besides creating a disturbance of the quiet and dignity of the city, for which she received a night's lodging in the dog house and a reception at the police court next morning, the expense of which was about $20. Wyatt Earp was assessed the lowest limit of the law, one dollar." This news account no doubt entertained the masculine readers of Dodge City, but it was certainly not amusing to the dance hall girls.[14]

What may have been one of the first strip teases in a frontier dance hall was reported by a Scottish poet, James Thomson, author of "The City of Dreadful Night." Thomson worked for a Colorado mining company during the 1870s, and while off duty at Central City he attended a "prostitutes' ball." According to Thomson, prizes were offered for the best dancer, and after the same girl won four times, she refused to accept the fifth award, and instead undressed down to the stockings and garters. She danced to the lively music for "five wonderful minutes," and concluded her performance with a bit of chanted doggerel: "Here's the leg that can dance, and here's the arse that can back it up!" After that she put her clothes back on and danced with the others until daylight.[15]

And what of the ordinary women of a frontier town who might occasionally want to visit a saloon to view the action and perhaps have a drink? There was very little of that, the males having divided females into two classes, the reputable and disreputable, the good and the bad. Eventually, however, in some of the larger towns, saloon proprietors outfitted "wine rooms" into which reputable women were admitted through a side entrance. A few establishments went so far as to install roulette wheels in the wine rooms, so that women customers could gamble there, but as one woman complained, "It was a very tame affair...and you got only a rumble from the front, where things were really doing."[16]

Results of the division of frontier women into "good and bad" was manifested in typical fashion at Alamosa, Colorado, when a drunk wandered out of a saloon and molested a lady on the street. Next morning his hanged body was swinging above the sidewalk with a large placard attached:

ALAMOSA PERTECKS HER WIMMEN

Like many great institutions throughout history, the saloons and dance halls gradually passed their prime and went into a decline with the ending of the nineteenth century. On January 10, 1897, the *Anaconda* (Montana) *Standard* printed this observation about one of the leading drinking places in the state's capital city of Helena: "At the upper end of Main Street is a one-horse beer hall, called by courtesy a concert garden, where a pianist and violinist have performed so far without getting shot. Occasionally a woman, whose face would stop a freight train and a voice that would rasp a sawmill, comes out and assists the pianist and violinist in increasing the agony."

During the early years of the twentieth century, temperance advocates and prohibition laws began drying up entire towns. Armed with a hatchet, a muscular six-foot-tall, 175-pound woman named Carry Nation invaded saloons to intimidate bartenders and their customers. She smashed bottles, barrels, mirrors, and paintings of nude courtesans.

In 1907 a Ponca City, Oklahoma, saloon proprietor—condemned to close his bar by a local prohibition law—summed up the situation by posting this sign above his entrance door:

HUSH LITTLE SALOON
DON'T YOU CRY
YOU'LL BE A DRUG STORE
BY AND BY.[17]

CHAPTER FOUR

Making the Calico Crack

OF ALL THE MERRY-MAKINGS on the frontier, dancing was the most popular because it was inexpensive and quickly created an aura of friskiness in the midst of straitened environs. Dancing also afforded men and women opportunities for close encounters with each other, although this was not essential at gatherings of miners and cowboys. Whether women were available or not, the frontiersmen *would* dance, half of them tying bandannas around their arms to signify female roles in the dance. This enabled the square-dance sets to proceed smoothly when the caller cried out: "Gents to the right, ladies to the left, promenade to the bar" or "Last dance, gentlemen, before the girls go home."

Although dancing was frowned upon by some religious sects, it was incorporated into the practices of others. Brigham Young considered dancing an "innocent amusement" and encouraged the Mormons "to go forth in the dance in an acceptable manner before the Lord."

In 1792, Archibald Menzies, a naturalist traveling with the explorer George Vancouver, attended a dance at the Spanish governor's house in Monterey, California. The agility of the Spanish ladies fascinated Menzies. "They danced some Country dances," he reported, "but even in this remote region, they seemed most attached to the Spanish exhilarating dance the Fandango, a performance which requires no little elasticity of limbs as well as nimbleness of capers & gestures. It is performed by two persons of different sex who dance either to the Guittar alone or accompanied with the voice; they traverse the room with such nimble evolutions, wheeling about, changing sides and smacking with their fingers at every motion; sometimes they dance close to each other, then retire, then approach again, with such wanton attitudes and motions, such leering looks, sparkling eyes & trembling limbs, as would decompose the gravity of a Stoic."

Before Menzies and Captain Vancouver came to California, they had visited the Sandwich Islands (present-day Hawaii) and invited a party of the islanders to travel with them to America. At the suggestion of the Englishmen, the islanders exhibited to the Spaniards their manner of singing and dancing, which was probably some variation of the hula. "It did not appear to afford much entertainment to the Spanish ladies," Menzies said. "Indeed I believe they thought this crude performance was introduced by way of ridiculing their favorite dance the Fandango, as they soon after departed."[1]

About half a century later, a Frenchman named Ernest de Massey came to California and found that dancing was still the rage: "The Spanish–Americans are fond of dancing, and music furnished by the mandolin and guitar is always in evidence. The whole place is thus kept in an uproar and everyone appears to be either angry or drunk. This lasts until midnight; it is enlivened by a few fights and frays."[2]

In 1846 Edwin Bryant noted that the California ladies danced with much ease and grace. "The waltz appears to be a favorite with them. Smoking is not prohibited in these assemblies, nor is it confined to the gentlemen. The *cigarita* is freely used by the señoras and señoritas, and they puff it with much gusto while threading the mazes of the cotillon or swinging in the waltz."[3]

During this same period, dancing was as popular along the Mississippi valley frontier as it was on the West Coast, although the styles and settings were of a much earthier sort. In 1838, Friedrich Gerstäcker, a German traveler and hunter, attended a Fourth of July frolic in the foothills of the Ouachita Mountains:

"The sound of a solitary fiddle had been perceptible at a distance, and sure enough, when I arrived, I found dancing going on amongst the younger folk, in one of the wings of the double house. I had never succeeded in acquiring the dances of my own country, much less the extraordinary movements of those of America; so I amused myself with looking on, and watching the arrivals ... A great number of the young women were light and had graceful figures, and looked very interesting on horseback, their cheeks flushed with their quick ride. But they seemed as if they were going on a pilgrimage, instead of coming to a ball—for each fair dame had a bundle of tolerable size at her saddle-bow …

"I sauntered about among the various groups, and occasionally visited the ballroom—if the interior of a log-house, about sixteen feet by twenty, can be so called. The air within was hot, almost to suffocation, but the sight was at times too pretty, at times too comic to be quickly deserted. Indeed, most of the girls, beating time with their little feet in jigs, reels, and hornpipes, were pretty enough to chain to the spot any worshipper of natural beauty."

Gerstäcker was fascinated by the fiddler, the sole musician in action, who passed "abruptly from the wildest allegro to the most dolorous of the dolefuls, and then breaking off suddenly to ask me for a quid of tobacco." When Gerstäcker replied that he had no tobacco, the fiddler complained that he had received only two bottles of whiskey for his performance, and had drunk both, but his throat was still dry. He looked wildly round, began to cry, and fell sobbing on the neck of a thin man in a blue coat, burying his head in the man's large cravat. Thereupon, some of the disgruntled male dancers seized the drunken fiddler by the arms and legs and unceremoniously carried him out into the yard.

"Dancing, of course, ceased during this little intermezzo, and one of the party offered to find a sober fiddler; but as the amusement would have been interrupted too long by waiting for him, a tall lad placed himself in front of the chimney, turned up his sleeves with the utmost gravity, bent his knees a little, and began slapping them in time with the palms of his hands; in two minutes all was going on with as much spirit as before.

"At length the promised musician arrived, not however in the promised condition; but a connoisseur near me remarked that he would do till twelve o'clock.

"To my astonishment, I observed several of the young ladies in white dresses, whom I was almost sure I had seen in dark dresses; but, as I never paid much attention to such things, I thought I must have been mistaken."

Gerstäcker was not mistaken, however. As he soon discovered, some of the women had changed dresses more than once. The bundles he had observed each "fair dame" carrying at her saddle-bow upon arrival contained the spare costumes.

"Some changed their dresses five times between noon and the following morning. It would be as incorrect to dance for a whole night in the same dress as in Europe to appear without gloves, which latter articles were thought quite unnecessary here.

"A little after twelve ... the second fiddler was carried out and laid on the grass, while a third was soon found to take his place. By this time I was tired and sleepy, so I stretched myself under a tree, with my head on an old grindstone, and in spite of the hard pillow and squeaking fiddle, I slept soundly till morning.

"When the sun sent his hot rays over the trees into the clearing, dancing was still going on, and the ground was covered with sleeping figures. Preparations were soon made for departure. The horses, which had been tied to the bushes or fence, or driven into an enclosure, and had been well supplied with maize, were quickly saddled, and troop after troop of men and women disappeared in the thick green forest."[4]

A quarter of a century after Gerstäcker's Fourth of July dance, James Pike, traveling north from Texas in 1861, was invited to a wedding dance in the same area. Pike found the dancing to be as vigorous as his predecessor had described it, with perhaps a bit more style added to the performance.

"Forty or fifty stalwart men—real men of the forest—were there, with checkered coats and what had been linen standing collars on heavy cotton shirts with no bosoms; but alas! exercise in a hot climate in midsummer generates sweat, and sweat will tell upon standing collars; and theirs were clinging to the neck like wet rags; they likewise had on striped home-made pants, and very heavy cowhide boots.

"Some of the girls were truly handsome. I never was much of a critic of ladies' clothing, and therefore, I will not here undertake to describe the outline, except to say that the dresses were of very costly material, and made after the very latest rustic fashion, and each one was highly pleased with her appearance.

"On a kitchen table sat a very big, and certainly, a very black negro, playing the violin, and calling off, in mellifluous sing-song tones, tuning his voice to the music of the instrument, perfectly. There were two cotillions on the floor, whirling and twirling, to the giddy mazes of the dance ... By the side of the fiddler sat a veteran banjo picker, who added much to the effect of the music ...

"The dance was exceedingly amusing. The girls moved very lightly and with considerable grace; but the men made a tremendous lumbering over the loose puncheon floor. When it came to the 'balance all,' the heeling and toeing of those heavy boots was positively horrifying, but the 'swing' was rendered with such a hearty good will, and the girls seemed to enjoy it so well, that I almost wished I was a dancer myself.

"The bride showed us to the supper room ... We did justice to the viands, and then went back to the dance. The bride was anxious to dance with me; at least her uncle told me so; and I felt considerably abashed, when I told him I could not dance. Not to be able to dance, in Arkansas, is as bad as to be no horseman in Texas. The bride went through one set with her uncle, who appeared to be about the best dancer in the house. The girls all seemed to vie with her, which made me conclude that they wished themselves in her place; while the lady herself acted and looked as pretty as she knew how.

"The fiddler threw all his powers into his playing and his stentorian voice ... It was a complete and graphic picture of good old fashioned social life. Indeed the dancers exerted themselves so long, and well, that the puncheons seemed to take up their spirit, and appeared as if endeavoring to extemporize a hornpipe on their own hook. I had often heard the old story of the man in Arkansas who gathered up half a bushel of toe nails on his floor, after a dance; and I was scarcely inclined to doubt its truth, after what I witnessed on that night.

"We enjoyed ourselves hugely, till after twelve o'clock, when we went back to my friend's house."[5]

In Virginia City, Nevada, during this same period of the Civil War, twenty-six-year-old Mark Twain was having his troubles with the Virginia reel, trouble caused mainly by the long trailing dresses of his partners in the dance. "When the ladies were ordered to the center," he said, "two of them got there and the other two moved off gallantly, but they failed to make the connection. They suddenly broached to under full headway, and there was a sound of parting canvas. Their dresses were anchored under our boots, you know. It was unfortunate, but it could not be helped. Those two beautiful pick dresses let go amidships, and remained in a ripped and damaged condition to the end of the ball."

After an intermission for dinner, Twain returned to the fray, determined to master the Virginia reel, which he described in military terms in the account he wrote for his newspaper, *The Territorial Enterprise.* "The dancers are formed in two long ranks, facing each other, and the battle opens with some light skirmishing between the pickets, which is gradually resolved into a general engagement along the whole line; after that you have nothing to do but stand by and grab every lady that drifts within reach of you, and swing her. It is very entertaining, and elaborately scientific also."

In concluding his account, Twain saluted the fiddler. "We consider that the man who can fiddle all through one of those Virginia Reels without losing his grip, may be depended upon in any kind of musical emergency."[6]

During the bustling years after the Civil War, the Army followed the frontier westward, exposing many a simple-hearted young American to unfamiliar customs. In the Southwest a fandango was no longer the particular animated dance that had delighted visitors to California half a century earlier. A fandango was now an entertainment, or sport as one observer called it, an evening's amusement that included several Mexican dances as well as some that were introduced by United States soldiers, all accompanied by certain social procedures and considerable consumption of strong drink.

In 1870 a young officer stationed at Fort Reynolds, on the Arkansas River in southern Colorado, was highly amused by the whole process of creating and staging a fandango in the nearby village of Huerfano. An Indian scout for the Army, Bill Autobey, ran the village with the help of his three sons. When the notion struck the Autobeys, they would buy a couple of gallons of cheap whiskey, two or three pounds of candy, and a box of candles. They would then invite young and old in the nearby communities. Autobey himself would pass the word around Fort Reynolds: "Boys, a fandango tonight."

According to the young officer, "The boys apply for a pass and generally get one from retreat of today until reveille tomorrow. You go down to the Huerfano and enter a dirty-looking and dilapidated hall, made of adobes, and lighted up with eight candles, a bar at one end, the fiddler in the other, two rows of benches on each side of the hall, and one side filled with Mexican ladies, and the other with citizens and United States soldiers.

"The fiddler strikes up, the men go over to the girls and ask them to dance. They never speak, but nod their heads, signifying 'Yes' or 'No,' but generally 'Yes.' Then the dance commences, the soldiers generally preferring to dance quadrilles, waltzes, polkas, and schottisches, because they know them the best, while the Mexicans prefer their own native dances, such as the coonda, mendita, and slow waltz. After you get through the dance the woman leaves you very abruptly, you following for your hat, she for her shawl. She hands you her shawl, turns her back to you, and you adjust the shawl upon her shoulders and then she sits down. You then rush up to the bar, call for one glass of whiskey, one glass of water, and some candy. The whiskey costs you twenty-five cents, the water nothing. The articles are placed upon a salver, and you go to the lady and tell her to help herself. She generally takes the candy, and you of course drink the whiskey. The fandango is kept in this way all evening, until it breaks up in a row, which it generally does before twelve or one o'clock. The row sometimes is among the 'boys in blue,' but more generally among the Mexicans.

"The Mexicans are very cute.* They never spend money for dancing, but rather too freely indulge among themselves. Uncle Sam's boys pay the whole bill for fandangos. I have known a Mexican woman to fill her pockets with candy, given her by soldier admirers and other women, and then go around by the back door and hand it to the proprietor to resell.

"There is much fun to see at these fandangos in the fore part of

---

* Used in the contemporary sense—sharp or acute.

the evening. The women are gayly dressed, and consider themselves 'some pumpkins'…The fandango is a great institution, and, as I said before, it generally breaks up in a row. Some Mexican getting knocked over, knives are drawn, women scream and rush out of the window, pistols are fired, and the 'boys in blue' leave for camp, pretty full, and nobody hurt. Thus ends a Mexican fandango in Colorado Territory. It is the only sport among Mexicans and soldiers upon the plains."[7]

During that same lively decade of the 1870s, Captain John G. Bourke was stationed in the Southwest, as aide to General George Crook. He attended his first Mexican ball in Tucson, where the women "sat upon wooden benches extending around the room, and without backs, so that to save dresses from the lime on the walls it was necessary to sit bolt upright."

No introduction was necessary to obtain a dancing partner, Bourke discovered. "If a gentleman wished to dance with a lady, he asked her, and she accepted or declined at her option. After each dance it was de rigueur to invite your partner to partake of 'dulces,' or refreshments, and in all cases those invitations were accepted, not that the young lady always ate what was purchased for her; frequently she would take the 'pasas' (raisins), 'bollos' (sweet-cakes) or other refection, wrap them up in her handkerchief and keep them to take home. Those who wished it could have 'mescal' or 'wine.' In Arizona this 'wine' is mostly 'imported' and a viler decoction of boiled vinegar, logwood, alum, and copper as never was bottled.

"The ladies had a curious method of expressing their preference for a gentleman; this was done by breaking a 'cascarron' (literally 'eggshell'), or eggshell filled with cologne water or finely cut gold paper. The recipient of this delicate compliment had to return it in kind and then to lead the young lady in the dance. The energetic musicians extorted something like music from their wheezy mouth-organs and tinkling harps. This is my recollection of a Tucson 'baile,' barren and meagre enough it looks to me now, but there was a time when my companions and myself thought nothing of staying at one of them all night and of going to six in a week if we could."[8]

In the mining communities of the West, the only places with enough floor space for dancing were the saloons. Consequently that popular form of recreation was soon combined with gambling, prostitution, and hard drinking. Among other names, these places were called hurdy-gurdy houses, cantinas, whoop-ups, or plain dance halls.

"Representatives of almost every dancing nation of white folks may be seen on the floor of the Hurdy-Gurdy houses," Thomas J. Dimsdale said of those he frequented in the gold rush town of Virginia City, Montana, in 1863. The dance hall women themselves were called "hurdy-gurdies," and sometimes they danced in a uniform of sorts, although the more popular ones could afford to wear fine clothes, and dressed in the most fashionable of costumes.

Dimsdale described one of the latter: "There she stands at the head of the set. She is of middle height, of rather full and rounded form; her complexion as pure as alabaster, a pair of dangerous looking hazel eyes, a slightly Roman nose, and a small and prettily formed mouth. Her auburn hair is neatly banded, and gathered in a tasteful, ornamented net, with a roll and gold tassels at the side. How sedate she looks during the first figure, never smiling till the termination of 'promenade, eight,' when she shows her little white hands in fixing her handsome brooch in its place, and settling her glistening earrings. See how nicely her scarlet dress, with its broad black band around the skirt, and its black edging, sets off her dainty figure. No wonder that a wild mountaineer would be willing to pay—not one dollar, but all he has in his purse—for a dance and an approving smile from so beautiful a woman."

The "wild mountaineers" did pay a dollar in gold for each set, and they usually danced in their knee boots equipped with spurs, and seldom removed their wide-brimmed hats from their heads, or their loaded revolvers and sheath knives from their belts. Dimsdale described a typical male dancer: "In the corner of his mouth is a cigar, which rolls like the lever of an eccentric as he chews the end in his mouth. After an amazingly grave salute, 'all hands round' is shouted by the prompter, and off bounds the buckskin hero, rising and falling to the rhythms of the dance, with a clumsy agility, and a growing enthusiasm testifying his huge delight. His fair partner, with practiced foot and easy grace, keeps time to the music like a clock, and rounds to her place as smoothly and gracefully as a swan.

As the dance progresses, he of the buckskins gets excited, and nothing but long practice prevents his partner from being swept off her feet … "[9]

Across the West during the years of railroad building, of increased military activity, of repeated gold and silver strikes, and of trail drives to numerous cowtowns along the railroads, the dance halls became a considerable industry. Because they provided a high return of profit to their owners, rivalry for customers was often keen. As one cowboy put it, "If you did not come in to dance, they would grab you and pull you in, whether you wanted to dance or not. All the girls acted glad to see you. Round after round of drinks, then all hands would dance."[10]

CHAPTER FIVE

Stringing the Greeners

EVERYONE WHO WENT WEST was in the beginning a tenderfoot, greenhorn, or pilgrim, the nomenclature for newcomers varying by time and place. They were the most frequent targets for practical jokes and elaborate confidence games—in other words, sources for black comedy.

One tenderfoot arrived from the East in a frontier mining town to find himself in a poker game with a grizzled old prospector. Luck was with the tenderfoot, who won most of the hands. After being dealt a super hand, he said apologetically: "This is downright robbery. I don't want to bankrupt you, sir. But here goes." He threw down four aces and reached for the money in the pot.

"Hold on," his opponent the miner cried. "Hold on. I'll take care of that pot, if you please."

"But look, I just threw down four aces—see."

"Well, what of it," said the miner. "I've got a looloo."

The stranger was dumbfounded. "A looloo? What's a looloo?"

"Any three clubs with two diamonds. I guess you ain't accustomed to our poker rules, pilgrim. Looky there." And he pointed to a pasteboard sign on the saloon wall which read: A LOOLOO BEATS FOUR ACES.

"All right," said the tenderfoot. "I'm still game." A few minutes later a big smile lit up his face. He bet heavily, and put down his cards. "There's a looloo," he said. "Three clubs and two diamonds."

The miner shook his head. "This is really too bad, stranger," he said. "You just don't understand the rules out here, do you? Look up there on the wall behind you." The greenhorn turned and looked, and there was another pasteboard sign that read: THE LOOLOO CAN BE PLAYED BUT ONCE IN A NIGHT.[1]

Now that was a double sting, quite prevalent in the tenderfoot humor of the West.

Teasing susceptible young women was also a favorite sport of veteran frontiersmen. William A. Wallace, Texas Ranger and Indian fighter, generally known as "Big Foot" Wallace, was a notorious teaser. He so loved the ladies that during the Civil War instead of going east to fight Yankees he stayed on the Texas frontier, dedicating himself to the protection of the womenfolk of the absent Confederate soldiers.

Big Foot once warned an impressionable belle from Kentucky to beware of a varmint in west Texas called the "Santa Fe." It was much worse than the tarantula, Wallace told her. The creature was equipped with a hundred legs and a sting on each one, two lethal stings in its forked tail, and fangs as large as a rattlesnake's. A person stung only with the Santa Fe's legs might live an hour, Wallace said, but if stung by all stingers, the victim would live no more than twenty minutes.

Observing the expression of dread on the face of his young listener, Big Foot built upon his story. Anyone struck by the Santa Fe's fangs would turn blue, he continued, then yellow, and finally a beautiful bottle-green, after which the victim's hair and fingernails would drop off.

"Oh, my, Mr. Wallace," cried the belle from Kentucky, "how have you managed to live so long in that horrible country?"

"Why, you see, Miss," he replied, "with my tarantula boots made of alligator skin, and my centipede hunting shirt made of tanned rattlesnake's hides, I have escaped pretty well, but these don't protect you against the stinging scorpions, cow-killers, and scaly-back chinches that crawl about at night when you are asleep. The only way to keep them at a distance is to chaw tobacco and drink whisky, and that is the reason why the Temperance Society never flourished in Texas."

"Oh," said the young woman, "what a horrible country that must be, where people have to be stung to death, or else chaw tobacco and drink whisky. I don't know which is the worst."

"Well," said Big Foot, "the people out there don't seem to mind it much; they get used to it after while. In fact they seem to like it, for they chaw tobacco and drink whisky even in the winter time when the cow-killers and stinging lizards are all frozen up."[2]

Tormenters of tenderfeet occasionally found the tables turned upon them, especially if the intended victim was as foolhardy as a young English remittance man who fell into the clutches of some Texas gamblers in San Antonio. Although the naive Etonian was virtually robbed of his total wealth of four hundred pounds at a roulette table, he gamely went out upon the streets and peddled fruit until he earned twenty-five cents. As that amount was sufficient to admit him to the gambling house for one cut of the cards, he returned. On the first cut, the dealer won by palming a card so carelessly that the young Englishman caught him at it.

"You thief! You cheated me!" the boy shouted.

From the table drawer before him, the dealer lifted a revolver and pointed it at his accuser. "Do you know what we do to people who use that word in Texas?" he asked coldly. "We kill them!"

The bold young Englishman flung himself across the table, pushing his head against the end of the dealer's revolver barrel. "You thief!" he repeated so loudly that everyone in the casino heard him. "I say you cheated me!"

With a gesture of disgust, the dealer dropped his revolver back in the drawer, and flung a ten-dollar gold piece across the table to the boy. "Here," he growled. "That'll help take you home to England. You're too damned tough for Texas."[3]

Before Theodore Roosevelt became President of the United States, he spent a considerable amount of time in Dakota Territory, eventually acquiring a ranch and trying to live the life of a cowboy. When he first went west Roosevelt was in his early twenties, unprepossessing in appearance with a pale dyspeptic face and a short moustache over a mouthful of big teeth. Teddy's weak eyes regarded the world through thick round lenses with an expression that reminded the Dakotans of an owl. The cowboys called him "Four Eyes" and laughed openly when in his high piping voice he would cry out: "Dee-lighted!" Teddy was the archetype of all tenderfeet, a perfect target for practical jokers.

One day Roosevelt rode into a small Dakota town, dismounted, tied his horse to a hitching rack, and went about his business. While he was inside the trading post, some cowboys slipped out of the saloon, unsaddled his horse, led the animal off to a livery stable, and put in its place a wild bronco that bore considerable resemblance to Roosevelt's mount.

After a few minutes, the near-sighted Teddy returned, untied his supposed steed, coiled up his rope, led the bronco out a step or two, climbed into the saddle, and headed up the street. The waiting cowboys hurried out of the saloon, grinning expectantly.

In a moment the bronco was boiling over, crowhopping and crawfishing, and then breaking into a straightaway buck as animal and rider disappeared in a cloud of dust. A quarter of an hour later the pair reappeared, the bronco subdued and sweat-covered. In front of the saloon Teddy, minus his eyeglasses, dismounted calmly.

"Forget something?" inquired an apparently disinterested cowboy.

"No," Roosevelt replied with a toothy smile. "I didn't forget anything. But you know it isn't good range manners for a man to ride another fellow's horse. I'll take mine now, please, and look for my glasses which came off near the edge of town."[4]

With these actions, the young man from the East shed his tenderfoot status. Drinks were on the cowboys that day, and not long afterward, when Roosevelt used his New York boxing skill to punch out a drunken bully in the bar of the nearby Cattlemen's Hotel, he was accepted as one of the boys.

Another well-known Easterner, Thomas A. Edison, was once set up for a practical joke while visiting Wyoming. In company with several scientists, the young inventor traveled to Wyoming for an advantageous view of an eclipse of the sun. After the eclipse the visitors hired a pair of local guides and went for a hunt near Rawlins. At day's end their total bag consisted of one sparrow hawk, and they began straggling back toward town quite disappointed, and pretending not to hear sotto voce remarks from the guides, deriding their marksmanship.

One of the guides, hurrying ahead, placed a stuffed jackrabbit alongside a patch of greasewood near the trail. Edison, who was well in front of his companions, saw the rabbit first and fired four quick shots at it before realizing he'd been hoodwinked. "That's one on me, all right," he called to the guide, who was waiting at the railroad track. When the guide retrieved the rabbit he was surprised to find that all four of Edison's shots had struck it, indicating that the poor results of the hunting expedition might be blamed on the inadequacy of the guides rather than on the marksmanship of the visiting Easterners.

As has been noted, the tall tale was surely a product of the harshness and boredom of frontier life. Many originated around campfires or at other gatherings and were transmitted by the spoken word in changing forms until someone put them into writing. Sir Richard Burton, the British explorer and author who ventured into the American West in 1860 was struck by the "inflamed imaginations of frontiersmen." He attributed this to the scenery and climate, the difficulty and danger, all of which combined had turned the white intruder into a remarkable resemblance to the wild Indian. "He is a liar," Burton wrote, "like his prototype the aborigine."

Burton went on to say that he had heard of a man riding eighty miles in order to enjoy the sweet delights of a lie. "His yarns and stories about the land he lives in have become a proverbial ridicule...he has seen mountains of diamonds and gold nuggets scattered like rocks...I have been gravely told of a herd of bison which arrested the course of the Platte River, causing the waters, like those of the Red Sea, to stand up, wall fashion, whilst the animals were crossing."[5]

Mark Twain in *Roughing It* included a number of exaggerated tales then circulating in the West, such as the effects of the continual 120-degree heat of Fort Yuma, Arizona. A very wicked soldier died at Fort Yuma and went straight to the hottest part of hell. The punch line is that the next day he telegraphed back to Fort Yuma for his blankets.

Jim Bridger's whoppers have become so much a part of our popular culture that a number of them are now stereotyped, even in their variations. Bridger told so many tall tales about mountains of pure glass and other phenomena that when he tried to describe the wonders of what is now Yellowstone Park, nobody would believe him.

One of Bridger's oft-repeated stories is about immense herds of buffalo freezing to death in a seventy-day blizzard near the Great Salt Lake in Utah. When spring came, Bridger tumbled the frozen buffalo into the lake and had enough pickled meat to supply him and the whole Ute tribe for years. Another of the old mountain man's stories concerns a flat-faced butte so distant from an army camp, where he was serving as scout, that an echo would not return for six hours. At midnight Bridger would shout a wake-up call that came echoing back promptly at reveille time.

Bridger's fur-trapping associate, Moses (Black) Harris, liked to tell of the occasion when he approached a beautiful grove of green trees only to discover that the forest was petrified. So sudden had been the process of petrification, the leaves remained green, and the birds that had been singing on the tree limbs still had their bills open.[6]

Almost everybody who was anybody in the Old West had a favorite tall tale or two. Charley Russell, the cowboy artist, told one that was based on the buffalo herds' migration patterns—southward across the Great Plains in winter and then northward in springtime. A rancher on the Yellowstone River caught a pair of yearling buffalo, yoked them like oxen, and hitched them to a sod-breaking plow. "It's springtime, and they don't mind going north," Russell said, "but the rancher can't turn them. They started north and that's where they're going. Streams don't stop them, and when he quits the handles they're still plowing north."

Through a friend late that summer, the rancher heard from his buffalo—they were north of the Teton River, but they had turned and were now plowing south. If the rancher could find a country with seasons no longer than the reach of his land, Russell explained, the buffalo would make a fine driving team. Or if he could spend his winters in Mexico and his summers in Canada, they'd be just the thing.[7]

One of Davy Crockett's favorite amusements was bragging to strangers about his hunting prowess. "I discovered a long time ago that a coon couldn't stand my grin," he would say. "I could bring one tumbling down from the highest tree. I never wasted powder and lead when I wanted one of the creatures.

"Well, as I was walking out one night, a few hundred yards from my house, looking carelessly about me, I saw a coon planted upon one of the highest limbs of an old tree. The night was very *moony* and clear and old Ratler was with me; but Ratler won't bark at a coon—he's a queer dog in that way. So, I thought I'd bring the lark down in the usual way, *by a grin.* I set myself—and, after grinning at the coon a reasonable time, found that he didn't come down. I wondered what was the reason—and took another steady grin at him. Still he was *there.* It made me a little mad, so I felt round and got an old limb about five feet long, and planting one end upon the ground, I placed my chin upon the other, and took *a rest.* I then grinned my best for about five minutes, but the cursed coon hung on. So, finding I could not bring him down by grinning, I determined to have him—for I thought he must be a droll chap. I went over to the house, got my axe, returned to the tree, saw the coon still there, and began to cut away. Down it came, and I ran forward, but damn the coon wasn't there to be seen. I found that what I had taken for one, was a large knot upon the branch of the tree and, upon looking at it closely, I saw that *I had grinned all the bark off, and left the knot perfectly smooth!*"[8]

Thanks to *Spirit of the Times*, a popular periodical published in New York during the nineteenth century, the tall tale came early into print. That publication emphasized hunting, fishing and horse racing, and favored colorful reports on these and other subjects from the Western frontier. The editors encouraged exaggeration whenever applicable, if done with some literary skill.

An example of early *Spirit of the Times* tale-spinning is Thomas Bangs Thorpe's "The Big Bear of Arkansas." The story inspired a string of bear yarns that followed the frontier westward and created what was known as "the big bear" school of humorists. Thorpe's tale is told aboard a steamboat by one of those "half-horse and half-alligator species of men" peculiar to the Mississippi Valley frontier of the 1840s. The narrator boasts of the rich delta soil of his Arkansas clearing where travelers mistook his potato hills for Indian mounds and his beets for cedar stumps. The soil was so rich he declared, that planting was downright dangerous.

"I had a good-sized sow killed in that same bottom land," he explained. "The old thief stole a ear of corn, and took it down where she slept at night to eat. Well, she left a grain or two on the ground, and lay down on them. Before morning the corn shot up, and the percussion killed her dead." Because of this, the settler said, he had stopped planting crops, believing that nature meant for his land to be a hunting ground.

And at that point he begins the bear story, perhaps the king of all tall tales of frontier hunters in pursuit of wild game. For days, man and beast challenged each other, the giant bear tantalizing his pursuer while the latter and his dogs trailed after "the damnedest bear was ever grown"—an animal eight inches taller than any of his species previously measured. "But wasn't he a beauty, though," the narrator declared in admiration. "I loved him like a brother."

After a chase to an island in a lake, the hunter engages the bear in a desperate underwater fight only to discover that he has killed the wrong bear. A few days later, however, he is startled to see the big bear climbing the fence outside his cabin. "The way he walked over that fence…he loomed up like a black mist, he seemed so large, and he walked right towards me." The bear is killed, and there the tall story ends philosophically, the tale teller expressing wonder as to why the great bear came in as though willing to be killed. "My private opinion is that that b'ar was an *unhuntable* b'ar, and died when his time come."[9]

Some of America's greatest writers were probably influenced by that tall tale. Herman Melville may have read it during the decade preceding his creation of Moby Dick, transforming the big bear into a white whale. Mark Twain must have read it because it is in the style he perfected, and William Faulkner re-created the mythological creature in the very region where T.B. Thorpe first conceived it.

Another example of *Spirit of the Times* frontier characters is "Old Singletire, the Man That was Not Annexed," an invention of Robert Patterson, who mined the same Southwestern area favored by Thorpe. Old Singletire was typical of the frontiersmen of that time and place, fiercely independent, distrustful of laws and authority, exploiting passersby with crude confidence games and outright robbery. He viewed travelers and visitors as invaders of his privacy.

Old Singletire built his cabin so that it was bisected by the boundary line of the Republic of Texas and the State of Louisiana.

"He slept, one half in the United States, and the other half in Texas, for he lay at right angles to the line."

Lawmen from both sides frequently found him in that position, but as they sought an entire individual they were not content to arrest one half of him. "A great deal of courtesy was at time exhibited by the officers, each pressing the other to break the forms of international law by pulling Old Single bodily over either side of the line. Each...feared the other wished to trick him, and declined the effort which might cause a rupture between Texas and the Union."

In 1845, Old Singletire's clever means of avoiding the force of law and order was threatened by the United States's annexation of Texas. The American government now surrounded him on all sides, and the regulators and bully boys of the area assembled to rout Old Singletire from his cabin.

Fearing the tricky reprobate's deadly rifle, and declaring that bloodshed was useless, they offered Singletire an opportunity to escape. If he could reach and cross the Red River, the boundary of Arkansas, before they could stop him, he could have his freedom.

"The old fellow led the crowd, hallooing at his topmost voice as he gained the river—'Hoopee! Hurrah!—I *aint* annixated!—*I'm off—I aint nowhar—nuther in the States nor Texas,* BUT IN ARKAN-SAW!!!' He swam to the opposite shore, fired a volley, gave three cheers and retired victorious."[10]

Following the example of *Spirit of the Times*, many frontier newspapers took up the tall tales tradition, with reports of fantastic animals, wondrous hunting feats, outlandish weather, or remarkable crops. For example, the *Omaha Nebraskan* of May 5, 1860, printed a story about an enormous catfish caught near the mouth of the Platte River. On being dissected the catfish was found to contain one raccoon, one first-class bulldog, an otter, and a small yawl boat, all supposed to have been swallowed by the catfish in moments of hunger.

Another story in the same newspaper is reminiscent of the Arkansas bear hunter's anecdote about the rapid growth of spilled grains of corn. The editor reported the amazing results of some turnip seeds planted in the rich soil of the Platte Valley. One of the turnips grew so large that it was hollowed out and "used for a military academy and did very well for years to house the boys." Another turnip was used as a railroad depot at Omaha, and another as a winter shelter for a huge herd of sheep.

To rival those turnips, an Ozark farmer named John Byrd grew pumpkins so enormous that they broke down his neighbor's fence rails and changed the courses of streams. After settling the resulting dispute with his neighbors, Byrd found a useful purpose for his pumpkins. He planted some of the seeds around a granary and a barn that needed moving. As the pumpkins grew they lifted the buildings off their foundations. Then the granary and barn were rolled along as if they were on ball bearings.[11]

Frontier insects could be as gigantic as the vegetables, according to the *Rocky Mountain News* of August 27, 1859. A group of travelers journeying across Colorado in a stagecoach saw in the distance what they supposed was the frame of a log house. On approaching, they found it to be the skeleton of a mosquito that had starved to death, the flesh having fallen from the bones.

Tall tales about the Pecos River were popular with explorers, soldiers, and cowboys, all no doubt culminating in the creations of a modern folk hero called Pecos Bill. One old-timer said that when he made coffee from Pecos water he used quinine for sugar. "The river," he added, "would give a killdee that flew over it diarrhea." And its course was so crooked that a cowpuncher claimed he could leave his garb on the bank, swim with the current for half a mile, and come out where he had left the clothes. A rancher once shot a wild longhorn that he thought was on the opposite bank, but when he swam across to get the beef he found that the steer was on the same side he'd shot from.[12]

Among Peter Hertzog's collected quotations from the New Mexico territorial press is what may be the first report of a flying saucer in America. The account was published in the *Santa Fe Daily New Mexican* on March 28, 1880. Datelined Galisteo Junction, New Mexico Territory, the story bore a large headline:

GALISTEO'S APPARITION
A Mysterious Aerial Phantom Appears at the Junction

The telegraph operator there, and two or three friends, were taking a short walk before bedtime, when they were startled to hear voices evidently coming from above them. At first they thought it to be a trick of the atmosphere bringing the sounds from a nearby mountain, but on looking above them they were astonished to see a large fish-shaped balloon coming from the west.

The construction of the balloon was entirely different from anything of the kind ever seen by any of the party, being in the shape of a fish, and at one time was so low that fanciful lettering on the outside of the car, which appeared to be very elegant, was plainly seen. The air machine appeared to be entirely under the control of the occupants and was guided by a large fanlike apparatus.

The party seemed to be enjoying themselves, as laughter and occasionally strains of music were heard. A few articles were dropped from the car as the balloon passed over the Junction, but owing to the imperfect light the only thing which was found was a magnificent flower, with a slip of exceedingly fine silk-like paper, on which were some characters resembling those on Japanese tea chests. One article which from its weight when thrown from the car, seemed to be a cup or some other piece of earthenware could not be found tonight, but diligent search will be made for it in the morning. The balloon was monstrous in size, and the car, as near as could be judged, contained eight or ten persons. Another peculiar feature of the air machine was that the occupants could evidently sail at any height they chose, as soon after passing the Junction, it assumed a great height and moved off very rapidly toward the east.

A follow-up story the next day reported the finding of the cup dropped from the air machine, "a cup of very peculiar workmanship, entirely different to anything used in this country."

A second follow-up story, which appears to have ended the incident, told of a traveler through Galisteo Junction who had offered such a sum of money for the flower and the cup that they were immediately sold to him. "He gave it as his opinion that the balloon must have come from Asia, and thinks it possible it came from Jeddo."[13]

Sometimes the line between the sweet delights of a humorous

lie and an outright confidence game ran rather thin, especially when the objective was to fleece a greener. One of the notable practitioners of lucrative shell games was Jefferson Randolph Smith, who operated in the Denver area where gullible prospectors brought their silver and gold in from the Colorado diggings.

Smith claimed to have started his working life as a Texas cowboy, but he soon discovered that gambling was more profitable. He specialized in the old thimblerig trick of three nutshells and a pea in which the bettor tried to guess where the pea was hidden. (Davy Crockett, while en route to Texas, encountered just such a gambler on a Red River steamboat and immediately saw through his sleight-of-hand tricks.)

After honing his skills, Jeff Smith moved on to Denver in the 1880s, only to find that the shell game's popularity had faded in the gambling establishments. Always resourceful, Smith purchased a quantity of unwrapped soap for two cents a cake and set up shop in an old wagon alongside a busy sidewalk. Well-dressed, sporting a neat Vandyke beard, and crying his wares in a silvery persuasive voice, he soon attracted a large crowd.

In full view of his audience, Smith began wrapping the soap in ten and twenty and fifty-dollar bills, around which he then folded a plain paper wrapper. "Soap! Superlative soap for bathing! Only five dollars a cake!" he shouted, and the crowd pushed forward, every man certain he would obtain a cake of soap wrapped in a fifty-dollar bill, or at least a ten-dollar bill.

At this stage in his career, Smith was already using two or three confederates in his flimflam games, and of course his confederates were the buyers who found the fifties and proudly displayed them to the crowd. Once in a while one of the dupes would find a ten, just often enough to keep the others paying five dollars for two cents worth of soap.

From that day to the end of his life, Jeff Smith was Soapy Smith, a super con man with a sense of humor. After each big sale, he and his associates would disappear for a day or so, long enough for a fresh crowd of miners to pour into Denver, and then he would set up shop again.

With his easy profits, Soapy Smith soon opened a gambling

house called the Tivoli Club. When one of his dealers plucked fifteen hundred dollars from a pair of traveling Californians, the latter sued the Tivoli for dishonest dealing. Acting as his own defense counsel, Soapy claimed that the Tivoli was an educational institution offering a cure for the gambling habit in the same way that the Keeley Institute provided a cure for the drink habit. "In my games," Soapy declared, "the player cannot win. I really should be recognized as a public benefactor." The court ruled in Soapy's favor.

On another occasion a Denver parson who had been highly critical of Soapy Smith's activities asked the gambler to speak to his church's Bible class. Soapy was astounded, but when the parson assured him that a man of his experience ought to have something worthwhile to say, he accepted the challenge.

"I am here, not as a preacher," Soapy told his audience, "but as a bad example." He warned the members of the class against gambling, and advised them to listen to what the parson told them. "Keep away from evil. Look at me."

Eventually Soapy and his expanding gang of confederates became too unruly for Denver. They moved on to the mining town of Creede, where they bullied and corrupted the local officials and took over the town. Among their partners in crime was Robert Ford, the man who shot Jesse James in the back.

When news came of a gold strike in Alaska, Soapy took his organization there, expecting to swindle the miners at Skagway and Juneau. Evidently the lawless Coloradans were too bold with their violent assaults and outright thievery to suit the hard-bitten Alaskans. In the summer of 1898, a group of outraged vigilantes shot Soapy Smith to death on the Juneau wharf, and drove his gang out of the area.[14]

Almost a generation before Soapy Smith began his career, a more benign pretender was entertaining the citizens of San Francisco with his jaunty make-believe. Joshua Norton was his name. He came to California during the gold rush and soon amassed a fortune, which he lost while trying to corner the California rice market. According to some of his contemporaries, the shock of financial disaster drove Norton over the brink into a gaudy sort of madness. Others said he was crazy like a fox. In 1857 he announced that he was Emperor of California and expected tribute to be paid to him by his subjects. At first, compliance was negligible, but he was such an ingratiating performer that he was soon dining free of charge at the best restaurants in San Francisco and was receiving donations of money sufficient to keep him clothed and sheltered.

In 1859 he extended his realm from the Pacific to the Atlantic by circulating a printed proclamation:

> At the peremptory request and desire of a large majority of the citizens of these United States, I, Joshua Norton, formerly of Algoa Bay, Cape of Good Hope, and now for the last 9 years and 10 months past of San Francisco, California, declare and proclaim myself Emperor of these United States; and in virtue of the authority thereby in me vested, do hereby order and direct the representatives of the different states of the Union to assemble in Musical Hall, of this city, on the last day of February next, then and there to make such alterations in the existing laws of the Union as may ameliorate the evils under which the country is laboring, and thereby cause confidence to exist, both at home and abroad, in our stability and integrity.
>
>

NORTON I
Emperor of the United States
16th February, 1859

With his added responsibilities, Emperor Norton adopted a resplendent costume—a military cap embellished with red ribbons, a navy blue coat cut military style and adorned with a profusion of brass buttons and huge gilt epaulettes. Later on, one of his subjects presented him with a tall beaver hat decorated with a cockade of feathers and a rosette. Variations of this served as his regal headgear for many years.

As head of the nation, the Emperor believed it his duty to communicate with leaders of other countries. He composed long cablegrams that occasionally contained threats of belligerent action upon nations that he thought were not behaving properly. No international crises resulted, however, because the telegraphers sent none of the messages. Being loyal subjects and not wishing to discompose their ruler, they prepared suitable replies to each cablegram, and had them delivered by messenger to the Emperor's quarters in the Eureka Lodging House or Metropolitan Hotel.

To lend dignity to his financial affairs, the Emperor ordered his own currency printed in the form of notes bearing his portrait; they were to be redeemable in gold in 1880. He used the notes to pay for his modest wants, and made gifts of them to needy persons. On those occasions when he required U.S. currency, he exchanged his notes at banks, which rarely turned him down. Other holders of the Emperor's paper money, however, were seldom able to redeem them. Emperor Norton I died on January 6, 1880. Ten thousand San Franciscans attended his funeral, bringing so many bouquets that his casket was covered by a "wilderness of flowers."[15]

In those free and easy days of journalism on the frontiers of the Old West, imaginative hoaxes often sprang from the pens of collaborating newspaper writers. The Pikes Peak Prevaricator was the creation of a windy sergeant of the U.S. Signal Corps who was spurred on by journalists in Colorado Springs and Denver. During the 1870s the newspaper writers spread the sergeant's prevarications across the gullible Eastern states.

At that particular period the Signal Corps operated the Weather Bureau, and to gather meteorological data the corps established at the top of Pikes Peak a station equipped with telegraphic equipment. Sergeant John T. O'Keefe arrived at that lonely outpost in January 1876 to record wind velocities, precipitation, and temperatures, and to perform other repetitive duties.

Apparently O'Keefe's tall tales were meant to relieve the monotony of his assignment, but when he began telegraphing and relating his stories to Colorado Springs newspapermen, they published them locally and then sent them to other papers in the state. In a short time O'Keefe's yarns were being printed in papers all over the United States. The farther away from Pikes Peak they appeared, the more likely they were to be accepted as factual.

Sergeant O'Keefe's Pikes Peak rat story was probably the most widely circulated. How much of it was in O'Keefe's words, how much the work of an anonymous reporter is not known, but the pair together exhibited the ingenuity of the twentieth-century writer of horror tales, Stephen King. As it appeared in the *Colorado Springs Gazette* and the Denver *Rocky Mountain News,* the story is tinged with the black humor that was typical of many early frontier tall tales.

"The vast number of rats inhabiting the rocky crevices...at the summit of Pikes Peak," O'Keefe's tale began, "have recently been formidable and dangerous." Feeding upon a mysterious saccharine gum percolating through the pores of the mountain's rocks, they threatened the existence of the weather station and the lives of its operators.

"Since the establishment of the station at the altitude of nearly 15,000 feet these animals have acquired a voracious appetite for raw meat, the scent of which seems to impart to them a ferocity rivaling the starved Siberian wolf. The most singular trait in the character of these animals is that they are never seen in the daytime. When the moon pours down her queenly light upon the summit, they are visible in countless numbers, hopping among the rocky boulders that crown this barren waste, and during the summer months they may be seen swimming and sporting in the waters of the lake, a short distance below the crest of the Peak, and on a dark, cloudy night their trail in the water exhibits a flowing, sparkling light, giving to the waters of the lake a flickering silver appearance.

"A few days since, Mr. John O'Keefe, one of the government operators at the signal station, returned to his post from Colorado Springs, taking with him a quarter of beef. It being late in the afternoon, his colleague, Mr. Hobbs, immediately left with the pack animal for the Springs. Soon after dark, while Mr. O'Keefe was engaged in the office, forwarding night dispatches to Washington, he was startled by a loud scream from Mrs. O'Keefe, who had retired for the night in an adjoining bedroom, and who came running into the office screaming, 'The rats! The rats!'

"Mr. O'Keefe, with great presence of mind, immediately girdled his wife with a scroll of zinc plating, such as had been used in the roofing of the station, which prevented the animals from climbing upon her person, and although his own was almost literally covered with them, he succeeded in encasing his legs each in a joint of stovepipe, when he commenced a fierce and desperate struggle for his life with a heavy war club preserved at the station among other Indian relics captured at the battle of Sand Creek.

"Notwithstanding hundreds were destroyed on every side,

they seemed to pour (with increasing numbers) from the bedroom, the door of which had been left open. The entire quarter of beef was eaten in less than five minutes, which seemed only to sharpen their appetites for an attack on Mrs. O'Keefe, whose face, hands and neck were terribly lacerated.

"In the midst of the warfare, Mrs. O'Keefe managed to reach a coil of electric wire hanging near the battery, and being a mountain girl, familiar with the throwing of a lariat, she hurled it through the air causing it to encircle her husband, and spring out from its loosened fastening making innumerable spiral traps, along which she poured the electric fluid from the heavily charged battery. In a moment the room was ablaze with electric light and whenever the rats came in contact with the wire they were hurled to an almost instant death.

"The appearance of daylight, made by the coruscation of the heavily charged wire, caused them to take refuge among the crevices and caverns of the mountain, by way of the bedroom window, through which they had forced their way. But the saddest part of this night attack upon the peak is the destroying of their infant child, which Mrs. O'Keefe thought she had made secure by a heavy covering of bed clothing, but the rats had found their way to the infant (only two months old), and had left nothing of it but the peeled and mumbled skull.

"LATER—Drs. Horn and Anderson have just returned from the peak. It was first thought that the left arm of Sergeant O'Keefe would have to be amputated, but they now believe it can be saved."

There was not a word of truth in Sergeant O'Keefe's horror tale, yet it created such a sensation that newspapers everywhere demanded more stories from the Prevaricator of Pikes Peak. O'Keefe and his journalist friends complied with a bulletin announcing that Pikes Peak had become a volcano. Their descriptions of crater explosions, lava flows, and showers of ashes were so graphic, however, that some Colorado newspapers hastily published denials of the story's veracity in order to calm the alarm of their credulous readers.

In his later published prevarications, Sergeant O'Keefe told of how he carried out government orders to whitewash all of Pikes

Peak. He introduced a dog named Seldom Fed, and a government mule named Balaam (that in real life was used to carry supplies up the peak to the weather station). O'Keefe endowed Balaam with magical powers that enabled the animal to subdue mountain lions and perform other wondrous feats.[16]

One cannot help but wonder what fate would await a sergeant like John O'Keefe in the humorless, unimaginative, paunchy and overfunded military organizations of this late twentieth century. None of his stories could be publicly released until cleared by the Pentagon; at first receipt of one of the sergeant's tall tales, the bureaucratic brass would transfer him off Pikes Peak, and copies of his personnel file would be forwarded to the psychiatric division of the Medical Corps, to the CIA, the FBI, and the NSC.

We do not know why Sergeant O'Keefe did not choose to reenlist. At any rate, the creation of legends by the Prevaricator of Pikes Peak came to an end in 1881 with John O'Keefe's return to civilian life. His admirers banqueted him handsomely, offering numerous outlandish toasts to their favorite raconteur before sending him off to a more prosaic life as a telegraph operator in Denver.

By the end of the nineteenth century the frontier was passing, and with it the oral tradition of yarn spinning. From the inventive imagination direct to print was the last refuge of the tall tale. Because of their ready access to print, newspaper writers made frequent attempts at humorous hoaxes and tantalizing whoppers. One of the more fecund tale spinners was John G. Maher, who served as correspondent from Nebraska for James Gordon Bennett's *New York Herald*. Publisher Bennett knew that his newspaper's readers loved fanciful stories of the Wild West, and he encouraged his correspondents in the West to invent and exaggerate. John Maher was quite willing to satisfy the demand.

One of Maher's more sensational hoaxes was a petrified man, and he spent considerable time and effort in preparing for the discovery. To give the event some scientific authority, he chose a site south of the Black Hills near Chadron, Nebraska, where a team of archaeologists from the East was searching for fossils.

With the help of a friend and a very tall black soldier of the

Ninth Cavalry at nearby Fort Robinson, Maher set about his task. He first made a plaster cast of the soldier, flattening the man's feet with a pair of shingles because Maher had read somewhere that prehistoric men were flat-footed. Then with a mixture of cement and Badlands sand, he filled the cast and thus created his petrified man.

Under cover of darkness, the conspirators loaded the concrete statue into a dray wagon and hauled it out to the place where the archaeologists were digging. There they buried the petrified man in a bank of clay leaving one hand exposed.

As Maher had hoped, the statue was discovered a few days later, on October 10, 1891. Two local brothers, Ed and Clyde Rossiter, who were digging for the archaeologists, found the planted fake, and summoned everyone in the vicinity to come and see the startling discovery. By nightfall the brothers had cleaned up the petrified man and placed him on exhibit in the Rossiter Hotel in Chadron.

"The face resembles that of a Negro," declared the *Dawes County* (Nebraska) *Journal* for October 14, "but his shapely heels indicate caucasian blood...The medical fraternity and all others who have seen the specimen laugh at the idea it is not genuine. It is undoubtedly the most perfect specimen of the kind ever discovered, and is worth many thousands of dollars. Mr. Rossiter intends taking it to the Chicago World Fair." The newspaper went on to describe the geological formation in which the petrified man was found, stating that the presence of other fossils proved the immense antiquity of the find.

After a few scientific tests, the petrified man was declared genuine, and off he went on a tour of Nebraska. Then, as John Maher spread news of his hoax across the country, the petrified man became a national celebrity, drawing crowds wherever he was taken. Eventually he fell into the hands of a carnival operator, and ended up somewhere back in Nebraska.

For Maher, however, one good hoax deserved another. Over the next few years he "found" the man who blew up the battleship *Maine*, "discovered" a British naval force on the Niobrara River in search of Irish Fenians, faked a health spa by pouring sacks of soda into an ordinary hot spring, and created a fearsome sea monster in a Sheridan County lake.

Maher kept his "man who blew up the Maine" hoax running in newspapers for several months. He invented a name for him, Captain Manuel de Silva Braga of the Cuban Army, and kept him on the run in various parts of western America. Maher wanted to let the fictitious man disappear, but the *Herald* insisted on more stories. Finally, when exposure by the government seemed imminent, Maher reported that the mysterious Spaniard had barricaded himself in a gold prospector's abandoned cabin, deliberately set the place on fire, and burned himself to ashes.[17]

John Maher lived long past frontier days. His hoaxes died out during the era of the "muckrakers" early in this century, when journalistic magazines by the dozens were reforming everything, including the newspapers. Were Maher alive today he might be contributing to those sensational weeklies that clutter supermarket checkout counters across America. More likely he would scorn their feeble hoaxes, all of which appear to be unsupported by careful planning and a sufficiency of planted evidence. In other words they bear little resemblance to the elaborate hoaxes of the American frontier.

Having Fun with the Phenomena

THE FRONTIER OF THE GREAT PLAINS and the Rockies, more so than other sections of the nation, offered an abundance of afflictions upon those who first came there unprepared—excruciating heat and cold, blasting winds, plagues of insects, epidemics of disease, hailstorms, ice storms, blizzards, floods. Travelers and settlers survived by turning misery into a kind of dark folk laughter. They converted disaster into comedy in which they jeered at blizzards, northers, chinooks, and other vagaries of weather and environment. Often they exaggerated the phenomena of the pitiless natural world, or they related their painful experiences in wry homespun vernacular. After one of the most frightening storms endured by a frontier town, a nameless editor described it: "A windstorm that sat down on its hind legs and howled and screeched and snorted." Newspaper editors often set the comic attitude for their communities. They knew that merriment was necessary for survival.

The first white venturers into the West, the Spaniards, overstated their experiences. They drove away fear by creating legends. Living in their world of fantasy they easily accepted the lies of the Indian guides who promised there would be gold for them somewhere over the horizon.

These early explorers tried to make light of the flatness of the earth, the unending rim of the sky. This country, "so level and smooth," seemingly was empty of everything but buffalo, and "the sky could be seen between their legs." During the three centuries that followed the coming of the Spaniards, hundreds of men, and more women than men, were driven mad on the Great Plains because they could not accept the reality of vast space. They lost the ability to bare their teeth in laughter at the insensibilities of the environment in which they found themselves.

The folklore they created seems dated now in an age of technology that erases space and collapses time and swathes human bodies with instant warmth or coolness, and offers diversion through invisible waves of sound and light. Unless by choice, no one is isolated on the Great Plains anymore, and if madness comes, it comes not from the topography but from other circumstances.

Some folktales survive in memory. In windy places they tell of log chains used as velocity indicators. When fastened to a post or tree, the heavy chain hanging at 45 degrees indicated a mild breeze. If the chain was in a horizontal position, then the wind could be said to be blowing. Chickens trying to lay with their tails turned toward the wind sometimes layed the same egg four or five times.

In arid places they tell of rivers so dry that steamboat passengers could not see the banks for clouds of dust raised by paddle wheels. Chickens hatched in the dry heat came out of their shells already cooked, and snakes were so desiccated they could not bend their bodies.

Cold weather sometimes generated amazing tales. One of the oft-told ones concerned a pair of cowboys caught in a sudden blizzard. Their shouted words froze in the frigid air, and weeks later when the thaw came, travelers were frightened by sudden outbursts of profanity coming from empty air.

During the great January blizzards of 1886, a group of train travelers was trapped by huge drifts in the town of Kinsley, Kansas, near Dodge City. While waiting for snowplows to rescue them, a few creative members invented some folklore of their own. They printed it in a four-column, four-page newspaper with a bold masthead: *The B-B-Blizzard*, Vol. One, Number One. These headlines introduced the lead story:

TERRORS OF THE PRAIRIES!!!
Locked in the Embrace of the Grim Frost King
Terrible Sufferings of a Snowbound Raymond
Excursion Party. Hope Not Yet Wholly Abandoned.

In the exaggerated manner of Baron Münchhausen, the writer of the news story related how the tops of the Pullman cars were twelve feet below the surface of the snow; how the marooned travelers had consumed all their crackers and cheese, and drunk all the spiritous liquors that they had brought with them for medicinal purposes; and how they were reduced to subsisting on polar berries and mosses dug out from the snow with incredible labor. Some brave souls had attempted to seek assistance in a sledge drawn by reindeer, but had failed.

And so was the fury of a frontier blizzard overcome by merry tales printed on a press in the baggage car that was meant to furnish the excursionists with daily news bulletins. There was no follow-up issue of *The B-B-Blizzard*, but presumably the trapped travelers were eventually rescued.[1]

During this same blizzard the wind blew such a gale that passenger cars rocked as though they would leave the tracks. One traveler who got through to Meade Center, Kansas, found that town paying no attention to the snowstorm but gaily celebrating its selection as county seat. "The citizens of the town, assisted by a few cowboys...proceeded to paint the town red, and they got on the finest and richest coat of vermillion I ever saw. If there was a sober man...he was not in evidence at the hotel."[2]

In his reminiscences of early-day Gunnison, Colorado, George Root told a factual story about his tuba in below zero weather that approaches the apocryphal. During the winter of 1883, the Gunnison band was asked to play for a political rally on a street corner, and Root was there with his tuba. The temperature was well below zero.

"The music started with a vim," Root said, "the players all being pretty well drilled and putting in their best licks to work up a circulation. After playing a few bars I made the discovery that I was out of tune." The band leader also immediately noticed the situation, and brought the music to a halt.

Observing that the valves were frozen on the tuba, the leader sent Root into a nearby bakery to thaw out the instrument, and at the same time reminded him to return in time for his solo. Holding the tuba close to a red-hot stove, Root soon had it in working order. He stationed himself at the front door of the bakery, listening to the piece being played. "Timing myself so that I would not have more than a minute to wait, I hustled out through the freezing air to take my place. Alas, before I had a chance to show off, my old horn had again frozen so solid the valves wouldn't turn for love or money."[3]

So many exaggerated tales of blizzards were sent to Eastern newspapers by traveling correspondents that some local editors tried to outdo their rivals, who were being paid by the column inch for their highly imaginary lucubrations. In February 1886, the editor of the *Estelline Bell* in Dakota Territory composed a piece that he headlined BLIZZARD LIE, and dispatched copies to newspapers elsewhere:

"Varieties of the Western Roorback—for the East. Our Own Northwest Blizzard Lie. Storm extends from Butte City, Montana, to Chicago; raging with unprecedented fury. Snow one hundred feet deep. Stock on Western ranges all dead. There will be no more immigration to Dakota. Railroads will take up all tracks west of Chicago in the spring. Everybody, including the oldest inhabitant, dead, the news being brought by a traveling man who was the only person who escaped."[4]

The ability to find black humor persisted even in the worst of weather disasters. A settler in west Texas during the great drouths of the 1880s finally abandoned his claim, leaving this notice scrawled in charcoal on the door of his shack:

One hundred miles to Water
Twenty miles to wood
Six inches to hell
God bless our home
Gone to live with the wife's folks.[5]

Frontiersmen had various ways of explaining outrageous phenomena. A westbound traveler and his son passing through Arkansas in a wagon during the time of the Civil War had to cross an unbridged creek fed by a spring of very hot water near Hot Springs. Unaware of the stream's high temperature, he drove his horse into it, and the animal plunged and kicked furiously, almost overturning the wagon before reaching the opposite bank.

Surprised by his horse's unusual spirit, the traveler got down from the wagon, and for the first time noticed curls of steam rising from the surface of the creek. He walked back to the bank, kneeled, and thrust one hand into the water. Immediately he sprang to his feet and rushed to the wagon, shouting to his son: "Drive on, boy, fast as we can! Hell—hell's too close by!"[6]

Recourse to prayer was frequent among sinners and saints alike. A group of overlanders heading for the California gold fields in 1850 ran out of water. When their teams failed, they left their wagons and went forward on foot, hoping to find a water hole. At last one of the more religious members of the group fell to his knees and began to pray: "Lord Almighty, send us just one drop of rain."

A few minutes later to everyone's surprise, from a pair of fleecy clouds raindrops began falling. Someone quickly unfolded a rubber blanket, spreading it to catch the water, but only about ten drops fell before the clouds dispersed.

"The damn fool," a member of the party said of the man who had prayed for rain. "He might just as well have prayed for a barrel of water as for a drop, for he got ten times as much as he asked for."[7]

Rain may have been the object of most prayers on the dry frontier of the West, and some merriment occasionally was afforded listeners when the praying was done in public. During a serious but spotty drouth in the Sulphur Springs valley of New Mexico in 1887, the stockmen elected one of their number to intercede for them with the Almighty at a public gathering. His name was Dan Ming, and he approached the task by first reminding the Supreme Being that he had never asked for anything before. But the range was in a hell of a terrible condition, he continued, and the cattle and ponies needed water badly.

"Oh, Lord, if you do not grant us our prayer," he continued, "for Christ's sake stop it from raining on Joe Hampson's range, for all our cattle are going over there. Hampson, oh, Lord, is a powerful sinner and undeserving of such goodness from you…Yes, oh, Lord! we pray you to stop the rain on Hampson's range, at least until we can send him our marks and brands."

According to the *Chloride* (New Mexico) *Black Range*, which chronicled Dan Ming's prayer, Sulphur Springs valley three days later was blessed with one of the heaviest rains ever recorded there.[8]

Earthquakes seldom occur on the Great Plains, but Nebraska and Kansas were shaken severely on April 24, 1867. A train on the Kansas Pacific Railroad was stopped, the engineer and fireman jumping off because they feared the engine must be on the point of exploding.

Among the more entertaining phenomena of the far western frontier were fantastic visions seen in the boundless sky. Rare in the pollutant-ridden air of the present day, mirages then were so common and sometimes so startling that numerous travelers described or at least made mention of them.

Elizabeth Custer saw one the morning her husband marched away forever from Fort Abraham Lincoln with the Seventh Cavalry—high in the sky a winding column of wagons and horsemen and marching men. Sitting Bull may have seen one in his vision of many blue-coated soldiers falling from the sky with their heads down and their hats falling off. Neither Mrs. Custer nor Sitting Bull was entertained by these mirages; instead they were awed by them.

Marian Russell, who as a child traveled westward on the Santa Fe Trail, recalled mirages that "beckoned and taunted." Sometimes they were parties of mounted Indians; again they would be tall castles, or blue lakes that would disappear only with the sun's setting.

In Montana in 1864, a man named Fisk reported seeing the mirage of a lake, so real that his thirsty horses whinnied at the sight. A prospector named Harris, traveling on foot through an Arizona desert and suffering from lack of water, saw in the sky a vision of a camel drinking at a watering hole. Convinced that he had gone mad from thirst, the prospector almost abandoned hope, but he eventually discovered that the mirage he had seen was reality. Over the horizon there *was* a watering hole, and the camel was one of those used in the U.S. Camel Corps and then abandoned during the Civil War.

Dr. Josiah Gregg, who traveled the Santa Fe Trail several times as a trader, called mirages "false ponds" because he was deceived by visions of water that receded whenever he approached. He was fascinated by the frequent inversions of trees and hills. Surmising upon the prevalence of water in mirages, Gregg concluded in 1844 that the visions were reflections from a gas emanating from the sun-scorched plain. He came close to the modern scientific explanation that mirages are formed by refraction of light rays passing through layers of air of varying density, sometimes causing optical inversions.

What Heinrich Lienhard believed to be a huge sea serpent writhing in the sky turned out to be a mirage—a column of travelers with their horses and mules and oxen. While crossing the Colorado Desert, John Ross Browne, a writer of frontier experiences, was delighted when he saw a mirage of a railroad track on pilings, surrounded by brilliantly plumed water birds and a silvery lake.[9]

To Edwin Bryant, the mirage he saw near Salt Lake was "one of the most extraordinary phenomena" he had ever witnessed. The figures of fifteen or twenty men and horses of "gigantic stature" appeared almost in front of him and his party "as if they were rushing down upon us."

At first sight, Bryant thought the horsemen might be a hunting or war party of Ute Indians, but dismissed the supposition because of the trail's location. Bryant, who was several yards in advance, called for one of the men in his party to come forward, and shortly afterward they were both astonished to see the fifteen or twenty figures multiplying into three or four hundred and at the same time accelerating their movement forward.

Bryant and his companion agreed that the oncoming column might be Captain John Fremont and members of his expedition, but soon rejected that possibility. More likely, they decided, what they were watching was an optical illusion, a mirage. In that day, the magic of the fata morgana was fairly common knowledge.

"It was then, for the first time, so perfect was the deception, that I conjectured the probable fact that these figures were the reflection of our own images by the atmosphere, filled as it was with fine particles of crystallized matter, or by the distant horizon, covered by the same substance. This induced a more minute observation of the phenomena, in order to detect the deception, if such it were. I noticed a single figure, apparently in front in advance of all the others, and was struck with its likeness to myself. Its motions, too, I thought, were the same as mine. To test the hypothesis…I wheeled suddenly around, at the same time stretching my arms out to their full length, and turning my face sidewise to notice the movements of the figure. It went through precisely the same motions. I then marched deliberately and with long strides several paces; the figure did the same...The fact then was clear. But it was more fully verified still, for the whole array of this numerous shadowy host in the course of an hour melted entirely away...The figures were our own shadows...But this phantom population springing out of the ground as it were, and arraying itself before us as we traversed this dreary and heaven-condemned waste, although we were entirely convinced of the cause of the apparition, excited those superstitious emotions so natural to all mankind." And, he might have added, offered the rarest sort of entertainment to all concerned.

Several days later Bryant was again amazed by the sight of what he described as a mirage of "great perfection, a wide cascade or cataract of glittering, foaming, and tumbling water," a cruel deception in this case because he and his party were virtually starving for water.[10]

The crystal clear air of the frontier West—before man and his machines befouled it—charmed many travelers. After Josiah and Sarah Royce passed through the Wasatch range, they were overwhelmed by their first view of the Great Salt Lake Valley through the remarkably pure and transparent atmosphere. "We paused to take breath," Sarah later recalled, "and faced each other with mutual looks of wonder, we agreed that we did not know each other; and it was not until after free use of the pure valley waters aided in some instances by the hot mineral springs that we recovered our identity."[11] Modern psychologists would probably describe the Royces' experience as Stendhal's syndrome—too much wonder all at once.

CHAPTER SEVEN

Violence and Cruelty
beneath the Laughter

MIXED INTO THE MERRIMENT of the frontier were elements of violence and cruelty. Looking back on the badmen and lawmen of the nineteenth century, it is often difficult to separate the two; in many cases the individuals were interchangeable. Yet there were some badmen–lawmen, blessed with a sense of the ridiculous, who managed to entertain themselves and others with their holdups and shootouts.

An example was Charles E. Boles (or Bolton), a mild-mannered schoolmaster from New York who came to the California gold mines after serving in the Union Army during the Civil War. His twenty-seven stagecoach robberies have gradually entered the realm of folklore so that it is difficult now to distinguish fact from fiction.

According to legend, Professor Boles became a holdup man by pure chance. He was walking home from school one day in Calaveras County when he saw a stagecoach approaching along a crooked trail. Recognizing the driver from the distance as an acquaintance, Boles decided to play a practical joke on him. He tied a handkerchief over his face, broke a stick into the shape of a pistol, and stepped into the middle of the road, signaling the stagecoach to halt. "Throw down the box!" Boles shouted in a gruff voice, and to his astonishment the driver obeyed. When the treasure box hit the rocky roadside, it broke open, and as Boles leaned forward to examine its contents, the driver took advantage of the momentary distraction and lashed his horses into a fast exit from the scene.

After the astounded schoolmaster counted up the coins, the bars of bullion, and sacks of gold dust, he decided that highway robbery was more profitable than school teaching. He resigned his post and moved to San Francisco, where he set himself up as a mining engineer.

Boles was not a greedy man and he did not rob another stagecoach until his money ran low. His modus operandi was simple. He always wore a linen duster, armed himself with an unloaded double-barreled shotgun, and concealed his face by cutting eyeholes in a flour sack and pulling it over his derby hat. He was also careful to stage his robberies in widely scattered places.

Being an amateur poet with a sense of humor, Boles began leaving bits of doggerel in the Wells Fargo treasure boxes that he emptied. He signed the verses *Black Bart the Po 8*. Wells Fargo's chief detective so admired the poems that he sometimes included them in the numerous WANTED posters offering rewards for the capture of Black Bart.

These were among the more widely distributed verses:

I've labored long and hard for bread,
For honor and for riches.
But on my toes too long you've trod,
You fine haired sons of bitches.

Blame me not for what I've done,
I don't deserve your curses,
And if for some cause I must be hung,
Let it be for my verses.

For seven years, Black Bart got away with his random holdups, never shooting anyone, never robbing passengers, but taking only shipments of the Wells Fargo & Company Express. But on a fine November day in 1883, when he was conducting one of his dignified holdups, between Sonora and Milton, a bold teenage boy took a shot at him. Confounded by this unexpected audacity, Black Bart fled, dropping in his confusion his hat, a magnifying glass, and a freshly laundered white handkerchief. When these items were turned over to the Wells Fargo detectives, they discovered a laundry mark on the handkerchief and eventually traced it to Professor Charles Bolton in San Francisco.

Although no one could believe that the dapper old gentleman with the gray handlebar moustache, Prince Albert coat, gold-headed cane, and derby hat could be Black Bart, he offered no resistance and did not deny his guilt.

After serving four years of a six-year sentence, Black Bart was released. Folklore maintains that Wells Fargo paid him a monthly pension of two hundred dollars to leave their express shipments alone, but more likely he went home to New York. Supposedly he died there in his late eighties sometime during the first World War. Black Bart was one outlaw who provided an enormous amount of entertainment for the western frontier at a modicum of expense.[1]

An equally resourceful road agent, who operated in the Southwest, stopped a stagecoach one night on the highway between Pueblo and Alamosa, Colorado. The robber had placed a log barricade across the road and built a small fire nearby to illuminate the obstruction. When the stage driver stepped down to remove the logs, he felt a rifle muzzle pushed into his back and heard a voice order all passengers to get down with their hands up. By this time the driver and passengers had observed in the firelight a row of rifle barrels resting on the log barricade and pointed directly at them.

The masked robber turned nonchalantly toward the barricade and shouted cheerfully: "Keep 'em covered, boys, while I go through the bunch!" In the face of such armament, passengers and driver readily handed over their money and watches and jewelry.

As soon as the highwayman vanished in the darkness with his loot, the driver turned the stagecoach and headed for Alamosa. There a posse was quickly formed and the men galloped back to the scene of banditry. Beside the road the fire still burned, and the rifles apparently were still aimed across the log. A moment's close inspection revealed that the menacing weapons were only willow poles. The holdup had been a solo performance. Even some of the victims could not help but join in the laughter when they realized how deftly they had been stung.[2]

On the frontier the plug hat, or stovepipe hat (sometimes worn by Abraham Lincoln) symbolized the effete, the tenderfoot, the snobbish. Such imposing headgear made their wearers targets for verbal or physical abuse. Although gamblers occasionally wore them, the fingers of lowlife gunmen often turned itchy in the presence of a tall silk hat.

One day while Ben Thompson, the English-born gambler, was town marshal at Austin, Texas, he received a report that a certain cowboy had shot a bullet hole through the high hat of a visiting Easterner. Aware that this particular cowboy was trying to establish a reputation as a gunslinger, Thompson borrowed a plug hat from a friend and strolled quietly into the saloon where the cowboy was boasting of his prowess.

"I hear," Thompson said to him, "that you are shooting plug hats here today. Perhaps you would like to take a shot at mine."

Thompson then raised his revolver and shot a tiny piece off the cowboy's ear. "I meant," he said, "to hit your ear. Did I do it?"

The cowboy indignantly showed proof that his ear had been hit. "Well then," continued Thompson, "get out of here." He grasped the would-be gunman by the cartridge belt and hurled him out upon the street, ending whatever local reputation the cowboy might have acquired as a dangerous desperado.[3]

Thompson later operated a saloon in Abilene, Kansas, during that railhead's heyday as a cowtown, and he probably encountered the same problem there with plug hats. According to J.B. Edwards, a young man who peddled river ice to Abilene establishments, almost every Texas cowboy who came up the trail to Kansas was dangerously free with his sixshooters. "If his fancy told him to shoot," Edwards said, "he did so—into the air or at anything he saw. A plug hat would bring a volley from him at any time, drunk or sober."[4]

Firing shots in saloons was a popular means of amusement. Newspaper correspondent Albert Richardson reported that in a Denver gaming saloon, the firing would send everybody pell-mell out of the room, but the shots seldom wounded anyone. "One day I heard the bar-keeper politely ask a man lying upon a bench to remove himself. The recumbent replied to the request with his revolver. Indeed firing at this bartender was a common amusement among the guests. At first he bore it laughingly, but one day a shot grazed his ear, whereupon, remarking that there was such a thing as carrying a joke too far and that *this* was 'about played out,' he buckled on two revolvers and swore he would kill the next man who took aim at him. He was not troubled afterward."[5]

While "Mysterious Dave" Mather was a lawman in Dodge City, he fired a shot in a saloon that created more than the usual commotion. Mather was one of those frontier gunmen who divided his career between being an outlaw part time, and a peace officer part time. One afternoon he was playing a game of seven-up with a gambler of low principles in the Long Branch Saloon. Apparently the two men fell into argument and when the gambler drew his weapon, Mysterious Dave drew his, and both fired at the same instant. The gambler was dead; Mather's head was grazed quite bloodily.

According to John Callison, who was present and later wrote about the incident, the bullet went through the gambler, struck the stove, went through it and killed one of James Kelley's dogs, a bitch named Flora, in the rear of the saloon. Kelley was a restaurant owner and occasionally the mayor of Dodge City.

"Such little things as that happened so often in Dodge," Callison recalled, "that nothing was said about it until someone found the dead dog in the other end of the saloon. Kelley had only a hundred dogs that he kept to chase jack rabbits, antelope, and coyotes. Certain men sometimes called him 'Dog Kelley'...Someone slipped out and told Kelley that Mysterious Dave had killed one of his favorite dogs. Without stopping to ask any questions as to how it happened, he grabbed up his old sawed-off shotgun and started to hunt up the man that had the nerve to do such a thing. When Kelley reached the place where it happened, Mysterious Dave had gone out to get his head fixed up. The men in the saloon told Kelley it was an accident, and was done without malice aforethought. Kelley would not listen to anything. He even said Mysterious Dave had no business shooting his gun off without first looking to see if there were any dogs of his in the saloon. He went up and looked at the corpse, swore a few swears, and said he would bury that dog with military honors next day, and if there was a man in the town who did not attend the funeral he would hunt him up with that old sawed-off shotgun."

Although no inquest was held on the dead gambler (he was buried without ceremony in Boot Hill cemetery), Kelley insisted on a jury to weigh the evidence in the death of his bitch Flora. Several witnesses swore that the dog had no business in the saloon, that she should have been out chasing jackrabbits or at least had one eye on Mysterious Dave whose gun sometimes went off unexpectantly. "Other witnesses swore that Dave's gun hung fire, and if the dog had been on her guard she would have jumped out the window. The jury brought in a verdict that the dog...came to her death by a bullet fired from a gun in the hands of Dave Mather, better known as Mysterious Dave...and that the shooting was done in self-defense and was perfectly justified, as the dog had no business going to sleep in a booze house in Dodge City."

That evening a number of leading businessmen met and made arrangements for the grandest funeral ever held in the town. The Mayor declared a holiday so there would be no excuse for not attending the funeral. The cortege was headed by Dodge City's famous cowboy band, a squad of mounted police, and fire companies. When they reached Boot Hill, several men took turns speaking a few farewell words for the departed. Removing their hats, they recited the Lord's Prayer, and then all joined in singing several verses of "The Cowboy's Lament":

> *Beat the drum slowly, play the fife lowly,*
> *Play the Dead March as you bear me along.*
> *Take me to Boot Hill and throw the dirt over me*
> *I'm but a poor cowboy, I know I done wrong.*[6]

Whenever a shootout occurred in a barroom, the survivor or survivors immediately began claiming self-defense. Frontier juries almost always freed any gunman with such a plea, provided there were supporting witnesses. One evening in Denver, three men of doubtful reputations were drinking in a private anteroom adjoining a main barroom. One of them suddenly collapsed—dead from a heart attack. The remaining pair immediately panicked, fearing that because of their records, and with no proof of self-defense, both might be accused of his murder.

After a few moments they calmed each other down, and then walked casually into the main room which was empty except for a bartender. Knowing that cigars were kept in the office, they asked the bartender to bring some out to them. As soon as he was out of sight, they hustled the dead man out of the anteroom, seated him in a chair at a table, and then rested his head in his hands on the table as though he were sleeping off a drunk.

When the bartender returned, they motioned to the man at the table, and said that he would pay for the cigars. They then walked out of the saloon and prepared to depart Denver.

As closing time approached, the bartender went over to the man at the table, shook him by a shoulder, and asked payment for the cigars. To his consternation, the man fell off the chair, and rolled upon the floor. Almost at that very moment, two local lawmen making their rounds entered the front door. The bartender, realizing that he was standing over a dead man, immediately shouted to the lawmen: "Damn it, I did it in self defense!"[7]

In dealing with outlaws, officers of the law had to be fleet-footed as well as fast on the draw. The *Wichita Beacon* of May 12, 1875, reported an incident involving the famous Wyatt Earp who was serving as peace officer there. On his rounds through the town, Earp recognized a man named W.W. Compton who was wanted for horse stealing.

"Earp took him in tow, and inquired his name. He gave it as 'Jones.' This didn't satisfy the officer, who took Mr. Jones into the Gold Room, on Douglas avenue, in order that he might fully examine him by lamp light. Mr. Jones not liking the looks of things, lit out, running to the rear of Denison's stables. Earp fired one shot across his poop deck to bring him to, to use a naughty-cal phrase, and just as he did so, the man cast anchor near a clothes line, hauled down his colors and surrendered without firing a gun. The officer had hold of him before he could recover his feet for another run, and taking him to the jail placed him in the keeping of the sheriff. On the way 'Jones' acknowledged that he was the man wanted."[8]

The only man in Tucson who wore a stovepipe hat was an eccentric gentleman known as "Major" Duffield. "He carried about with him a small-sized arsenal of revolvers and pistols of all calibers," wrote John G. Bourke. "If my memory is not entirely at fault I think he never had less than ten or eleven about his person at one time."

Arriving at Tucson one day on a train from Texas was Waco

Bill, a teamster with dreams of becoming a top western gunfighter. While slaking his thirst in a saloon he learned of Major Duffield's reputation as the local object of dread. "Gents, I'm Bill from Texas," he boasted. "Blood's my color, I kerries mee korfin on mee back, kin whip mee weight in bar meat and the hummin' of pistol balls is mu-u-u-u-sic in mee ear—Whar's *Duffield?*" The last words had just left his mouth when he found himself sprawling on his back, leveled to the ground by a lightning blow from the horny hands of his opponent. True to his instincts, the Texan as he rolled grasped his revolver but before the weapon could be drawn, Duffield had shot from out of his coat pocket and a pistol bullet lodged in the groin of the unfortunate Waco Bill. "My name's Duffield," said the distinguished Arizonian with a statesmanlike wave of the hand, "and then eer's mee visiting keerd."[9]

The formal duel with its seconds and its rigid code of conduct—which was fairly common in the East—was gradually superseded on the trans-Mississippi frontier by the gunfight or shootout. Both antagonists were supposed to be equally armed at the time of showdown. Shootings in the back were definitely frowned upon, but otherwise the rules were rather loose.

A westbound traveler in 1858 told of how he got into a duel at Fort Laramie. "One of the teamsters struck me at Scotts Bluff, and as he had his revolver by his side and I was unarmed I had to take the blow without resenting but when I got to Laramie I challenged him. He chose Colts Revolvers 12 steps. At the first fire I gave him a severe flesh wound in the shoulder and his ball cut the rim of my hat about 2 inches from my head. By this time friends interfered and I confess I was willing enough to stop. My adversary has a pretty sore shoulder and cannot use his left arm much but is doing well."[10]

Such violent activities made badmen and lawmen nearly as symbolic of the frontier as cowboys and Indians. Local newspapers often furthered the images by proudly printing or commenting on reports of western gunplay. Many such reports were reprinted in eastern newspapers.

"But one man has died at Cheyenne with his boots off since the town first sprouted," the *Boston Globe* declared, "and he had them in his teeth and was crawling out of a bedroom window when an avenging pistol ball let daylight shine through him."[11]

Local editors also became quite adept at writing headlines to arouse the curiosity of readers so that they would want to buy copies of the papers in order to learn the outcome of a wild shootout. In July 1884, a Montana newspaper, the *Mineral Argus*, reported a gunfight involving two notorious horse thieves, Rattlesnake Jake and Long-Haired Ed Owen, under these headlines:

PERFORATED THEM!

The Way the Citizens of Lewistown
Celebrated the Fourth

Two Desperate Characters Attempt
to Hold Up the Town

Charles Owen and Charles Fallon
Will Steal No More Horses

A Lively Fourth That Will Go Into History as the First
in Lewistown, and the Most Thrilling
in the United States in 1884

They Tackled the Wrong Town

Only a reading of the full text in small print reveals the fate of the two outlaws and an innocent bystander. All three were "perforated" and all three expired.[12]

While visiting Carson City, Nevada, in 1864, Artemus Ward added his bit to the hyperbole of badmen and lawmen. "Shooting isn't as popular in Nevada as it once was. A few years since, they used to have a dead man for breakfast every morning. A reformed desperado told me that he supposed he had killed enough men to stock a graveyard. 'A feeling of remorse,' he said, 'sometimes comes over me. But I'm an altered man now. I haven't killed a man for over two weeks! What'll yer poison yerself with?' he added, dealing a resonant blow on the bar."[13]

Hangings were the inevitable results of gunfights that were

judged unfair. Once they began to be supported by court decisions, executions became formalized, and "hanging days" were often the high spots of the social season in frontier towns. People traveled for miles to county seats or wherever a hanging was held, bringing food and drink and organizing sportive picnics from the tailgates of their buggies and wagons somewhat as modern college alumni tailgate from their automobiles before attending football games—which may have replaced hangings as jolly social events in our time.

Reporting the hanging of Morgan Williams on the Arkansas frontier in 1835, a newspaper described the incident as full-scale entertainment for a large number of spectators. Williams began his "last words" by reading a prepared story of his life. He then made a speech to vindicate himself, sang a song he had composed for the occasion, and bade each of his friends goodbye individually by name. All this required a considerable amount of time, but devotees of hangings evidently appreciated long drawn-out executions.[14]

The prevailing attitude toward hangings is indicated by this entry in the 1860 diary of a Denver express clerk: "About three o'clock went down to see the 'German' hung. The gallows was erected a short distance below the Kansas House. There was a great crowd and a good many ladies present. He was very cool to the last moment. Had a prayer and his confession read. Did not make a struggle after he dropped. Everything about the hanging went off quiet. Took a walk after tea."[15]

Not all hangings were public, and black humor usually accompanied the apocryphal accounts. More often than not they concerned horse thieves, as was the case with One-Eye Hogan. One-Eye was suspected of stealing rancher Jack McCarthy's best quarter horse. McCarthy organized a posse of neighboring ranchers and they tracked One-Eye down in a draw where he was asleep, with the horse hitched to a cottonwood. One of the tree's lower limbs looked quite suitable for a necktie party.

One-Eye's defense was that his own mount had gone lame and he had only borrowed the quarter horse, leaving his crippled animal in McCarthy's corral. Being reasonable men, the ranchers decided to accept One-Eye's story.

"There is one more thing, though," McCarthy said. "Did you

stop to eat at my cabin this morning?"

One Eye replied that he had done so.

"Can you read?'

"I can read," One-Eye replied.

"Did you read my sign on the wall over the dining table?"

"I noticed a sign, yeah, but I never troubled to read it."

McCarthy motioned for his posse members to gather round and they whispered together for a few minutes. In complete agreement, they turned then toward One-Eye and announced their verdict: One-Eye Hogan must hang.

After stringing up the condemned man, the ranchers followed McCarthy back to his ranch cabin where he showed them the dirty plates, cups, and utensils left on the table by One-Eye, and the sign on the wall that the culprit had neglected to read:

All are welcome to my grub
Take anything you wishes
But 'fore you leave my little shack
Be damn sure you wash the dishes.

As open and free as the frontier was, minorities were frequently the butt of rough practical jokes. And whenever a lawbreaker wanted to cover his transgressions, it was usually convenient to blame the Indians.

A lazy tightwad squatter who had failed to register his claim learned suddenly one day that a party of land speculators were coming to survey unclaimed plots in the area. Fearing the loss of his land and house, the squatter mounted his horse and galloped toward the surveyors, loudly shouting: "Indians! Indians! They're murdering and scalping everybody in the valley. Help! Help! Ride for help!" The frightened land speculators turned their horses quickly and rode as fast as they could to the nearest town.

While almost everybody in the town and countryside forted up to await the attack, the squatter rode into the county seat and registered his claim.

The Indians themselves, awed by and not understanding the technical and scientific advantages enjoyed by white frontiersmen, were often the sport of explorers, fur trappers, Army officers, and others who came in close contact with them.

Captain John G. Bourke, who for many years was aide-de-camp to General George Crook and author of a number of substantial works on the western frontier, delighted in playing practical jokes on his associates. The tricks sometimes rebounded. While stationed at Fort Robinson, Nebraska, in the 1870s, Bourke began tinkering with one of the crude electrical apparatuses of that day—a battery, a pail of water, and a revolving handle to generate electricity.

Setting up his equipment in an entry to the officers' messroom, Bourke dropped a few shiny coins into the charged pail of water and stood nearby to watch the astonished faces of those who attempted to retrieve the coins. The electric current was strong enough to repel most attempts, and Bourke gradually added to the value and number of coins in the pail.

Indian chiefs who lived on the adjoining agency were frequently invited to dine at the officers' mess, and some of them were enticed into a try for the coins. Word soon spread around the agency that Captain Bourke possessed a "medicine box" so powerful that neither Spotted Tail nor Dull Knife could overcome it. Several medicine men from the Sioux and Cheyenne tribes also came to try their spells upon it, and failed. High Wolf, one of the most renowned of the Cheyenne medicine men, at first declined any attempt to overcome the mysterious instrument and win the wealth at the bottom of the pail. Not until after Captain Bourke challenged him personally, and several women of his tribe chided him into action, did High Wolf venture a visit to test the power of electricity. When news spread that High Wolf was preparing to pit his "medicine" against Bourke's contraption, a considerable crowd of Indians and military men began gathering. For this great occasion, the more confident of the officers dropped several extra silver dollars into the pail.

High Wolf brought along some fresh stems of sweet grass, balled them around a small stone, and placed the magic object in his mouth. After obeisance to the sun and the four directions, he began humming his "medicine song," gradually increasing the volume of sound.

Meanwhile Captain Bourke had been busy spinning the handle

of his battery's generator. When High Wolf began chanting, Bourke attempted to counter this power by launching into a rendition of his favorite ballad, "Pat Malloy." At last High Wolf was ready to plunge one of his brawny arms into the pail of water.

"I am not prepared to say exactly how many hundred thousand volts he got," Captain Bourke later recalled, "but worst of all, he couldn't let go. He was strong as a mule and kicked like a Texas congressman, smashing the poor rickety battery all to pieces." To Bourke's surprise, High Wolf was neither humiliated nor defeated. The medicine man demanded a second try, a request that Bourke could not honorably refuse. The captain patched up his contraption but was unable to produce enough electrical current to prevent High Wolf from easily fishing the silver and gold coins from the pail. And thus were the tables turned upon a practical joker. Not only did the proposed victim, High Wolf, win the prize, his reputation as a powerful medicine man was enhanced.[16]

Shortly before the Civil War, Colonel Charles May, a dragoon commander in the Southwest, obtained a quantity of chloroform for medicinal use. One day a group of Indians visited the dragoon encampment, and May told them that he had the power to kill a man and then restore him to life. He asked for a volunteer among the visitors. None responded, but one man offered his dog for the experiment.

The colonel took the dog into a nearby tent and after a few minutes returned with it, apparently lifeless in his arms. To further convince the Indians that he had killed the dog, May placed it on the ground and cut off a piece of its tail. As the animal showed no signs of life, the Indians agreed that it must indeed be dead.

May then carried the dog back into his tent, returning a few minutes later to drop it in front of the Indians. With a loud yelp the recovered dog scurried out of the circle, whereupon the Indians leaped to their feet in fright to follow the tailless animal. Along with the dog they put as much space as possible between themselves and the diabolical soldier-chief May.

Several months later, Colonel May was leading a troop of dragoons across the southern Plains when he sighted a small party of Indians. He ordered his men up a low knoll to face the Indians on a similar mound, each group trying to determine if the other was friendly or hostile.

Eventually the leader of the Indians began gesticulating and brandishing a small object above his head. He then clasped his hands in a sign of friendship. He had recognized Colonel May, and when he led his followers out to meet the dragoons, he held up the dried tail of the dog that the officer had "killed" and brought back to life. What Colonel May had meant as an amusing practical joke had unexpectedly made him into a white chief with great magical powers.[17]

Black men on the frontier were also objects of derisive pranks, entertaining perhaps to the perpetrators but rarely ever to the victims. While John Bratt was working as a trader at Camp Mitchell in western Nebraska, his black handyman, John Duval, came to him and declared that he was in love with Puss Garner, a young half-blood Sioux who was a frequent visitor to the trading post. Duval wanted to make Puss his wife and take her back with him to Missouri.

At first Bratt advised Duval not to pursue his courtship, warning him that the girl's Indian grandmother did not like black men, that she had a violent temper, and had threatened to use her butcher knife on any man she did not like who came near her granddaughter.

Duval was persistent, however. "He had $600," Bratt said, "and would give it all to get her and begged me to see what I could do...I told him he might give her and her relatives every dollar he had and then not get her, but he did not care and wanted me to go ahead."

Conniving with the post surgeon, Bratt arranged a mock marriage. He told Duval to present Puss with two white or spotted ponies, a fine saddle, two red blankets, looking glasses, beads, paints, moccasins, and shawls, and to obtain numerous other presents for her relatives and friends. In addition he would have to arrange for a big feast. Duval agreed to these requirements even though they would surely cost him his entire savings.

"Puss hesitated a long time before consenting to even a mock marriage," Bratt said, "and old Grandma Antelope invested in another whetstone to make her knife doubly sharp for John...The officers of the Post were taken into the secret and entered into it with much zeal. Dr. Cunningham, the post surgeon, was to perform the ceremony."

After John Duval left his presents outside Puss's tepee, she came out and unsaddled the ponies and took the other things into the tepee—a gesture of acceptance of the proposed marriage. At this point, however, Bratt decided to inform Duval that this was only a mock marriage and that it was up to Puss to decide whether she wanted to go to Missouri to live with him. Duval still wanted Bratt to arrange the ceremony.

Collecting numerous candles and lanterns, Bratt lighted the scene of the wedding ceremony brightly. Soldiers, Indians, bullwhackers and muleskinners crowded into the trading post, and Ben Holladay's stagecoach delayed its departure so that its passengers could witness the ceremony. Bride and groom were dressed in their finest.

"At last, all being ready, the ceremony proceeded. The doctor read some lines from one of Shakespeare's plays, made John jump several times backwards and forwards over a long stick, made him stand on his head, crawl on his knees, walk on his hands and feet, bark like a dog, meow like a cat, bawl like a cow, howl like a wolf, yell like an Indian, give the war whoop, and do many stunts that created much merriment, but John took for granted it was all a part of the ceremony. After the ceremony came the marriage feast, which all relished, except the whites when it came to the dog soup and dog meat which the Indians present enjoyed very much."

Sometime before two o'clock in the morning, Puss slipped quickly away, and when the party ended, Duval asked what he should do next. Someone told him to go to her tepee and see if she would allow him to enter. Mustering up his courage, Duval followed the suggestion, but when he raised the tepee flap, Grandma Antelope came charging out with her butcher knife. Duval took off running, pursued by the old woman and a pack of barking dogs.

Next morning the disillusioned handyman returned to the trading post. According to Bratt's story, Duval never again went near the tepee to claim his bride. Bratt managed to recover some of the presents for him, but not the ponies. A few days later Duval joined a train of freight wagons bound for Missouri and was never seen again at Camp Mitchell. John Duval was a victim of frontier attitudes, now fortunately less accepted than in the past.[18]

Wherever there were hangings there were usually undertakers, and their black costumes suited the dark jesting that surrounded their activities. In the early boom days of mining in the West, undertakers usually made arrangements with saloons and gambling establishments to remove bodies immediately after violent altercations and shootouts. An enterprising Denver cabinetmaker named McGovern developed just such a practice. He also owned the cemetery, and would always place the victim in one of his hand-hewn coffins before driving out to the burial ground. If no one followed the hearse—and usually no one did—the undertaker would dump the body out of the casket into the grave and make use of it again.[19]

In more sophisticated places such as San Francisco, undertakers held elaborate funerals for those who could afford them. Hearses were quite fancy, and to relieve the blackness of the plumes and palls and wreaths, teams of pure white horses were used to pull the vehicles. Further relief was provided by hired grooms dressed in black but wearing bright-colored plumage in their hats as they walked on either side of the hearse.

Friends of the deceased were often quite creative in their efforts to provide entertaining epitaphs for inscriptions on grave markers. A San Diego newspaper printed this narrative epitaph seen at the Sparta Diggings during the California gold rush:

> *Here lies the body of Jeems Humbrick*
> *who was accidentally shot*
> *on the bank of the pacus river*
> *by a young man*
> *He was accidentally shot with one of*
> *the large colt's*
> *revolvers with no stopper for the cock*
> *to rest on it*
> *was one of the old fashion kind brass*
> *mounted and of*
> *such is the kingdom of heaven.*

James Clyman, one of the more literate of the fur-trading

Mountain Men, composed an epitaph for his friend Moses (Black) Harris:

> *Here lie the bones of old Black Harris*
> *who often traveled beyond the far west*
> *and for the freedom of equal rights*
> *He crossed the snowy mountin Hights*
> *was free and easy kind of soul*
> *Especially with a Belly full.*

A troop of cavalry following the Santa Fe Trail west halted near a grave marker: HERE LIES SANDY MCGREGOR, A GENEROUS FATHER AND A PIOUS MAN. "That's just like the Scots," declared one of the Irish troopers. "Three men in one grave."

This oft-quoted epitaph is said to be in a cemetery in Ouray, Colorado:

> *Here lies Charlotte,*
> *She was a harlot.*
> *For fifteen years she preserved her virginity*
> *A damn good record for this vicinity.*[20]

J.S. McClintock observed this one, inscribed on a single marker above three graves in the Black Hills:

> *Here lie the bodies of Allen, Curry and Hall.*
> *Like other thieves they had their rise, decline and fall;*
> *On yon pine tree they hung till dead,*
> *and here they found a lonely bed.*
>
> *Then be a little anxious how you gobble horses up*
> *For every horse you pick up here, add as sorrow to your cup;*
> *We're bound to stop this business, or hang you to a man,*
> *For we've hemp and hands enough in town*
> *To swing the whole damned clan.*[21]

An epitaph that appears to have been used more than once for victims of gunfights was short and to the point:

> *He had sand in his craw*
> *But was slow on the draw*
> *So we planted him 'neath the daisies.*

Inscriptions used so often that they became banal sometimes

attracted postscripts from critics:

> *Remember me as you pass by*
> *As you are now so once was I*
> *As I am now so you must be*
> *Prepare for death and follow me.*

Below that inscription left on the Oregon Trail in 1849 a passerby scrawled:

> *To follow you is not my intent*
> *Unless I know which way you went.*[22]

Lawyers as Entertainers

THE FRONTIER COURTROOM was theater, the only stage that many of the smaller settlements had, and the players from the judges down to the lowest functionaries made the most of every opportunity to create merriment in their performances.

During Dodge City's heyday as a wild cowtown, a local *Times* reporter described a scene in the police court:

> "The Marshal will preserve strict order," said the Judge. "Any person caught throwing turnips, cigar stumps, beets, or old quids of tobacco in this Court, will be immediately arranged before this bar of Justice." Then Joe [a local policemen] looked savagely at the mob in attendance, hitched his ivory handle a little to the left and adjusted his moustache.
>
> "Trot out the wicked and unfortunate, and let the cotillion commence," said his Honor.
>
> City vs. James Martin—But just then a complaint not on file had to be attended to, and Reverent John Walsh of Las Animas, took the Throne of Justice, while the Judge stepped over to Hoover's [a saloon].
>
> "You are here for horse stealing," says Walsh.
>
> "I can clean out the damned court," says Martin. Then the City Attorney was banged into a pigeon hole in the desk, the table upset, the windows kicked out and the railing broke down. When order was restored, Joe's thumb was "some chawed," Assistant Marshal Ed Masterson's nose sliced a trifle, and the cantankerous originator of all this, James Martin, Esq., was bleeding from a half dozen cuts on the head, inflicted by Masterson's revolver. Then Walsh was deposed and Judge Frost took his set, chewing burnt coffee, as his habit, for his complexion. The evidence was brief and pointed.
>
> "Again," said the Judge, as he rested his alabaster brow on his left paw, "do you appear within this sacred realm, of which I, and only I am high muck-i-muck. You have disturbed the quiet of

our lovely village. Why, instead of letting the demon of passion fever your brain into this fray, did you not shake hands and call it all a mistake. When the lion and the lamb would have lain down together and white-robed peace would have fanned you with her silvery wings and elevated your thoughts to the good and pure by her smiles of approbation; but, no you went to chawing and clawing and pulling hair. It is $10.00 and costs, Mr. Martin."[1]

Similar courtroom antics were reported some years earlier in a Missouri newspaper, the writer describing how the spectators interrupted the proceedings with whistles, by whittling away at tables and chairs, and cracking walnuts on the wood-burning stove: "A double-fisted fellow...appeared desirous to get a fight; 'hell's afloat, and the river's rising,' said he. 'I'm the yaller flower of the forest; a flash and a half of lightning; a perfect thundergust. Who wants to fight?'"[2]

The famous Benton–Birch trail in Missouri attracted so many lawyers that it became a legal circus. After Thomas Hart Benton and James Birch fought a fierce campaign for the U.S. Senate, Birch charged Benton with slander for saying that Birch had beaten his wife and knocked out all her teeth because she objected to his liaison with another woman. On another occasion, Benton allegedly described Birch as a sheep-killing dog.

Both men had personal and political friends among the lawyers of the Missouri frontier, and many of them came to speak for one side or the other. Waldo Johnson, a supporter of Benton, spoke so eloquently that he brought one spectator to his feet shouting, "Go it my little Johnson! Rise and shine, honey; live in the milk and die in the cream!"[3]

Benton's supporters were certain he would win the case, and openly placed bets on a verdict in his favor. During the closing hours of summation, however, Birch's lawyer made such a silver-tongued appeal to the jury's emotions that some members wept openly, and after due deliberation awarded Birch five thousand dollars, a considerable fortune in those days.

In the early 1880s the Marquis de Mores, a Frenchman who had married an American heiress, established a large ranch in the Dakota Badlands. In order to have a shipping point for his cattle, the marquis built a small town along the Northern Pacific Railroad and named it Medora in honor of his wife. As there were several other large ranches in the area (including one owned by Theodore Roosevelt) the town of Medora became the center for the requirements of what was largely a cattle-raising economy.

One of Medora's first courtroom comedies concerned a cattle rustler, a disbarred lawyer named Simpson, and a profane bailiff named Bill Jones who had recently immigrated from New York City where he had been a fireman. The only lawyer willing to take the rustler's case was the disbarred Simpson, who was given permission by the court to remain just outside the courtroom and transmit messages to a young assistant inside.

As there was no courthouse in Medora, the trial was held in a schoolroom. On the morning the court opened, a group of cowboys wearing their best boiled shirts came into town for jury duty. They were met by bailiff Bill Jones, known as "Foul-Mouthed Bill," who instructed them in proper courtroom behavior. "When the judge comes in," Jones told them, "you all stand up and don't sit down until the judge sits—that's the way we do it in New York."

Meanwhile Simpson was organizing a command post outside on the front steps of the schoolhouse. From there he could coach his untrained assistant on the points of law in the cattle rustler's case.

After the jury was empaneled and the evidence taken, Simpson sent a message inside to his assistant, instructing him to object to everything the other side did. The young man followed orders. In the Badlands cattle country, however, the trial of a cow thief seldom lasted very long, but in this case, according to one witness, representatives for both the prosecution and defense delivered "fiery, frothing addresses" to the jury.

When they were finished, the judge gave his charge, and then asked "Foul-Mouthed Bill" the bailiff if he had a proper place where the jury could retire for consultation and where they could not be approached.

"I have, your Honor," replied Bill Jones. "I've been in New York and know all about these things." The jury then filed out of the schoolroom, with Jones in close attendance. He led them down the street to a saloon, entered the barroom and ordered everyone out except the bartender, whom he warned not to have any conversation with members of the jury. "Now sling out a drink for all of us," he added, "and charge it to the county."

After the foreman of the jury had downed his whiskey, he suggested that they return to the courtroom and finish the business.

"No," replied Bill Jones.

"Well," said the foreman, "we have convicted him."

"I know that," said Jones. "I heard you decide he was guilty as you came over here, but you've got to put up a bluff at chewing the rag before you go back, or the judge will think that you don't know nothing, and you don't." One member of the jury wanted to know how long they would have to wait. "Well, said Bill, "I couldn't let you go in less than half an hour."

"Can we smoke and drink while we're waiting?"

"Yes, said Bill, "you can smoke and liquor up a little at your own expense, but I got to get you back sober."

Half an hour later, Jones ordered the bartender to sling another round of drinks at the expense of the county. He then told the foreman how to deliver the verdict, and instructed the rest of the jury to respond only with bobs of their heads when they were asked: "So say all of you?"

After the verdict was delivered, Lawyer Simpson's associate rushed out to the schoolhouse steps to inform him of the result. "I knew he was guilty," the disbarred lawyer replied, "but go back and take an appeal. Tell the judge that we have two very important witnesses that were held up by high water and couldn't get here."

The judge took the appeal under advisement, delivered a congratulatory address to the jury, and then adjourned the court.[4]

Some frontier judges could be as unprincipled as the accused who were brought into their courts, and were less interested in justice than in the fines they levied and often put into their pockets. Judge R.C. Barry, known as the "Texas Bantam Cock," held court in a saloon in Sonora, California, while it was still a raw mining camp. On one occasion Barry fined a mule thief a hundred dollars and costs. When he learned that the thief had no gold dust to pay the fine, Judge Barry ruled that the original owner of the mule, George Work, would have to pay the fine if he wanted his mule returned. Work's lawyer made a strong protest, too strong in fact, as the judge's written memorandum of the case reveals:

> H.P. Barber, the lawyer for George Work insolently told me there was no law for me to rool so I told him that I did not care a damn for his book law, that I was the law myself. He jawed back so I told him to shet up but he would not so I fined him 50 dollars and comited him to gaol for 5 days for contempt of Coort in bringing my roolings into disreputableness and as a warning to unrooly citizens not to contradict this Coort.[5]

In Cheyenne, Wyoming, during the railroad track-laying days, Colonel Luke Murrin served as city magistrate and judge. Everyone charged with gunplay who was brought before Judge Murrin was fined ten dollars "whether he hit or missed." To these standard fines the judge always added twenty-five cents:

"Your fine is ten dollars and two bits."

"Yes, your Honor, but what's the two bits for?"

"To buy your honorable judge a drink in the morning."[6]

While visiting the Nevada mining towns in 1860, Sir Richard Burton noted: "A mining discovery never fails to attract from afar a flock of legal vultures—attorneys, lawyers, and judges. As the most valuable claims are mostly parted with by the ignorant fortunate for a song, it is usual to seek some flaw in the deed of sale, and a large proportion of the property finds it way into the pockets of the acute professional, who works on half profits."

Several of the judges encountered by Burton had committed murder and other crimes themselves, and their courtroom rulings were sometimes surprising: "A man was convicted of killing his adversary, after saying to the bystanders, 'Stoop down while I shoot the son of a bitch.' Counsel for the people showed *malice prepense;* counsel for defense pleads that his client was *rectus in curia,* and manifestly couldn't mean a man, but a dog. The judge ratified the verdict of acquittal."[7]

The epitome of frontier judges was Roy Bean, whose life was filled with more adventures than the heroes of the wildest Western dime novels. During the last half of the nineteenth century he participated in a variety of shootouts and duels in Mexico and California. He was even hanged once, but survived with a permanent scar where the rope burned into his neck. He was a blockade runner for the Confederacy, and after the war operated saloons in San Antonio. In the 1880s he drifted out to the Pecos River country of west Texas where he became a justice of the peace and began dispensing the law to prisoners brought in by the Texas Rangers.

For a courtroom, Roy Bean used his saloon, often hearing cases on the front porch. He fancied Mexican sombreros, wore bandannas around his scarred neck, and let his shirttail hang out. Frequently he served and drank beer during court sessions.

Many of Judge Bean's court decisions have become intermixed with legend. Perhaps best known is the case of the man charged with carrying a concealed weapon. Bean's 1879 edition of the *Revised Statutes of Texas* told him the accused had violated the law, but he also found another statute that permitted travelers to carry arms packed out of sight. Since the man was walking when arrested, Bean ruled that he was a traveler and therefore not guilty. On another occasion he fined a dead man forty dollars for the same offense, declaring that he was not able to walk or ride and therefore was not a traveler.

Like Roy Bean, a Tucson judge named Meyers had no legal training, but unlike Bean he was not able to obtain any books of territorial statutes to guide him. Before his appointment, however, Judge Meyers had been a pharmacist. To lend dignity to his office he placed his largest volumes of materia medica, dispensatories, and military hygiene, as well as a copy of Webster's dictionary on his desk. Whenever a difficult case came before him, Meyers would consult one of these books, deliberate a few moments, and then render a verdict.

A Colorado contemporary of Roy Bean used the same sort of informality in his dealings with lawbreakers. He was Jim Barker of Blue Lizard Gulch in El Paso County. One of the first cases brought before him was a complaint by a traveling preacher, one Elder Slater, against Zimri Bowles, charged with stealing Slater's one-eyed mule.

Zimri was arrested while in the act of forcing the mule down Mad Gun Mountain with a lariat fastened to the animal's tail. The proof against Zimri Bowles was conclusive, and although he was a friend of Judge Barker, the latter proceeded to sentence him to a year in the Territorial penitentiary.

"An' now, Zim," continued the judge, "seeing as I'm about out of things to eat, an' as you will have the [court] cost to pay, I reckon you'd better take a turn among the Foot Hills with your rifle, an' see if you can't pick up some meat before night, as you can't start for the Big Canyon before morning."

Soon after nightfall Zim brought the judge a black-tail deer and a rabbit. On the following morning, Constable Mike Irving, mounted on a bronco, and the prisoner Zimri Bowles, mounted on the one-eyed mule, kindly lent him by Elder Slater, started on a two-day journey through the mountains to the penitentiary. By the time they arrived there, the bronco and the mule were loaded with deer, antelope, and bear. After selling the game to the warden, Mike and Zimri divided up the money, and then the constable handed over his prisoner and a written message from Judge Barker:

> To the hed man of the Colorado prison, down at the foot of the Big Canyon on the Arkansas—Take Notice:—
> Zimri Bowles, who comes with this here, Stole Elder Slater's one-eyed mule, and it was all the mule the Elder had, and I sentenced him officially to one year in the Colorado prison, and hated to do it, seein as Zim once stood by me like a man when the Injuns had me in a tight place an arter I sentenced Zim to one year for stealing the Elder's mule, my wife, Lizzy, who is a kind o' tender hearted critter, come and leaned her arm on my shoulder, and says she, "Father, don't forget the time when Zim, and his rifle, covered our cabin from Granite Mountain, and saved us from the Arapahoes, and Father, I have heard you tell that arter you was wounded at Sand Creek, an helpless, it was Zimri's rifle that halted the Injun that was creeping in the grass to scalp you." An then there was a tear fell splash upon the sentence I was writing and I changed my mind sudently as follows: seeing the mule had but one eye, and wernt mor'n half a mule at that, you can let Zim go at about six months, an sooner if the Injuns should get ugly, an, futhermore, if the Elder shud quiet down an give in any times, I will pardon Zim out instanter.
> Witness my official hand and seal,
> JAMES BARKER, J.P.[8]

Judges who were sent out from the East by the federal government were sometimes slow to accept local customs. One such was a

Judge Fitzgerald, appointed to Tucson, Arizona Territory. Fitzgerald forbade smoking, tolerated no loud talking or other disturbances, and required attorneys and jurors to wear suit coats in his courtroom.

One day when a jury filed into the box, the judge noted a brawny miner dressed in a shirt and overalls.

"What do you mean, sir," Fitzgerald shouted, "by appearing in this courtroom in your shirt sleeves? Where is your coat?"

"At home, Judge," replied the juror.

"Then go and get it. Not a word from you, sir, or I'll commit you for contempt!"

The miner went silently. He did not return that day, nor the next, and Judge Fitzgerald, after swearing in another juror, issued a bench warrant for the miner's arrest.

Several days later, the man appeared in the courtroom, dressed as he had been ordered. To the angry judge, he explained that his home was down near the Mexican border, more than a hundred miles by horseback—information he had been unable to impart because the judge had silenced him.[9]

In the beginning of another trial in Arizona Territory, a judge noticed after two hours of preliminaries that there were only eleven jurors present. "Where is the twelfth juryman?" he demanded.

"Please, your honor," replied one of the eleven, "he had to go back to his ranch. But he left his verdict with me."[10]

Just before hearing a case in frontier Oregon, the judge summoned the opposing lawyers into his chambers. "I have a problem," he told them. "Last night the plaintiff sent me $200 to decide the case in his favor. Then this morning the defendant sent me $300 to decide in his favor."

"Under these circumstances," asked the plaintiff's lawyer, "are you going to return the $200 to my client?"

"No," said the judge. "No, I figure I'll just give $100 back to the defendant, and then we'll try this case on its own merits."

When outside the courtroom, some of the severest and most solemn judges occasionally displayed tendencies toward humor. In 1878, Charles Thomas accompanied Judge Bowen, a stern adjudicator, to the Colorado town of Parrott City. Thomas and the judge found rooms in a boarding house, and on the day of their arrival an entire sheep, minus its head, appeared on the dining table in a huge dish filled with melted grease. "We were there for a week," Thomas recalled, "with the sheep present at every meal. Efforts were occasionally made to eat parts of it, but our stomachs were unequal to it. At the end of the last meal, Judge Bowen told the landlord that court would adjourn that afternoon. 'But before adjournment,' added the judge, 'I intend to discharge that damned sheep of yours on his own recognizance.'"[11]

During the intermittent wars of the 1880s between cattlemen and rustlers around Tombstone, Arizona, judges were not immune to threats and acts of violence. Soon after Judge Wells Spicer found the Earp brothers and Doc Holliday not guilty in the famous gunfight at the O.K. Corral, he received an anonymous letter. Spicer immediately gave the letter to the *Tombstone Epitaph* to publish, along with an accompanying reply.

> TO WELLS SPICER—Sir, if you take my advice you will take your departure for a more genial Clime. as I don't think this One Healthy for you much longer. As you are liable to get a hole through your coat at any moment. If such sons of Bitches as you are allowed to dispense Justice in this Territory, the Sooner you Depart from us the better for yourself. And the community at large you may make light of this But it is only a matter of time you will get it sooner or later So with these few gentle hints I will Conclude for the first and last time.
>
> A MINER.

In his reply Judge Spicer turned his frontier wit upon the anonymous threat and made merry with it:

> I much regret that the writer of the above did not sign his true name or at least inform me what mine he works in, for I would really be pleased to cultivate his acquaintance, as I think he would be an amiable companion—when sober.
>
> A close examination of the chirography of the above love letter reveals the fact that it was written with a stub pen, in a backhand, with the intent to disguise the handwriting, and must have been written by some one who attended both the spelling and writing school.
>
> As I cannot have the pleasure of a personal interview with

the amiable "Miner," will you allow me the privilege of replying to his charming epistle, and say to him that I have concluded not to go, nor would I ever notice his disinterested advice on the subject were it not for the fact that similar threats have been made by others, and that the threats would be carried into execution if they only dared to do it...

I am well aware that all this hostility to me is on account of my decision in the Earp case, and for that decision I have been reviled and slandered beyond measure, and that every vile epithet that a foul mouth could utter has been spoken of me, principal among which has been that of corruption and bribery...

In conclusion I will say that I will be here just where they can find me should they want me, and that myself and others who have been threatened will be here long after all the foul and cowardly liars and slanderers have ceased to infest our city...

WELLS SPICER[12]

On the frontier, as now, judges seldom rated very high with the people they were supposed to be serving. Except for the few federal authorities sent from the East, judges were usually ordinary folk, not necessarily lawyers. Any show of pomposity or power that judges might attempt to display was promptly put down.

Hank Monk, the stagecoach driver who frightened Horace Greeley on his ride over the Sierras, was not one to take lightly a threat from a mere judge, such as the swellhead who tried to bully him during a similar rough ride from California into Nevada. For several minutes, Hank paid no attention to the admonitions of his arrogant passenger—until finally the judge shouted at him: "I will have you discharged before the week is out! Do you know who I am, sir?"

"Oh, yes!" replied Hank, "Perfectly well. But I am going to take this coach into Carson City on time if it kills every one-horse judge in the state of California."[13]

After a well-known lawyer became a judge somewhere in Texas, he decided to have his portrait painted. The artist, proud of his work and hoping to obtain more commissions, invited various people of means into the courthouse to view the painting.

"That's not a good likeness of old Joe," one man said bluntly.

"What's the matter with it?" asked the artist.

"He's got his hands in his pockets. They ought to be in somebody else's pockets."

On the Missouri frontier in the 1840s local jokelore held that when lawyers died, there were no burial expenses. They were simply laid out at night in a room with one window open and the door locked. Next morning they were always gone, leaving a strong odor of brimstone in the room.[14]

Frontier judges were likely to lose patience with lawyers who spent too much time arguing over points of law. During a bitter altercation in a Texas court, one lawyer shouted at the other: "You are a lying son of a bitch!" His opponent immediately shot back: "You are a lying son of a bitch yourself."

At this, the judge banged his gavel for order, then let silence hang over the room full of spectators who were certain he would levy a heavy fine upon the offending lawyers.

Instead, the judge leaned forward, fixing his gaze first on one and then the other of the attorneys, and said slowly: "Now that you gentlemen have got acquainted with each other, we will proceed with the argument."[15]

During steamboating days on the inland waters there were frequent explosions of steam boilers that brought on lawsuits. In 1851 *Spirit of the Times* reported the case of Mrs. Jones suing for the value of her husband and a trunk, both missing after the boiler blew up on the *Ol'Kentuck*. Counsel for the steamboat company decided the best course was to make his opponent prove that Mr. Jones was on board the boat when the boiler exploded. After all, no trace of Jones or his trunk had been found after the explosion. The lawyer called the only surviving eyewitness, a German immigrant named Dietmer.

"Did you know the *Ol'Kentuck?*" asked the lawyer.

"Yah, I wash blowed up mit her," replied Dietmer.

"Were you on board when she collapsed her flue?"

"When she bust de bile? Yah, I wash dere."

"Did you know Mr. Jones?"

"To be sure—Mr. Jones and I took passenger together."

"You did? When did you last see Mr. Jones on board the boat?"

"Well, I didn't see Mr. Jones aboard de boat last time!"

Here the defense lawyer was certain he had won his case, yet he asked the perfunctory question. "You did not? Well, Mr. Dietmer, when did you last see Mr. Jones?"

"Well, when the schmoke pipe and me was going up, we met Mr. Jones coming down."[16]

Frontiersmen spent considerable time attempting to outsmart the legal representatives of powerful establishments, particularly the early railroad. In a western Kansas town a dog was run over by a locomotive. Its owner went to see the railroad's lawyer to make a claim for damages.

"My dog, sir, was the finest dog in the state of Kansas," said the owner. "There's nothing that dog didn't know. I wouldn't take a thousand dollars in hard cash for that dog if he was alive today."

"So your dog knew a good deal, did he?" replied the railroad official. "A smart dog?"

"I tell you, sir, that dog would remember everything I told him, and I had to tell him only one time. I wouldn't take a thousand dollars for him this minute."

"If your dog was so damned smart," asked the railroad representative, "why didn't he have sense enough to get off the track when the train was coming?"

Without blinking an eye, the dog's owner responded: "You changed your time-table a couple of days ago, didn't you?"

"Yes, but what's that got to do with it?"

"Well, that's just it. I never saw the new time-table, neither did my dog. If you had sent one around to my place, I would've told the dog what time the fast express was due, and he wouldn't have been on the track."[17]

Frontier lawyers were the cleverest of actors, however, and knew how to turn a case in a client's favor by the use of dramatic devices. If a lawyer could bring a jury to tears, he had a good chance of a favorable verdict. A certain Missouri lawyer was so good at this, he could lead an entire jury into sobbing over the fate of a stolen horse or cow. Flowery language, accompanied by a few Latin phrases, was also a powerful force in swaying untutored jurists. In courtroom theater it was almost a requisite for one of the attorneys to paint the other as a villainous liar and cheat, an evil and malicious human being, and do it with such flamboyant oratory that guilt or innocence no longer mattered.

In western Missouri, a settler was accused of repeatedly inching his rail fence over onto his neighbor's land until he had gained an extra acre. His attorney declared that an act of God had made his client cross-eyed, and that if there had been an encroachment it was an honest mistake. With this point established, the defense then went on the attack, stating that his cross-eyed client was an honest man who would never have even thought of such a scheme. Only a shady lawyer, he said, such as the opposing counsel, would have conceived of such a crooked way to acquire land. After that, the verdict was predictable.[18]

If a person charged with a crime had no money to hire a lawyer, judges sometimes appointed one, the assignment usually falling upon a greenhorn attorney. In December 1847, the *Santa Fe Republican* reported the case of an indigent accused of theft. The judge instructed a neophyte lawyer to withdraw with the prisoner, confer with him, and give him such counsel as would be best for his interest. The lawyer and his client withdrew, and in fifteen or twenty minutes the lawyer returned to the courtroom.

"Where is the prisoner?" asked the judge.

"He is gone, your honor," replied the young lawyer. "Your honor told me to give him the best advice for his interest, and as he said he was guilty, I thought the best counsel I could offer him was to 'cut and run' which he took at once."[19]

From the earliest days of the Republic, most American politicians began their careers as lawyers. For a generation or so after the founding of the nation, the citizenry allowed their lawyer-politicians a period of grace, but by the middle of the nineteenth century elected officials were becoming the butts of barbed jests and colorful insults, especially from the thinly settled frontier where they were known personally by many of the voters who elected them to office. Mark Twain, a child of the frontier, observed that there was no distinctly American criminal class except Congress. Will Rogers, who grew up in the last years of the frontier, was certain that politicians would never permit a newly discovered truth serum to be put on the market because it would ruin the foundations of political government. "If you ever injected truth into politics," he said, "you have no politics."

A visiting English clergyman, S. Reynolds Hole, was shocked by this attitude, and did not agree with a Denver acquaintance that members of the U.S. Congress seemed somewhat inferior to members of the British House of Commons. "I must dissent," he said, "from the cruel distinction made by a quaint gentleman of Denver, when he said, that as the cream was formed upon the milk, as in England the best men were sent up to Parliament, but as in boiling potatoes the scum rose to the surface, so in America the worst men were sent to Congress."[20]

According to that old Mountain Man, James Clyman, the politicians of early California were held in a tight rein. Much has changed since Clyman made his observations: "In speaking of the government of California, I must say that it is the most free and easy government Perhaps on the civilized globe. No Taxes are imposed on any individual whatsoever. I saw nor heard of no requirement for Road Labour no Military tax no civil department to support, no Judiciary requiring pay and in every respect the people live free. You may support Priest or not at your pleasure and if your life and property are not Quite so safe as in some other countries you have the pleasure of using all your earnings."[21]

Politicians were viewed not only as objects of comic entertainment but as providers of monetary largesse by the citizens of Helena, Montana, the capital where the state legislature assembled regularly to tax and spend. "The saloon keepers are complaining that this is the bummest legislature they ever saw," reported a newspaper correspondent in January 1897. "The members are so slow in getting down to the business of blowing in the stuff...The saloon men recall with fond recollections the palmy days of the session of 1893 when it was nothing unusual for certain members who had been properly seen to blow in from $100 to $200 a night apiece. For the next generation by some men in Helena every legislature will be gauged by its saloon propensities, the famous session of 1893 being taken as the standard of perfection."[22]

Politicians who did not imbibe were the exceptions, one of the more notable being William Jennings Bryan of Nebraska. Although he abhorred liquor and spoke against it in his campaign speeches, Bryan was not averse to seeking votes from drinkers in saloons. During his first run for Congress, he would often drink sarsaparilla in barrooms while canvassing for votes. In this way Bryan encountered an old Democrat who admitted he could not hold his liquor, and asked the politician for advice on how to break the habit.

"When you get all the liquor you want," said Bryan, "why don't you call for sarsaparilla?"

"But Mr. Bryan," replied the old gentleman, "when I get all the liquor I want, I can't say sarsaparilla."[23]

Losers of political races were inclined to be sensitive to post-election criticism. After being defeated in a contest for sheriff in Ford County, Kansas, the famous lawman, Bat Masterson, was attacked in print and charged with threatening to whip every "son of a bitch" who voted against him.

Masterson retaliated by placing an advertisement in the *Dodge City Times* of November 15, 1879. "In answer to the publication made by Bob Fry of the *Spearville News*, asserting that I made threats that I would lick any s— of a b—— that voted or worked against me at the last election, I will say it is as false and as flagrant a lie as was ever uttered; but I did say this: that I would lick him the s— of a b—— if he made any more dirty talks about me; and the words s— of a b—— I strictly confined to the Spearville editor, for I don't know of any other in Ford County."[24]

Similar losers in politics made frequent use of newspaper columns to express their indignation. "Another terrible calamity has befallen our unfortunate Territory," declared the editor of the *Arizona Miner* of November 26, 1870, "the will of whose citizens has just been defeated at the ballot box...Mr. McCormick the Vile, and his backers, the contractors, Federal office-holders, monopolists and their retainers, have again stuffed the ballot boxes with fraudulent votes."

And during this same period the *Arizona Sentinel* attacked the city of San Francisco for sending to the U.S. Congress "the biggest fool of them all, Senator Hagen," who was guilty of describing Arizona Territory as "nearly worthless country." The *Sentinel* editor asked rhetorically what the senator knew about Arizona, and answered: "Nothing. He is totally ignorant of the Territory and its resources, and to make such a barefaced gratuitous lying assertion is disgraceful to the country and to his constituency..."[25]

There was always an affinity of sorts between frontier lawyers and the early post office. Lawyers were usually literate and were likely to receive more mail than ordinary citizens. With their political ties they found it easy to obtain appointments as postmasters, giving them a small but steady income between law cases.

Before the Civil War period, private enterprise carried the mail from the Missouri border to the sparsely settled West, and charged twenty-five cents for a letter. After the federal government took over mail deliveries, the price dropped to two cents and remained there until the inflationary rises of modern times.

Quite often postage was not prepaid on letters sent to the West, the recipients being expected to pay the costs. Many sly receivers of letters would return them to the postmaster after reading them, claiming they must have been meant for some other person with a similar name and demanding that the postage they had paid be returned. To stop this practice a Colorado postmaster refused to deliver letters until the addressee stated from where and from whom he expected his mail to come. In case of doubt the postmaster would open the letter and read a few lines.

In one such instance, the postmaster started reading: "Your wife has been raising hell ever since you left—" At this point the man interrupted: "Hold on, I think that is my letter." He took it, paid for it, and went on his way.[26]

On the early frontier there were some illiterate postmasters— who may or may not have been lawyers. A letter to the *Batesville* (Arkansas) *News* in 1839 told of a postmaster at a certain crossroads village who could not read or write. "He is driven to the necessity of measuring the mail—sending three pecks to Little Rock, and two pecks to Batesville, and dwindling down to a gallon when he comes to the *out* counties."[27]

Another problem with mail sent to the West was that everybody along the way wanted to read it—especially the newspapers. An army officer at a Wyoming fort complained that his mail was always being "looked over at the posts along the Platte as far down as Laramie and does not get enriched in the process." On a visit to one post, he said, he saw enlisted men go into the post office and examine all the letters and papers. "Nothing criminal is probably intended by this free-and-easy way of treating the mail, but it does not conduce to speed or to care in its delivery."[28]

At Fort Garland, Colorado, in 1862, the sutler who may also have been a part-time lawyer acted as postmaster in his spare time. On the front of the mail cage he posted a schedule of arrivals and departures:

> Monday—Eastern arrives
> Tuesday—Western arrives
> Wednesday—Eastern closes
> Thursday—Western closes
> Sunday—The Postmaster will put on clean clothes.
> N.B.—The above is subject to all and every change.

Beneath the sign some impertinent soldier scrawled a line: "The clothes? I doubt it!"[29]

During the Civil War, the postmaster at Pueblo, Colorado, certainly must have had other irons in his fire. When the mail bag arrived he would empty it in the middle of the floor and ask those who could read to pitch in and pick out what belonged to them. "What was left after this promiscuous sorting was put in an empty candle box and when people came to the postoffice they were told to go and look for themselves, and not be bothering the postmaster."

A Free but Cantankerous Press

PRINT WAS POWERFUL on the frontier, its only rivals being numerous writers of lengthy letters and a pack of orators who went about the West spreading the word about politics, religion, and the finer things of life. Most local editors lived precariously, however, and some grew quite peevish from continuous struggles with deadbeats, delinquent subscribers, and ruthless competitors. One editor described himself as "a poor fellow who empties his brain to fill his stomach." He spaced out his columns with one-liners about the ingratitude of neighbors, the recklessness of modern youth, and the boldness of frontier women.

"Hell is full of newspapermen who killed themselves blowing for some little one horse town," a Texas editor noted in 1893, "and that too without enough support to fatten a grasshopper. We have decided that it is a sin to lie anyway, and in the future we'll be found telling the truth."[1]

In a similar vein a Kansas editor reacted to constant complaint from his readers: "Whenever people learn to walk upon their eyebrows, to balance ladders on their chins and climb to the top of them —when fleas shall swallow elephants and elephants traverse space upon mosquitos—then, and then only, will an Editor be found whose items give pleasure alike to rich and poor, honest and false, respectable and low."[2]

Editors also had to contend with antiquated presses and shortages of type and printing supplies. An Arkansas printer told of how he overcame a deficiency of "I" and "1" types by substituting the heads of horseshoe nails, but he admitted the typographical appearance of his newspaper was not handsome.

In 1847 Walter Colton described his difficulties at Monterey, California: "The press was old enough to be preserved as a curiosity;

the mice had burrowed in the balls; there were no rules, no leads and the types were rusty and all in pi. It was only by scouring that the letters could be made to show their faces...A sheet or two of tin was procured and these, with a jack-knife, were cut into rules and leads. Luckily we found with the press the greater part of a keg of ink; and now came the main scratch for paper. None could be found, except that used to envelope the tobacco of the cigar smoked here by the natives. A coaster had a small supply of this on board, which we procured. It is in sheets a little larger than the common-sized foolscap...And this is the size of our first peper, which we have christened the *California*..."[3]

In some frontier towns, rival editors carried on constant wars of words with each other, priding themselves on the quality of their rich epithets and scatological insults. The practice became almost a literary art in Kansas and New Mexico, and there were masters of the colorful defamation of fellow scribes scattered through all regions west of the Mississippi.

Soon after Walter Colton started the *California* under great difficulties, he aroused the ire of the editor of the San Franciso *Star*, who derided him in print: "We have received two late numbers of the *California*, a dim, dirty little paper printed at Monterey, on the worn out material of one of the California war presses. It is published and edited by Walter Colton and Robert Semple, the one a lying sycophant and the other an overgrown lickspittle."[4]

In 1868, the editor of the Prescott (Ariz.) *Miner* engaged in a feud with the editor of the Tucson *Arizonian*. On one occasion he went so far as to attack his rival's portrait, which had been sent him by the photographer. "Mr. De Long looks well in a picture; his forehead is well suited for flattening out tortillas; his nose projects some distance from his face, and is, we think, large enough to 'smell a mice.' His mouth appears to have been well cut with some dull instrument, either a crevice spoon or a shovel, and the eyes—those glorious 'yorbs' look like empty egg shells.

"We mean to preserve this picture by having it framed with 'brass,' and mounted on a braying ass..."[5]

Six years later the *Miner* itself came under attack from the Yuma (Ariz.) *Sentinel*'s editor, who claimed to have seen his rival of the *Miner* dead drunk at a party in Prescott, "laid out in the refreshment room...with candles placed at his head and his feet, and a regular 'wake' held over him...It was then for the first time that we discovered Darwin's connecting link. As he lay, with his drunken slobber issuing from his immense mouth which extends from ear to ear, and his ears reaching up so high, everyone present was forcibly impressed with the fact that there was a connecting link between the catfish and the jackass. What we have here faintly described is the truth, to attest which there are plenty of living witnesses. Now dry up, or we will come out with some more reminiscences."[6]

The poet of the Sierras, Joaquin Miller, served for a time as editor of the Eugene (Oregon) *Democratic Register*. When he journeyed to Britain and charmed the Londoners, who named him "the Byron of Oregon," his fellow Oregon editors were not impressed. After Miller's first book of poems was published in Britain, the editor of the *Albany* (Oregon) *Democrat* offered no congratulations. "[Miller] has published a book of poems and become a man of fame in London. This fact makes me think no more of Miller but a lot less of the Londoners."[7]

An unnamed litterateur of New Mexico was put down in similar fashion in 1875 by the editor of the *Daily New Mexican* of Santa Fe. "The monkey, subscribing himself 'Rio Grande' of the *News and Press* continues to climb the literary pole."

The editor who delivered that mild insult was attacked in turn by the *Mesilla Valley Independent*: "The *New Mexican* man seems to be the victim of a troublesome infirmity; from the symptoms recently manifested we conclude that he is afflicted with the 'bots.' In sympathy we recommend a mild course of aloes and turpentine. This remedy is highly recommended in cases of other beasts of burden thus afflicted, and we see no reason why it should not prove equally effective in the case of any *ass*. Suffering of any kind, even of a brute, arouses our sympathies."[8]

A decade later, in the 1880s, the editor of the Las Vegas (New Mexico) *Daily Optic* was also denouncing the *New Mexican* editor for being an ass. "The writer of the second page of the Sante Fe *New Mexican* has about as much idea of the courtesy due a gentleman as an ass has of manners...When the fellow charges the *Optic* with being an 'organ of the New Mexico boodlers,' and having been bribed in its utterances...he lies in his throat!...Bobby Spradling, whose imbecility of mind is shown by the silly paragraphs he pens, at the bidding of his keepers, is painful evidence that he is a bound slave to onanism, and therefore the time server should not be held accountable for what he says or does. Outside of his office he is a man whom God hates (a sneaking coward) and in his office he is a blubbering fool, who is to be pitied and not blamed for his unjournalistic utterances."[9]

During this same period the *Gleaner* and the *News–Register* of Gallup were also battling with each other. The *Gleaner* had this to say of the *News–Register's* editor: "An evidence of the underhanded sneak, liar, ruffian, the two-faced scarecrow whose whiskers are leaking for need of a bath, is given in the last issue of the hyphenated bladder...it says we made anarchist [*sic*] speeches to the strikers and several other damphool statements."

The hyphenated *News–Register* came right back with matching invective: "May fortune flee from him, and evil cling to him all his days; may death rob him of family; friends forsake him; disease waste his flesh; ghosts of women haunt his sleep, and in the end poor, miserable, loathed of men and despised by God may the wretch sink into the grave and hell receive his soul."[10]

In El Paso, Texas, the denunciations were equally acrimonious, as illustrated in this blast from the *Lone Star* in 1883: "When the editor of the El Paso *Herald* shall have cleansed his columns of the filth that has for three years distinguished them—when he shall have returned to the city money he has stolen from the public treasury during the past two years and a half—then, and not till then, can he hope to rise near enough to the plane of respectable people to expect a gentleman to spit in his face."[11]

In 1889, the editor of the Cimarron (Kansas) *Jacksonian* turned his vituperative skills upon a competitor: "We are 'onto' the lop-eared, lantern-jawed, half-bred and half-born whiskey soaked, pox eaten pup who pretends to edit that worthless wad of subdued outhouse bung fodder, known as the Ingalls *Messenger*. He is just starting out to climb the journalistic bannister and wants us to knock the hayseed out of his hair, pull the splinters out of his stern and push him up. We'll fool him. No free advertising from us, Murphy. k.m.a."[12]

During months of controversy in 1887 over changing the county seat of Garfield County, Kansas, from Ravanna to Eminence, the editors of the rival papers engaged in a heated word battle. The Ravanna *Chieftain* described Eminence as a "nondescript collection of bug infested huts which its few and scabby inhabitants have the supreme gall to call a town." As for the editor of the *Eminence Call*, he was a "loathsome creature who sets type for an alleged newspaper in that God-forsaken collection of places unworthy to be called human habitations...he is the kind of man who sleeps on a manure pile from choice and whose breath has been known to turn the stomach of a veteran skunk."[13] (Largely as a result of this county seat squabble, Garfield County lost its identity by being absorbed into an adjoining county, and the two rival towns eventually disappeared from the plains of western Kansas.)

Rivalry between towns was quite common but did not always descend to bickering between editors. Leavenworth, Kansas, and St. Joseph, Missouri, were competitive from the days when they were both jumping-off bases for crossing of the Great Plains, and their newspapers were constantly mocking the opposite city's quality of life. In 1864, after praising Artemus Ward's speech in Leavenworth, the *Times* of that city noted that the great humorist would appear next in St. Joseph. "If the inhabitants of that benighted region do not receive a few grains of common sense," the paper added, "it will be because they are still endowed with their usual amount of stupidity."[14]

The record for the largest number of derogatory adjectives in a one-paragraph editorial may belong to the editor of the *Watonga* (Oklahoma) *Republican*, who was attacking the editor of his rival paper, the *Rustler*, on November 29, 1893. "The ignorant, egotistical, scrawny, miserable, contemptible, disgusting, measly, mangy, depraved, lying, hypocritical, blear-eyed, dough-faced, idiotic, dwarfed, pinched-up, quaking old numbskull of the ex-Rustler ghost still continues to impose himself upon a people who are even more completely disgusted with him than were the Nebraska people who compelled him to make a premature and hasty exit."[15]

Frontier editors managed to save some of their venom for attacks on politicians and local residents. Referring to the governor of neighboring New Mexico Territory, the El Paso *Lone Star* described him as an "old reprobate" with a peculiar faculty for wrongdoing and mischief. "He is the weakest, vainest, most ambitious, most unscrupulous, most unreliable, and most vacillating executive that, we dare say, any state or territory ever had. Besides, which, he is a constitutional liar and was at one time a 'visiting Statesman' [Republican carpetbagger]."[16]

Aroused by the mutilation of a horse, the editor of the Manzano (New Mexico) *Gringo and Greaser* penned this diatribe: "Some lousy, fistulous worm-eaten and otherwise deformed human miscarriage, walking on its hind legs and having a remote resemblance to the animal man, has added another to the horrid list of his infamous acts by cutting off the nose of a colt, the property of Nicolas Candelaria! Such a wretch ought to be mashed to a jelly between two limberger cheeses without benefit of clergy, and the remains of his hideous cadaver chopped into sausage and fed to the dogs."[17]

John P. Clum, who achieved some fame in the West as a humanitarian Indian agent to the Apaches, was one of the founders of the *Tombstone Epitaph* and served as its editor for a few years. During the 1880s Clum became involved in efforts to rid Tombstone of outlaws, and allied himself with Wyatt Earp and his brothers. Clum's newspaper rival was the *Nugget*, which Clum called the "Laughing Hyena," whose editor he accused of supporting cattle rustlers and highwaymen.

On October 26, 1881, three of the Earp brothers, with Doc Holliday, engaged in a grim duel with six outlaws on Fremont Street, not far from the *Epitaph*'s office. This encounter, known as "the fight at the O.K. Corral," soon achieved legendary status in Western lore.

Following the bloody gunfight, the outlaws drew up a list of fifteen Tombstone citizens and marked them for assassination. Editor Clum's name was on the list, but he continued attacking his challengers and the *Nugget*. "Its so-called reply to the specific charges made by the Epitaph," he said in an editorial on December

26, 1881, "as to the different classes of robbery its friends are engaged in are answered by billingsgate, which is universally conceded to be the rogue's argument. They cannot get around the fact that they stand on record as having endorsed the ten-per-cent steal, all the cattle stealing and stage robbing done by their cow-boy friends, the outrages committed by the rustlers, the turning loose of prisoners charged with murder and grand larceny, and other offenses too numerous to mention. They dare not deny that they have virtually endorsed every one of these acts, and as a consequence, answer by making faces at us. We can stand it if they can."[18]

Not long after Clum published that charge, his two partners outvoted him and sold the *Epitaph*, and he decided the time had come for him to leave Tombstone. He boarded a stagecoach, and on the road out of town his enemies fired upon him, but no shots took effect. The life of a frontier newspaperman was not always merry and bright.

Reviewing what he described as "traces of blood on the journalistic moon," a New Mexico editor listed various evidences of violence that had come to his attention. One editor was wearing a steel breast plate; another had acquired a loaded cane. In Albuquerque a woman went after the city editor of the *Democrat* with a strip of rawhide; in the same city another editor was recovering from bruises received during a beating.[19]

During its early years, Denver was a rough town for newsmen. Enemies of the editor of the *News* set fire to his office and burned his home. An indignant candidate for Congress confronted the editor of the *Herald* on the street and spat in his face. When a correspondent for a St. Louis newspaper aroused the ire of the Denver postmaster by exposing his political machinations, the postmaster lured the correspondent into the post office and closed and locked the doors. Then he placed a cocked revolver at the man's head and compelled him to write and sign a statement that he knew his published allegations were false and slanderous. When news of this strong-arm action leaked out, however, a group of outraged citizens of Denver seized the postmaster and threatened to hang him unless he signed a bond to desist from such practices.[20]

In later years in Denver, Eugene Field kept a special chair near his desk in the *Tribune* office for the benefit of threatening visitors. The cane seat of the chair had been removed, and over the hole Field placed an opened newspaper. Friendly visitors were warned away from the chair; those with fire in their eyes usually sat down unbidden, only to wind up with their bottom on the floor and their feet in their face.

People were not the only beings that harassed early frontier editors. Then as now, domestic animals could make life difficult, as the *Daily Monitor* of Fort Scott, Kansas, complained: "The individual who left three kittens, and a dog with a tin pan tied to his narrative, on our office stairs last night, can have them in a transfigured state by calling at the butcher shop. We would modestly suggest that we have no further call for such supplies."[21]

When the appropriately name *Huntsman's Echo* was established at Wood River on the Nebraska plains in 1861, antelopes, foxes, wolves, and buffalo became constant annoyances. Buffalo trampled editor Joe Johnson's garden and turned the grass around his building into dust and mud. "We shan't try to stand it, and give timely notice the the *echo* of fire arms will be a common thing in this neck of the woods, unless the fearfully frightful looking creatures desist from peeking into our office and discomposing our printer."[22]

Editors in rip-roaring boom towns often had lively visitors, among them roving reporters from big newspapers back east, searching for exciting stories. "A Chicago correspondent dropped in on us the other day for a brief visit," an anonymous editor wrote, "and after showing him our Washington hand press, six varieties of job type, and two bundles of print paper, we took him out for a survey of the town. The news had gone abroad that he was a Chicago detective, and it was laughable to note the effect upon our leading citizens. A dozen or more broke for the sage brush, without stopping for clean shirts, and so many others cut off their whiskers or donned false ones that we walked the whole length of Apache Avenue without meeting a man we could recognize at first glance.

"While there is nothing mean about us, this is a feature we are going to work about twice a month on this town. It will keep the boys unsettled and anxious, and may be the means of converting some of them from the error of their ways. It's an awful good feeling to feel that you are the only man in a town of three thousand people whose liver don't kick the breath out of him every time a stranger comes along and takes a second look at the bridge of your nose."[23]

Like most males in the nineteenth century, newspapermen tended to look upon women as second-class citizens. When frontier women by necessity began shaking loose from their centuries-old shackles, many editors viewed them with distrust, an uneasiness that soon grew into fear. To face down this intimidating change, the editors began blaming women for almost everything unpleasant that occurred, and ridiculed them at every opportunity.

In an account of a man's suicide at Fort Scott, Kansas, in 1872, a reporter for the *Daily Monitor* wrote that the coroner's verdict was suicide caused by a woman. "Some woman is always found to be an accomplice in all such scrapes," he concluded, "and we should think they ought to be banished from the community."[24]

Whenever a frontier woman became a public figure, she was likely to suffer a barrage of derision from the press. Calamity Jane, for instance, was a favorite target. The editor of the *Cheyenne Daily Leader* claimed that she responded to one of his tales about her by invading his office with a horsewhip, cracking it above his head, and threatening him until he had to flee the premises. When he returned half an hour later, he found his office wrecked, with tables, chairs, desks, and books scattered about the room. Tacked to the door was a note: "Print in the *Leader* that Calamity Jane, the child of the regiment and a pioneer white woman of the Black Hills, is in Cheyenne, or I'll scalp you, skin you alive and hang you to a telegraph pole. You hear me, and don't you forget it. CALAMITY JANE."

Of this story, Agnes Wright Spring, a pioneer woman herself and a historian of the region, was quite skeptical, pronouncing it a probable fabrication.[25]

Documented accounts of female retaliation against editors do exist, however. A bad review of a theatrical performance brought an actress into the Virginia City *Territorial Enterprise* office where she attempted assault with the point of an umbrella. In 1880, the editor of the *Short Creek* (Kansas) *Daily Republican* wrote an editorial about the painful state of affairs in his county. "What this community needs just now is a society for the prevention of cruelty to writing men, otherwise editors. There is entirely too much blood on the moon and the air is getting too fragrant with the smoke of battle. There are too many bloodthirsty women on the warpath and unless some steps are taken pretty soon to secure a cessation of hostilities, there is liable to be a number of vacant chairs.

"For three days a woman in a violent rage has been promenading the streets of this town, looking for the man who writes up articles for the Republican...She doesn't know him when she sees him, and thanks to a generous public, no one will point him out. She boils over at every street corner, and the object of her search hasn't eaten a hearty meal for three days, and besides his hair is rapidly turning gray."

The editor went on to tell of another woman who had brought suit for libel against the newspaper, and was probably armed with a whip, pistol or loaded cane. Somewhat disheartened, he then concluded: "We no longer have a free press. We have been muzzled, and that, too, by women who seem determined not only to rule but to ruin also."[26]

A story that circulated through western newspapers for several months may or may not have originated with the *Melrose* (Wisconsin) *Chronicle*. "It is reported that one of the fastidious newly married ladies of this town *kneads* bread with her gloves on. This incident may be somewhat peculiar, but there are others. The editor of this paper *needs* bread with his shoes on; he *needs* bread with his shirt on; he *needs* bread with his pants on, and unless some of the delinquent subscribers to this 'Old Rag of Freedom' pony up before long, he will *need* bread without a damn thing on, and Wisconsin is no Garden of Eden in the winter time." As was the custom, papers copied extensively from each other, and this play on words at the expense of a fastidious woman appeared in various versions until it was worn out.

Sometimes editors shifted sights and ridiculed marrying males, as in this account of a Texas wedding: "The groom was dressed in a black, two-button, tailored to measure wool suit, plain black tie and black socks with small embroidered silver stars which jetted vertically down the sides. The shirt was white cotton with french cuffs fastened with striking bold cuff links which matched the pin. Plain toed black calfskin shoes completed the very masculine attire. The bride wore the traditional white."

Like many other publisher–editors, Joe Johnson of the *Huntsman's Echo* was often in search of an assistant. In April 1861 he advertised for "an 'outdoor' partner, who don't drink, smoke or chew, can work all day at every business—from the hairspring of a watch up to feeding pigs and picking millstones, turning grindstone when it rains, preaching on Sundays, and doing all the editor's hard fighting."[27]

A "Wanted Immediately" notice in the *Arizona Sentinel* of October 5, 1872, carries a note of beleagured desperation. "A large, broad-shouldered, bulldog head, short-haired man, is wanted immediately at this office, to serve as fighting Editor for the Sentinel. We have tried to do our own work, besides 'playing the devil,' but when it comes that we have to fight battles, then we are not equal to the emergency. After mature deliberation, we conclude that engaging a fighting Editor is the cheapest. Applicants will please send weight—whether light or heavy—also the number of men he has 'chawed up.' Terms—half the profits. Blood pudding furnished everyday. None but the principal need apply."[28]

In 1874, the editor of the *Mesilla* (New Mexico) *News* advertised for a man to collect overdue subscriptions and other bills: "Wanted, at this office, an able-bodied, hard-featured, bad-tempered, not-to-be-put-off and not-to-be-backed-down, freckle-faced young man, to collect for this paper; must furnish his own horse, saddle-bags, pistols, whiskey, bowie-knife and cowhide. We will furnish the accounts. To such we promise constant and laborious employment."[29]

A young editor who was preparing to go west to found a newspaper on the frontier asked the famous Kentucky journalist, Henry Watterson, if he should always be careful to tell the truth in his news stories. "Lord, no," Watterson replied. "That would ruin us. Write something that everybody will read and that nobody can remember."

Truthfulness was certainly not the hallmark of frontier journalism.

Editors learned to give their readers what they wanted, and apparently that was entertainment. The tall tale told orally was at the heart of frontier humor, and after the printing presses came west, readers delighted in printed whoppers and big brags, along with dashes of scandal, and black humor mixed with merry quips. Factual news was usually relegated to a column of one-liners. Newspaper readers knew the difference. If Mark Twain's editor in Virginia City had restricted him to writing facts—who, what, when, and where stories—we probably never would have heard of Mark Twain. He learned his craft, along with several contemporaries like Dan De Quille (William L. Wright), by writing embroidered news for the Virginia City *Territorial Enterprise* and other frontier papers.

Bill Nye of the *Laramie* (Wyoming) *Boomerang*, who was a master of the exaggerated news story, made a great pretense of being shocked by the many variations in published reports of General Philip Sheridan's horse: "I found out that General Sheridan's celebrated Winchester horse was raised in Kentucky, also in Pennsylvania and Michigan; that he went out as a volunteer private, that he was in the regular service prior to the war, and that he was drafted, and that he died, on the field of battle, in a sorrel pasture, in '73, in great pain on Governor's Island; that he was buried with Masonic honors by the good Templars and the Grand Army of the Republic; that he was resurrected by a medical college and dissected; that he was cremated in New Orleans and taxidermed for the Military Museum of New York. Every little while I run up against a new fact relative to the beast. He has died in nine different states, and has been buried in thirteen different sites while his soul goes marching on. Evidently we live in an age of information. You can get more information nowadays, such as it is, than you know what to do with."[30]

Few limits were placed upon the prevarications of newspapermen in the Old West. Mark Twain's editor on the *Territorial Enterprise*, Joseph Goodman, asked that his reporters be responsible only for defending themselves. That was sometimes necessary. On one occasion Twain got into trouble over a piece he wrote about a group of women who were raising money for charity. The story was meant as a hoax, but the editor of the rival Virginia City *Union* defended the women and described Twain as a "liar, a poltroon, and a puppy." Twain challenged the man to a duel, probably also as a joke, but seconds had to be brought in to stop the potential bloodshed.

Ten years after his Virginia City experiences, Twain wrote in *Roughing It:* I let fancy get the upper hand of fact when there was a dearth of news." He went on to relate how he had interviewed several immigrants who had brought their wagons through hostile Indian country and had fared rather roughly. "I made the best of the item that the circumstances permitted, and felt that if I were not confined within rigid limits by the presence of the reporters of the other papers I could add particulars that would make the article much more interesting. However, I found one wagon that was going on to California, and made some judicious inquiries of the proprietor. When I learned, through his short and surly answers to my cross-questioning, that he was certainly going on and would not be in the city next day to make trouble, I got ahead of the other papers, for I took down his list of names and added his party to the killed and wounded. Having more scope here, I put this wagon through an Indian fight that to this day has no parallel in history."[31]

During Twain's Virginia City days, his older and more experienced colleague, Dan De Quille, outdid him in the production of hoaxes. Out of De Quille's inventive mind came "the Stones of Pahranagat Valley," a fake news report of the discovery of stones that possessed magnetic qualities and were controlled by electrical forces. If one of these stones was removed from the valley, it would begin rolling back to the magnetic center of the Pahranagat as soon as it was released. After numerous reprintings, the story reached Germany, exciting a group of physicists who were studying electromagnetism. They wrote De Quille for more information, and refused to believe him when he explained that it was all a hoax. P.T. Barnum also telegraphed an offer of ten thousand dollars if De Quille would bring some of the stones to his circus and museum for a demonstration.

Another De Quille story told of the inventor of a suit of armor equipped with a refrigerating device for use in crossing hot deserts. According to De Quille, on the first trial the refrigerating cut-off valve failed to operate, and the inventor was found frozen to death in his armor with a long icicle hanging from his nose in 117-degree heat. When this oft-reprinted tale reached England, the London *Times* accepted it as factual and recommended that Great Britain manufacture an improved model of the armor for issue to British army troops in India and other tropical regions of the empire.[32]

From the available contemporary sources, it appears that De Quille was the more popular of the rollicking pair of yarn spinners during their time together in Virginia City. In the 1950s when Lucius Beebe was researching for his book, *Comstock Commotion*, a man named Joe Farnsworth claimed to have known some of the reporters who worked on the *Territorial Enterprise*. Twain was regarded as "the prime s.o.b. of Virginia City," he said. "He was personally unclean; his mind and conversation was foul and he was forever trying to insinuate double meanings into his copy...He was notoriously a drink cadger and mean as catsmeat when it came to setting them up on the bar."[33] Farnsworth's information was hearsay, of course. He could have been only a small boy when he heard it, and was quite elderly when he told it, and everyone knows the unreliability of an old man's maunderings.

One of Twain's alleged practical jokes as a reporter approaches implausibility. A day or so after his editor, Joe Goodman, left Virginia City for a week of rest and recreation, Twain supposedly sent him a copy of the *Territorial Enterprise* that was filled with libelous statements about the leading citizens of the town and Nevada Territory, as well as disparaging comments about the virtue of certain local women. As soon as Goodman received the paper, he rushed back to town, determined to fire his young reporter and apologize to the maligned, only to discover that Twain had set the type and printed only one copy—the issue that Goodman held in his trembling hands.[34]

It is true that Mark Twain was an experienced typesetter, but anyone who has ever set even a paragraph of agate or six-point type, and then re-distributed it back into the proper boxes, knows the meaning of tedium. Mark Twain hated everything humdrum and he avoided wearisome tasks. He might have conceived just such a trick, but it is most unlikely that he carried it into action. The whole affair must have been a tall tale told about a teller of tall tales, probably by himself.

CHAPTER TEN

Masters and Marms

AS SOON AS SETTLEMENTS were built on the frontier and children began to appear, demands for schools and teachers gradually arose. Before the middle of the nineteenth century the frontier teacher was usually a male, and although poorly paid and of lowly status in the community, he was usually known as "perfesser." To obtain his position, the main qualification was a knowledge of Latin and Greek, and since few of his employers knew either language, the quoting of a few phrases in any unknown tongue was enough to pass the test.

Not everybody in a new town—especially those populated predominantly by single males—wanted a school or a schoolteacher. These resisters had journeyed west to escape all such concomitants of civilization. They were content with their saloons and dance halls, and resented any reversion to what they had fled, such as schools and churches, teachers and preachers.

Californian Lemuel McKeeby complained that the building of schoolhouses and the coming of teachers "meant that the miners should now put on a boiled shirt of a Sunday." The building of a schoolhouse and church, he added, required the miner to go into town "with his boiled shirt on twice a week or more, and help dance up enough money…he danced to build the school house, and he danced all around the school marm when she came…No night was too cold, too dark, or too stormy; the miners were there all the same."[1]

Schoolmasters varied sharply in their capabilities and their stores of knowledge; a few were well read, good mathmaticians, skillful at teaching. Others were almost as illiterate as their pupils (who were usually called *scholars* in that time.) Schoolmasters from this latter group were as fraudulent as confidence men, and only confirmed the low opinion some settlers held for "perfessers," who they viewed as being little more than necessary nuisances.

A visiting Easterner who was hunting wild game met a young man near a small town in the Southwest. "Could you tell me," asked the Easterner, "if there's anything to shoot around here?" "Not out here, sir," replied the young man, "but the schoolmaster lives over there by the schoolhouse. You're welcome to target him, if you like."

In a study of the frontier, Robert William Mondy cited a schoolmaster who had deserted from the British Navy. His schoolhouse had no stove, and during cold weather he "warmed his scholars by having them join hands and run round whilst he hastened their speed by the free use of a stick." In Texas, another schoolmaster used a technique that he called the "loud method" to make his students learn. During reading periods the pupils were ordered to read aloud at the top of their voices, the aim being for each one to drown out all the others. According to a contemporary traveler in the area, the noise of competing voices could be heard for a considerable distance from the schoolhouse.[2]

Other schoolmasters believed it their duty to shield their charges from pernicious influences of the outside world. During a tour of California in 1863, Artemus Ward was surprised to find the Santa Clara schoolhouse doors closed when he arrived there to give his lecture. He was even more astonished to discover that the schoolmaster had not locked him *out*, but had locked the pupils *in*, so they would not be exposed to the uncensored remarks of a so-called humorist from the East. Ward was forced to go to a grocery store, which more than accommodated his reduced audience.

In addition to having to live on scanty salaries and being treated like hired help by members of the community, schoolmasters were often hazed by unruly students. When Professor Maxwell Gaddis arrived at his one-room log schoolhouse one morning, he found the entrance blocked with benches. The students inside demanded a keg of cider and three bushels of apples as payment for admission. Gaddis refused, and when he realized that the students did not intend to relent, he turned away and started back home. Before he had taken a dozen steps, the students rushed out of the schoolhouse in full pursuit.

They were such a formidable and fast-footed mob, Gaddis decided to take shelter in the nearest house. His pursuers swarmed in after him, however, the ringleaders shouting that they would tie Gaddis's hands and feet with a rope unless he gave in to their demands for a keg of cider and three bushels of apples. By using a chair as barricade, Gaddis managed to stand off the students until help arrived in the form of their parents. A compromise was soon struck. The "scholars" would receive the apples, but instead of cider, they would be excused from classes for the remainder of that day. At the end of that term, Professor Gaddis did not ask for a renewal of contract.[3]

One "perfesser" who made a mark for himself in Colorado during the boom years of mining was Oscar J. Goldrick, graduate of Trinity College, Dublin. On an August day in 1858, he appeared in Auraria (now a part of Denver) driving an ox-drawn wagon. Goldrick was wearing a shiny plug hat, polished boots, an immaculate linen shirt, lemon-colored kid gloves, a Prince Albert coat, and a waistcoat embroidered with lilies of the valley, rosebuds, and violets. In a pocket of the waistcoat was his last coin, a fifty-cent piece.

In addition to wearing a fancy costume, Goldrick attracted attention with his method of driving oxen. Instead of shouting Anglo–Saxon profanity at his team, Goldrick used Latin and Greek phrases, or as he explained, "classical objurgations relished by the oxen." His demonstrated knowledge of those respected scholarly languages immediately earned him the title of "Perfesser" and the way was opened for him to pass around his hat for a collection to establish a school. According to a letter that he sent to a friend in the East, the schoolhouse was a one-room log cabin on Blake Street, and his first class consisted of thirteen pupils, "two Indian, two Mexican, and rest white, and from Missouri."

Not content with bringing culture to the young, Goldrick founded Denver's first library, naming it the Denver and Auraria Reading Room Association and starting it with one book from his personal collection. Goldrick also began contributing articles to the *Rocky Mountain News*, his efforts so impressing the owners that they made him an editor. In May 1864 a sudden flood down Cherry

Creek swept away bridges, habitations, the city jail, and the building housing the *News*. About twenty people lost their lives by drowning.

In his baroque schoolmaster style—which reveals what his pupils had to endure each day—Goldrick wrote up the event, using an extraordinarily long lead sentence to introduce the calamity:

"About the midnight hour of Thursday, the nineteenth instant, when almost all the town were knotted in the peace of sleep, deaf to all noise and blind to all danger, snoring in calm security and seeing visions of remoteness radiant with the rainbow hues of past associations, or roseate with the gilded hopes of the fanciful future—while the full-faced queen of night shed showers of silver from the starry throne o'er fields of freshness and fertility, garnishing and suffusing sleeping nature with her balmy brightness, fringing the feathery cottonwoods with lustre, enameling the house tops with coats of pearl, bridging the erst placid Platte with beams of radiance, and bathing the arid sands of Cherry Creek with dewy beauty—a frightful phenomenon sounded in the distance, and a shocking calamity presently charged upon us."[4]

When Bostonian Albert Pike, returning from a journey to Santa Fe, reached Fort Smith, Arkansas, in 1832, he found himself short of funds. Learning of a teaching vacancy on the Little Piney Creek near Van Buren, he decided to apply. Pike was twenty-four, in good physical condition, but the only clothing he possessed was what he was wearing—"leather pantaloons, scorched and wrinkled by fire, and full of grease, an old grimy jacket and vest, a pair of huge moccasins in the mending of which I had expended all my skill during the space of two months...a shirt made of what is commonly called a counterpane which had not been washed since I left Santa Fe; and to crown it all, my beard and mustachios had never been trimmed during the entire trip."

At the first cabin he reached on the Little Piney, he found a man playing a merry tune on a fiddle. He was dressed in leather somewhat like himself, and had also been to Santa Fe. The two became immediate friends. When Pike inquired about the school, the man replied that the prospects were good.

"I reckon thar might be a right smart chance of scholars got, as we have had no teacher here for the best of two years. Thar's about fifteen families on the creek, and the whole tote of 'em well fixed for children. They want a schoolmaster pretty much, too. We got a teacher about six months ago—a Scotchman, or an Irishman, I think. He took for six months, and carried his proposals 'round, and he got twenty scholars directly. It warn't long, though, before he cut up some *ferlicues*, and got into a *primary*, and so one morning he was found among the missing."

"What was the trouble?" asked Pike.

"Oh, he took too much of the essence of corn, and got into a chunk of a fight—no great matter, to be sure; but he got whipped, and had to leave the diggins."

"And how am I to get a school?" Pike next inquired.

"I'll tell you," replied the settler. "You must make out your proposals to take up school; tell them how much you ask a month, and what you can teach; and write it out as fine as you can (I reckon you're a pretty good scribe). In the morning there'll be a shooting match here for beef; nearly all the settlement will be here, and you'll get signers enough."

Next morning Pike went with his new friend to the shooting match, where he met the Little Piney settlers, and soon gained their approval by demonstrating his skill as a marksman. Before the day was over, he signed to teach twenty pupils and agreed on his compensation. It was to be paid half in money and half in hogs.[5]

Another schoolteacher on the Arkansas frontier, a Professor Anderson, used his fists to maintain authority. When two brothers named Madden kept bullying other students, Anderson decided to break up one of their fights. He seized Henry and Bud Madden from the mêlée and gave them both a hard paddling. When the Madden brothers went home they told their father what the "perfesser" had done to them.

Madden the father stormed down to the schoolhouse and demanded to know why Anderson had whipped his boys instead of the ones they were fighting. "Your boys were the aggressors," Anderson told him. "The others were fighting in self defense."

Madden retorted: "I'll whip you after school." For the rest of the day he waited out on the school grounds for classes to end.

After the last class, Anderson stepped outside and found Madden, as well as a considerable crowd of onlookers from the neighborhood, ready and waiting. For some time the two men pounded and wrestled each other until at last they were bruised and bloody and exhausted. The watching crowd called it a draw and separated them.

When Madden reached home that evening, bearing the marks of his fight, his wife asked if he was going to send his boys back to school if Professor Anderson remained as schoolmaster.

"Dag-goon yes," Madden replied. "Any man that can whip my boys then beat me up can teach my kids."[6]

During and after the California gold rush, which created a rising sweep of westward migration, males began leaving frontier schoolhouses in droves, and females were called upon to fill the vacated posts. Because so many New England males had left by land and sea, mainly for economic reasons, that area of the nation became the preferred hunting ground for female teachers. Towns along the western frontier ran advertisements in New England newspapers and magazines. "We want good female teachers, who could obtain constant employment and best of wages...We want them immediately and they would do much good."[7]

During the 1850s competition for teachers was so keen in Kansas that school authorities began offering special inducements. After Lyon County asked for "one hundred School marms who will pledge themselves not to get married within three years," the town of Manhattan made what its authorities believed to be a better offer: "We want one hundred in this county, between the ages of 18 and 21 *who will pledge themselves to get married within one year.*"[8]

The presence of women in the one-room schoolhouses could bring about considerable improvements in the surroundings. A teacher arriving in one western mining town was told that she would have to use her bedroom for the schoolroom. Each morning the bed had to be moved out and soap boxes and planks moved in, the process being repeated in reverse each evening. Within a few days the schoolmarm had the males busy at work on a log schoolhouse.

A young schoolteacher in Washington Territory during the Civil War demanded an outdoor toilet for the school and was called before the authorities to justify the need for it. "Now you see what comes of hiring someone from Outside," one of her critics declared. "Never had any trouble before, plenty of trees to get behind." She won her case by threatening to leave if the toilet was not built.[9]

To spruce up the drab walls of schoolrooms, the women teachers papered them with pages from magazines and newspapers, students' drawings, and for good measure, hand-lettered maxims of the times: NEVER SAY FAIL; LOOK BEFORE YOU LEAP; A ROLLING STONE GATHERS NO MOSS.

Before long the frontier schoolmarm became a stereotype, often a subject of fun for the popular scribes of the late nineteenth century. Henry Wheeler Shaw who wrote and lectured as Josh Billings described her this way: "I have never yet known a country schoolmarm to be over twenty-three years old. She remains right there for an indefinite period of time. She wears her hair either cut short or hanging in ringlets, and is as prim and precise in everything as a pair of improved Fairbanks Scales. She seldom ever smiles and was never known to laugh out loud, but when she does, she does it according to the rules laid down by Murray for speaking and pronouncing the English language correctly. She is the paragon of propriety and had rather be three years behind in styles than to spell one word wrong or to parse a sentence incorrectly…With all her concise foibles and idiosyncrasies, I have always had a tender spot in my heart for her. She is stepmother to more bad boys' children than anybody else and has the patience and forbearance of Job with naughty boys and stupid girls…She works the harder and gets the nearest to no pay for it of any person I know in a civilized and Christian land."[10]

J.L. McConnell, who sketched western characters in the 1850s, also had his say about schoolmarms:

"Her name was invariably Grace, Charity, or Prudence, and, if names had been always a descriptive of the personal qualities of those who bore them, she would have been entitled to all three…She was somewhat angular and rather bony. Her eyes were usually blue, and, to speak with accuracy, a little cold and grayish, in their expression—like the sky on a bleak morning in Autumn. Her forehead was very high and prominent, having an exposed look, like a shelterless knoll in an open prairie. Her mouth was of that class called 'primped,' but was filled with teeth of respectable dimension...She had, however, almost always one very great attraction—a fine, clear, healthy complexion...In manners and bearing, she was brisk, prim, and sometimes a little 'fidgety,' as if she was conscious of sitting on a dusty chair; and she had a way of searching nervously for her pocket, as if to find a handkerchief with which to brush it off...Though rigid and austere, I have never heard that she was at all disinclined to being courted; especially if it gave her any prospect of being able to make herself useful as a wife...She was careful of three things—her clothes, her money, and her reputation...Almost invariably, the western schoolmarm in the course of time became a married woman, but the man who courted her must do so in the most sober, staid, and regulated spirit."[11]

The very essence of the frontier, however, rendered such caricatures virtually meaningless. What was true in one settlement might be utterly false in another. Out in Mason County, Texas, the first schoolmarm was an "Irish woman who had the strength of a strong man and the typical fighting spirit of her race. She kept a quart of whiskey and a leather quirt in her desk. The whiskey was strictly for her own use, the quirt for use on the kids."[12]

That Irish schoolmarm was no stereotype, yet she exemplified the power of women that was to come out of thousands of one-room schools across the western frontier. The teachers were in the front lines of a conflict—sometimes merry, sometimes grim—with the males who wanted to keep everything the way it was back East, where they had always been top dogs—or thought they were.

And what of the students who attended the frontier schools? A letter written on April 22, 1871, by Jacqueline Watie, to her famous Cherokee father, Stand Watie, reveals that after more than a century little has changed in the attitude of students. Emotions, needs, and interests remain much the same.

Berryville, Ark.
April 22ond 1871

My Dear Papa
This eaveing is still and I will have no other chance to write to you, and I will give you as good a history of Berryville as I can.

Well Cap. Clarke has a very full school I don't believe I ever went to any better school than he has; for he makes his scholars study now just rite. He dont allow any sweet-hearts to be claimed so I just think he is rite about that. For I dont think its rite for students to have such things as they call sweet-hearts. The students are some of them very far advanced. Oh! I think Capt. Clarke is a splendid teacher. This place dont carry fashons to such an extent; for povity will not let them. But at the examination time we will have big to do. You will come wont you; I would rather you would come than any one else. I will need some money too; for I will have to get some things for the examination, for it will take me from now to get ready. Those folks carry fashons to an extence then; for they go well every Sunday. But every day as I told you above they go plane and I can keep up with them then. Papa you must send me some money; if it is not but $5, for I need it very bad and have been needing it a long time. But if you have $25, send it; for it will take that much to fix me for the exibition, and more too I expect. And I will need some between *now* and *then*. You told me to let you know what it cost; I will send you a sirceler and then you can setle with Clarke...Well Papa I think this is a very cheap school and good too. I would like to come back here if posable next session; but if it is exposing your povity I will not ask any more, but I think the boading place cant be beat for we are treated just like home folk. We are not treated like strangers. Capt. Clarke has the best mother or as good as ever was, for I like her as if she was kin to me. I am taking mucis lessons and hope to be able to play some for you if you come after me. You must bring Sister with you if you come. The school will be out in July. About the 3rd or 4th. You come about the last day of June and then you will see and here all that is to be heard. But you must be dressed now I tell *you*. For these people are mity sprucy them times.

Well Papa I expect you are getting tired reading my letter it is just filled up with nonsense. You may tell Stand William and Tobaco houdy for me. And David too. Well Papa send me some money just as soon as you get it if you have it now send it as soon as you get this. Good bye Papa answer this when you receive it...

Your affectate Child

Like many modern teenagers at some stage in their development, Jacqueline was dissatisfied with her name, and was experimenting with others. She signed the letter "Jessie" and asked her father to direct his letters to "J.W. Watie."

Stand Watie's reply a few days later, as these excerpted lines indicate, was comparable to that of any modern father writing to a daughter away in school:

Grand River, At Old Place
May 10th 1871

My dear daughter:

Your most affectionate and loving letter has reached me. I am happy and delighted to hear from you. You cant imagine how lonely I am up here at our old place without any of my dear children being with. I would be so happy to have you here, but you must go to school. I am glad you are pleased and like the school and your teacher. I am well acquainted with Capt. Clarke he is a fine man...I must try to come to Berryville at the examination. I shall do my utmost to send you back again next term....I will try to send the money you require...

Your affectionate father
Watie[13]

CHAPTER ELEVEN

Servants of the Lord
in a Turbulent Land

EUROPEANS WHO CAME FROM their native lands directly to the American frontier were sometimes surprised by what they saw and heard when they first enountered backwoods religion. While visiting Arkansas in the 1840s, Friedrich Gerstäcker stopped one evening to join a small group of people gathered in front of a log building. "We had not long been seated," he said, "when a tall, ceremonious, respectable looking man, buttoned to the chin in a long brown coat, arrived. He saluted us rather solemnly, then seating himself at a short distance, took a little book from his pocket, turned over the leaves, and, before I suspected any thing, he thundered out a hymn with a voice that astounded me. Not being used to such a proceeding, I looked first at one then at the other for some explanation, but they kept their eyes fixed on the ground, looking very solemn all the time.

"The voice of the singer became louder and louder. The good man seemed to have lost the end of his song; night came on, and it was rather cold—still he kept on, until at last his voice failed, and he was obliged to stop. I though this was all, but more people arrived, among them some very pretty young women, such as I never expected to see in the wilderness. The air being cold and damp, we entered the house, which was set out with benches, and looked like a school-room. The case was clear—I had stumbled on a Methodist meeting, and must take the consequences. The singing and praying lasted several hours, and I was heartily tired of it, as it did not agree with my habits and feelings."[1]

In spite of his reservations, Gerstäcker was later persuaded (perhaps by the pretty young women) to attend another camp meeting where the tall man in the brown coat delivered a sermon.

Gerstäcker said the preacher used his right arm like a windmill blade while his left, pressing a Bible against his side, was going up and down like a butcher's cleaver, hard enough to throw the arm out of joint.

"As I sat watching the preacher, there suddenly came a scream; and for the first time in my life I saw the spectacle of a woman so overcome by religious zeal that she was shouting, jumping about, and clapping her hands together, crying out, 'Oh Lord, glory, glory, glory, happy, happy, glory.' until she fell exhausted and faint to the floor. After the woman was quieted the sermon was soon ended, and according to custom a song was to signalize the conclusion of the service. We stood up, turned our backs, and had just finished two stanzas when another scene broke loose. This time it was a young widow, weighing I judge not less than one hundred and eighty pounds, who had begun to jump around so violently that the whole house resounded. It was well known that she was greatly admired by the shoemaker. He stood ready to catch her, and it was his good fortune to be short and stocky of build. Had he not been so, he would have been bowled over when she finally collapsed in his arms.

"The people believing that shouting and jumping are symbols of the possession of Divine grace; that it is a Heaven-sent preview, as it were, of the indescribable joy and happiness the faithful will know and experience when they come into Heaven. To me, however, the scene was depressing. That night I dreamed the tall, brown-coated preacher sat like an incubus on my chest, alternately patting my cheeks and singing hymns."[2]

Not long after Gerstäcker's Arkansas experience, a correspondent for *Spirit of the Times* reported on a church service he attended near Hot Springs: "The place of worship was well ventilated, being a new and well-built log house minus the 'chinking,' windows, and doors. It being rather a blustering day, the pastor labored under considerable difficulty in keeping his text before him, the leaves of the book blowing to and fro, as the breeze changed. To obviate this he drew his 'Bowi' from the back of his neck and deposited it on one side of the text book. But this would not suffice; the opposite side required 'holding down' likewise, and he was compelled to search for his 'Derringer' and lay that down also. Here was a spectacle, truly! but as all was well now, the pastor went on with the sermint."[3]

Worse distractions than strong breezes made life burdensome for God's servants in the wilderness. Frontiersmen usually possessed numerous hunting dogs that followed their masters wherever they went, including the Sunday meeting houses. The animals usually lay by the dozens beneath the slab benches, and sermons were continually interrupted by growling and barking that often culminated in a glorious dogfight.

And as was the case when schoolteachers first arrived in a community, there were some inhabitants opposed to preachers coming to challenge their free and sinful ways. Recalling the wild days of Uvalde, Texas, Sheriff J.C. Harkness said that when a certain Parson Potter announced that he was coming there to preach, the rowdies of the town warned the preacher to stay away.

Parson Potter paid them no heed. He rode into Uvalde and went directly to the building where he was to hold services. From around the countryside a large crowd had gathered there, its members more curious about Parson Potter's reception by the bravos and gamblers than in what he might have to say in a sermon.

"Parson Potter mounted the platform," said Sheriff Harkness, "opened his Bible, then pulled out his gun, a regular old 'hog-leg' cap-and-ball gun eighteen inches long, and laid it beside the Good Book.

"'Now,' said the parson. 'You fellows sent me word not to come, saying that I couldn't preach here. I've come and I'm going to preach. The first fellow that makes a move while I am preaching I'm going to shoot him right between the eyes, and I'm a good shot. You are the fellows I mean! You fellows right there !' He pointed his finger straight at some men sitting on one of the benches, and they never moved a muscle.

"That was the most attentive audience that a preacher ever had. Not a man stirred during the sermon."[4]

For special occasions such as the Fourth of July, settlements without churches would invite a circuit rider to come and add a bit of reverence to the day's events. These parsons on horseback usually rode regularly assigned circuits of towns that were too small to afford a full-time minister. In other situations the riders were free to choose the settlements in which they felt they could accomplish the most good works, or gain the most converts, or collect the most donations. They flourished on the early woodland frontiers; after the lines of settlement moved out to the Plains and Rockies, distances were usually too great for traveling preachers.

A young circuit rider, with but little experience, was invited to a Fourth of July celebration in the Ozark Mountains. After the political speeches, the square dances, and the footraces, the county judge asked him to offer a prayer before the picnic dinners were served. The young preacher hesitated a moment, then stammered: "But I don't know what to pray for at a gathering of this kind!" The circuit rider folded his hands, closed his eyes, and in a solemn voice prayed: "Lord, bless the hilarity of this occasion."[5]

Another Ozark circuit rider, Benjamin Harvey Greathouse, ran into the sort of predicament that occasionally happens to public speakers in our age of swift electronic communication. To save time and energy, Reverend Greathouse prepared only one sermon, which he planned to repeat at each of the churches on his circuit. After delivering it at a Sunday morning service in a mountain church, he saddled up and rode ten miles to the next church for an evening gathering where he expected a completely different group of worshippers.

"When I looked over my congregation," Greathouse said afterward, "there, lo and behold, were about half the folks I had preached to that morning. Choking down my surprise and even panic I preached a sermon strictly off the cuff—my first such."

Some time later, Reverend Greathouse joined with another minister in conducting a camp meeting. On the day he was to preach his first sermon, a community bully, well fortified with whiskey, entered the brush arbor with the intention of breaking up the meeting. He began shouting threats at Greathouse, finally growing so odious that the other minister seized the man and then asked Greathouse to assist him in expelling the intruder. Excusing himself from the pulpit for a minute or so, the circuit rider joined his associate. They forced the troublemaker outside the arbor and rammed his head against the trunk of an oak tree until he begged for mercy. When the man promised to behave himself forthwith and forever, he was released and Greathouse resumed the interrupted sermon.[6]

As the frontier moved into the Old Wild West, preachers adopted a uniform of sorts, not unlike that of the gamblers who followed the frontier westward with them—a long-tailed black coat or a black linen duster, with a white shirt and a black string tie. Only their hats varied—where the gambler wore a low-crowned wide-brim, the preacher sported a tall stovepipe.

For one reason or another, preachers, gamblers, and saloon-keepers joined forces on various occasions. The more persuasive transient preachers could talk saloon-keepers into permitting use of a bar-room early on Sunday mornings before the gambling and dancing commenced. Arrangements such as this led a traveling Frenchman, Paul Blouet, to observe in 1890: "The American is the only man under the sun...who can play poker and swear a blue streak one hour, and sing gospel hymns with just as much gusto the next hour."[7]

When the famous bishop, Henry Spalding, came to preach to the Colorado miners, he found a tent set up for him, with fresh sawdust on the ground and candles neatly arranged around a box that was used as a pulpit. The tent, however, adjoined a gambling hall, and all during the services the congregation could hear the clicking of poker chips and the voice of a dance-caller shouting "allemande left, ladies and gents walk to the bar."

Bishop Spalding's efforts to stop gambling and dancing during church services met with no success, but the proprietor of the establishment did order his customers to "plug up the kitty" and give the bishop the winnings of their next play. The result was a hatful of silver that was presented with due ceremony to the astonished bishop.[8]

In Denver during this same period, the Episcopal minister, Father J.H. Keller, decided to ask the gambling fraternity to aid him in raising money to build a proper church. He visited all the houses and invited everybody present to come to his log structure the following morning, telling them frankly that he had a favor to ask them.

Next morning a considerable number of sporting gentlemen

filed into the little temporary church and took seats near the pulpit. Father Keller wasted no time coming to the point. To build a church he needed $150 (a small fortune in 1860) but his congregation was too poor to raise such a sum. The gamblers discussed the problem, then consented to assist in their own professional way. Each man agreed to place his next bet at a monte bank in a gambling hall, all winnings to be contributed to Father Keller.

One gambler hit a streak of fantastic luck and ran his winnings up to three hundred dollars. As Father Keller had asked for half that, the winner sent him that amount and spent the other half on what was described a dozen years later by the *Rocky Mountain News* as "riotous living."

In recalling the incident, the newspaper further commented: "The fashionable worshippers at St. John's this morning may be shocked by the reflection that the sacred edifice was founded after this fashion, but perhaps the church would not now be in existence if there had been no monte banks in Denver at an early day."[9]

The success that preachers had with gamblers and tosspots brought an occasional flimflam artist into the play. One evening during the heyday of trail town Newton, Kansas, a man dressed in a long-tailed black coat entered a saloon filled with revelers. In a rich ministerial voice he asked permission to pray for the souls of the sinners present. At the bar a few men set their glasses down; the faro players paused in their betting. A hymn followed the prayer, the dance-hall girls joining in. Disregarding a noisy dogfight that swirled inside from the street, the man in the black coat launched into a brief but fervent sermon.

Closing the service with a benediction, he then passed his stovepipe hat around to collect a generous offertory. That night he departed Newton on the late train east. Not until next morning, when the drunks sobered up, did some of them recall they had seen the man before—in another trail town—a professional gambler down on his luck.[10]

The earnest preachers not only had to contend with outright resistance to their presence, but with the indifference of an unrooted population enjoying their loosened ties. "There is not many churches here yet," Ed Donnell wrote his brother from Arcadia, Nebraska, in 1877, "but I dont think it is any closer to hell than it is any place else for my new well is 125 feet to water and it is almost as cold as ice. I like to have churches and go to them, but I dont think God requires people to stay in a country where they…cant make a liven or have a home, just because they have churches."[11]

The editor of the *Dodge City Times* must have expressed the attitude of his readers in June 1878 when he announced that "the wicked city of Dodge" could at last boast of a church. "It was organized last Sunday week. We would have mentioned the matter last week but we thought it best to break the news gently to the outside world."[12]

Frontier evangelists of a century ago were equipped with attributes quite similar to those of their modern successors who use the electronic media of radio and television. They were genial, vigorous, and sometimes fanatic and over-ambitious males, and in that age before microphones they were endowed with fine-toned vocal cords and lungs like bellows. Evangelists were also among the first of the professions to use the burgeoning art of advertising that was beginning to sweep across America.

A Lawrence, Kansas, observer of a revivalist in 1872 described him as being "of a class of man who, while their labors relate almost exclusively to another world, enjoy a hearty laugh and a good dinner in this…He adopts the clerical suit of black and the white neckcloth, but further than that has little to mark him for a clergyman."

In efforts to publicize their presence in a town and attract possible converts, the revivalists boldly invaded saloons and houses or prostitution, inviting operators as well as patrons to attend the gospel meetings. In Atchison, Kansas, teams of hymn-singing children were taken into the saloons. Although some saloon-keepers refused to admit the children, most let them sing and depart in peace. Some bully boys of Atchison followed the young singers, however, shouting abuse at them and hitting them with sticks.[13]

Because there were so many gambling houses in frontier towns, the evangelists usually devoted one day of their protracted meetings entirely to sermons about the wages of sin at the betting tables. Sermons on "gambling day" almost invariably drew the largest crowds, sometimes making it necessary for the evangelists to move out of their tents or arbors into larger quarters or the open air. Why there was so much more interest in reformed gamblers than in sworn-off tipplers has never been explained. Perhaps everyone believed the salvation of the latter was only temporary.

A Kansas newspaper, in fact, reported the back-sliding of a Lawrence convert who was arrested in Kansas City for drunkenness one April evening in 1872: "He told several persons that his visit to Kansas City was to escape the importunity of the revival people in Lawrence, and to enjoy a quiet drunk."[14]

There were other opponents of revivalists—representatives of established churches or of factions within religious movements, or challengers of the evangelists' recommended methods for salvation, or eccentrics who followed them from town to town, demanding opportunities for public debate. Experienced evangelists tried to stay clear of these entanglements unless they saw a publicity advantage in such a confrontation, and then they would encourage their critics to challenge them in the pulpit.

An observer reported one such incident in which the preacher "made some allusions to Tom Paine, when a poor, lost blind sinner, by the name of Stine...openly and shamefully disturbed the religious meeting by calling the Rev. Mr. Paulson a liar."[15]

Sometimes different opinions led to violence. During a Topeka revival, a spirtualist requested permission of the evangelist to present his views on resurrection of the dead. When he was turned down, he started a campaign of writing open letters to newspapers, attacking the revivalists for condemning spiritualism as a monstrosity and refusing to let a spiritualist speak out in its defense. Soon after the first letter was published, a former spirtualist named Collingsworth gave testimony at the revival meeting, blaming all of his past sins on spiritualism.

To this the spiritualist replied with another letter to the press, insinuating that Collingsworth at some time in his past might have ruined the character of an unsuspecting girl. He then attacked all revivalists in general, saying that they lived as they pleased, then said a few prayers, and expected to "go into heaven on a white horse with a great flourish of trumpets." On the day following the appearance of this letter, the spiritualist chanced to meet Collingsworth on a Topeka street. Collingsworth gave the letter writer such a severe beating with his cane that the man had to seek medical attention.[16]

Another grievance against the evangelists was their practice of selecting certain well-known persons in a community and offering public prayers to convert them, sometimes accusing them of being heretics and vile sinners. One Topeka citizen protested in a letter to the *Kansas Daily Commonwealth:* "I was made the subject," he wrote, "of public exhibition and scurrilous attack which was utterly uncalled for, and without justification." He went on to compare the revivalists' methods with those of the Inquisition.[17]

Some newspapers also became critical of the traveling clergymen and, in the way of frontier journalism, used tall tales to make merry with them. "It appears that people become sinners at a very early age in this part of the country," the *Leavenworth Times* observed. "We heard of one yesterday only two and a half years old, who becoming convinced that he was a great sinner, and had been all his life, concluded to have prayers in the family thereafter. His father, being a very bigoted and over bearing man objected and told him that if he must have prayers it could not be in that house, and so the brave little christian went upstairs to pack his trunk."[18]

The promotion-minded revivalists learned how to deal with competition whenever it appeared—usually in the form of tent shows of all kinds—circuses, stage performers, and medicine shows. Alliances for mutual publicity were formed, representatives from one group being invited to the other so that hours could be adjusted and gatherings postponed to avoid conflicts.

A popular medicine show that traversed the West in several units—Hamlin's Wizard Oil, Blood and Liver Pills and Cough Balsam Show—employed male quartets that lent their talents to any traveling revival that might be encountered. Dressed in Prince Albert coats, gray pin-striped trousers, patent leather boots, and high silk hats, the members of the quartets sang hymns to churchgoers and then switched over to lively contemporary ballads for the buyers of wizard oil and liver pills. No doubt they increased attendance at both happenings.[19]

In efforts to attract more sinners and backsliders, some evangelists stepped up the quotient of sex in their sermons, the Old Testament being an excellent source for material on the subject. One preacher also borrowed from certain secular works until his presentations became so raunchy he held special meetings for men only. "The place was packed to the doors," one of his listeners reported. "There was a hymn or two, and then a sermon. At least, he called it a sermon. It was, in fact, merely a recital of page after page from Rabelais, the *Decameron* and the *Contes Drolatiques*, culled out by the parson and worked over to suit the taste of his customers. It suited me all right. I enjoyed it. Never anywhere, not even in the worst barrooms I have sinfully frequented, have I ever listened to as choice a collection of pornographic anecdotes. The preacher taught us things about women that I had never know of before—things extremely scandalous and surprising."[20]

The Temperance Movement, which eventually led to the Prohibition Act of the twentieth century, did not endear participating preachers to the hard-drinking frontiersmen. After attending a temperance meeting in San Francisco in 1848, Chester Lyman noted in his diary: "Mr. Hickok and Mr. Dunleavy spoke, nothing great. Mr. Hickok mouthed and murdered the Queen's English horridly, the other was a decent speaker, but people could not help thinking all the while how shockingly he beat his wife a short time since, a thing which he is in the habit of doing. Meeting too long, left at 10:45. 15 signed the pledge."[21]

Mining camps were prime targets for the Temperance Movement's spokesmen. They came in considerable numbers to booming camps such as Leadville, Colorado. The local press sometimes reported their activities in colorful fashion. The *Leadville Democrat* described a preacher named Campbell as "a heavy-set man of terrible power, who could convert a drunkard or knock down an ox with equal ease. One doesn't hear what he says, but feels it. His words go flying through the hall like red-hot balls of fire. Everybody is excited."

Less tolerant was the competing *Chronicle:* "All temperance lecturers take special delight in telling the rising generation how gloriously drunk they used to get. They fill an hour's lecture with anecdotes of how they used to cuff their poor wives about, break the hearts of girls who loved them, dishonor the sacred name of mother, and send her sorrowing to her grave. Very often these lecturers will tell how they used to lie, steal, pawn their wife's wedding dress, kick over the kitchen stove, drag their little daughter around by the hair, and cut other capers for which, had the law done its duty, they would be serving out a life sentence in some state prison in place of bragging about their crimes before really temperate men and women."[22]

CHAPTER TWELVE

Sawbones and Pill Rollers

MANY PHYSICIANS ON THE FRONTIER knew more about treating horses than they did about ministering to the luckless human beings who came under their control. Few of them had medical schooling and some were acknowledged self-taught amateurs with perhaps a medical manual or two for consultation. Most of them could set a broken bone and extract a bullet, but surgery and contagious diseases were pure guesswork. For their suffering patients they relied heavily upon camphor, calomel, castor oil, and other cathartics. Purge, puke, and bleed were the usual courses of action. A few smart ones learned the potency of herbs and borrowed formulas from the Indians.

Edwin Bryant, who was in charge of the medicines and acted as unofficial "doctor" for an overland expedition to California in 1846, believed that his policy of refusing large doses of strong pills and powders was the reason everyone survived. "The propensity of those afflicted by disease, on this journey," he said, "is frequently to devour medicines as they would food, under the delusion that large quantities will more speedily and effectively produce a cure. The reverse is the fact, and it is sometimes dangerous to trust a patient with more than a single dose."[1]

Doctors on the frontier tried to impress visiting patients with office displays of their instruments and bottled bits and pieces supposedly removed from ailing human beings. During the Civil War period, a doctor's office in Placerville, California, contained a large jar of leeches, a microscope, an array of splints, implements for surgery and dentistry, a few chemical retorts and alembics. Several bottles displayed organs removed from former patients and preserved in alcohol. The miners, according to one observer, "stood in awe of such matters and considered no doctor worth his salt who had not something curious wherewith to astonish them."[2]

Some years later, during the Central City, Colorado, mining boom, a doctor delivered of a prostitute a stillborn child. At the time he was in the process of building a bottled collection for his office; therefore he wrapped the tiny cadaver in a newspaper and took it home for preservation in alcohol. Proud of his acquisition, he invited a few of his cronies to see it before bottling. When he unwrapped the newspaper, he found that inked letters from a large advertisement were impressed upon the dead infant's abdomen. "Whose is it?" asked one of the men. "No doubt about it," replied the doctor, "it bears their brand." In reversed block letters on the skin were the names of two local tobacconists, advertising their wares.[3]

In 1857 the wife of a doctor, who had established himself in a California mining camp, visited his office for the first time and was shocked to find it unfloored, the medicines arranged along shelves "which looked like sticks snatched hastily from the woodpile." To decorate the walls, pictures had been cut from contemporary magazines.

Western mining towns could be financially rewarding locations for doctors, especially if they had a monopoly of an area. When Dr. Edward Willis arrived in Placerville, he discovered that another physician had already established an office there. Not wanting a rival in camp, the first doctor called upon Willis and demanded to see his diploma and certificates. Willis presented them, and the first doctor not only tore the papers to bits, he spat a jet of tobacco juice into Willis's face. Willis challenged him to a duel, killed him, and took over the monopoly for himself.[4]

On the Great Plains, doctors who made house calls usually had to travel long distances. Charles Reed, who lived in the sandhills of western Nebraska, once accompanied a Dr. Robinson out to a sod house to attend a woman suffering from a gall bladder attack. After deciding to operate, the doctor asked Reed to put extra leaves in the kitchen table, spread a sheet across it, heat some water, and bring a clean dishpan. "He not only located and deleted the offending gall bladder," said Reed, "but took out her appendix for good measure, with the comment that he didn't want to have to drive back up there for that. The patient recovered and outlived the doctor."[5]

Another physician in western Nebraska frequently had trouble after dark finding the homes of his patients. Dr. John W. Thompson was so hopelessly lost one night that he drove his buggy around aimlessly for hours, searching with his lantern for familiar landmarks. At last he stopped the buggy and stepped down only to be confronted by an angry man surrounded by several frightened children. "Get out of here," the man shouted. "What do you think you're doing! Get off my house." Dr. Thompson had stopped his team on the roof of a combination dugout and sod house—which as it turned out was the home of his patient-to-be.[6]

Doctors also had to deal with frontier superstitions, such as belief in the "evil eye." An aged woman, who was a patient of Dr. Charles Martin in Arkansas, became convinced that she had a frog in her stomach, the result of a dispute with a neighbor. She went to bed to die, and Dr. Martin's efforts to reason with her could not bring her to change her mind. It began to look as if die she would. On his next visit to the woman, the doctor carried a toad in his pocket. First he gave her a dose of ipecac and waited for results. At the proper time he transferred the toad from his pocket to the jar. When she had sufficiently recovered he showed her the results. In a short time she was up out of bed, singing the young doctor's praises.[7]

Popular remedies could be painful, as Lemuel McKeeby learned while traveling to California in 1850. In that age of horseback transportation, hemorrhoids could bring a rider to the ground, destroy a cavalryman's career, and limit the earning power of those who used saddles in their work. McKeeby's attack of swollen piles led him to ask an old colonel if he knew of a remedy. Turpentine, the army officer told him, adding a warning that turpentine would make him prance around a little while. "Before going to bed," McKeeby noted, "I made the first application, and it was some time before I went to sleep that night." Next day he felt better, and the hemorrhoids gradually went away so that he was able to ride horseback again.[8]

Charles Goodnight's remedy for hemorrhoids was a home-made suppository consisting of pure salt in a base of buffalo tallow. The famous cattleman and his wife, Mary, were ardent believers in the medicinal qualities of buffalo fat. They devised a buffalo soap that Goodnight claimed stopped soreness in a corn on his foot. "I am satisfied it will relieve rheumatism. Try it for tuberculosis. I do believe it will work. It is harmless. We do not know what we have found. Help us hunt it out. I believe it stands a fair chance to become the discovery of the age."[9]

Seidlitz powders were a popular laxative for a time, the effervescent salts giving authority even to a mild dose. In the early days of Hot Sulphur Springs, Colorado, John Stokes, who managed a general store, provided the powder for his customers. One day a Ute Indian came in, said he was "heap sick" and asked for a glass of the bubbling medicine. When Stokes gave him the usual amount, the Ute swallowed it in one gulp, then complained it was not enough to cure his sickness. Being busy at the moment, Stokes hurriedly spooned a double dose into the glass, but did not add the water. Neither did the Ute, and a minute later to Stokes's dismay the Indian began gasping for breath, his hands clawing the air, his eyes bulging. To the grocer, the Ute appeared to be swelling up, perhaps to the bursting point. At last he got his breath, nodded gratefully to Stokes, and went off quite satisfied with the treatment.[10]

During the 1850s, overblown accounts of Indian troubles kept travelers in wagon trains constantly alert. The appearance of even a small band of Plains Indians would quickly turn the wagons into bristling armed fortresses. One day a train of wagons traveling along the Platte route sighted a single Indian horseman approaching. The inexperienced immigrants convinced themselves that the oncoming Indian was a spy sent to estimate the strength of the wagon train and the size of the horse herd.

A doctor with the wagons immediately suggested a stratagem to fool the Indian. He took a young freckle-faced boy to the lead wagon, sprinkled his face lightly with flour so that his freckles appeared to be spots, and then put him into a bed with the wagon cover turned back so that he was in plain view of any horseman nearing the front of the train.

As soon as the Indian came up, saluting and halloing, the doctor pointed to the bed and announced loudly that the boy had smallpox. The Indian took one look at the boy's face, then quickly turned his horse about and raced away in the direction from which he had come. For two or three weeks no Indians came near that wagon train; they were too fearful of smallpox to want to trade.[11] This was probably more of a loss than a gain for the overlanders, who surely needed wild game, berries, and fresh horses, which they could easily have obtained from the Indians.

Some Indians were better physicians than the frontier army surgeons. When William Bent of Bent's Fort in Colorado Territory could get no relief for a sore throat so acute he could barely breathe or swallow, and could talk only in whispers, he sent for a Cheyenne medicine man. With the handle of a spoon, the Cheyenne examined Bent's throat, then went out on the prairie and collected several small sandburs. The burs were about the size of a pea and were covered with sharp barbs. Preparing a thread-sized sinew with a knot at one end, the Cheyenne used an awl to poke a hole through a sandbur, ran the sinew through to the knot, and then rolled the bur in marrow grease.

Asking Bent to open his mouth, the medicine man forced the bur down his throat, pulling it out and pushing it in several times until all the hard dry matter was removed. To Bent's immense relief he was now able to swallow soup and, in a day or two, was well enough to eat solid food.

William Bent probably did not know he was following the example Andrew Jackson had set a half century earlier on the Tennessee frontier. A gunshot wound became infected in Jackson's arm. The white surgeons wanted to amputate it, but the future President called in a Cherokee medicine man who saved it.

Most cures for frontier ailments were not nearly as practical as that of Bent's Cheyenne "doctor." Physicians from the East clung to ancient remedies, although those with inquiring minds were constantly fretting over the causes of disease outbreaks in the West. Year after year they consulted each other about the causes for malaria, never suspecting the pesky mosquito. Even the brilliant Dr. Walter Reed, for whom the well-known military hospital in Washington, D.C., is named, was baffled by malaria for more than a quarter of a century. While he was stationed at Fort Lowell, Arizona, in 1876 he decided the disease was caused by the sharp differences in temperature between day and night. He advised the fort's commander to delay reveille until after sunrise to lower malaria exposure to the men. The soldiers were undoubtedly delighted by the change in schedule, but the mosquitoes continued to carry the disease. Some years later Reed helped solve the mystery. His work with mosquitoes and yellow fever won him honors at the turn of the century.

Malaria was a major problem along the Texas coast where heavy rainfall left plenty of standing water for mosquito breeding. But not a single doctor before Walter Reed seems to have connected the prevalence of the disease with the prevalence of the insects. Some causes given in the contemporary press included bad air, bad food, overexertion, and too much sunshine. A Houston newspaper of 1843 declared a late autumn epidemic was caused by "the excitement of the elections." Popular remedies were bloodletting, tartar emetic, cold baths, or snow and ice packs when they were available. When asked what he gave for malaria, a Missouri physician listed calomel, quinine, and Mangum. As none of his colleagues had heard of Mangum, he had to explain that Mangum was the name of his brother-in-law, a local undertaker.

While at Fort Lowell, Dr. Reed did discover the cause of one mysterious case of diarrhea. Suffering from the ailment was a certain Private Kelly who spent much of his time in the post infirmary. Reed tried every medicine in his dispensary, but without success. Then one day he noticed that the castile soap he placed in the infirmary washroom kept disappearing. Since Private Kelly frequented the washroom more often than any other patient, Reed confronted him, and the soldier admitted he had been eating the soap to keep his diarrhea flourishing. Private Kelly was soon returned to duty.[12]

Cures for many other diseases were also based on folklore, trial and error, and old wives' tales. Some physicians drew off a cupful of blood at the first complaint of a patient, even before the ailment was diagnosed. Brown sugar was believed to be just the thing for smallpox. A Texas rancher posted a prescription for bad colds in his bunkhouse: ONE QUART OF WHISKEY AND A DOZEN LEMONS. DIRECTIONS: THROW THE LEMONS AT A FENCE POST AND DRINK THE WHISKEY.[13]

As early as 1856 frontier doctors were prescribing various cures for women suffering from backache. According to a San Antonio newspaper, a local physician was advising his female patients to wear less clothing. One of his patients was "induced to adopt hooped and light skirts instead of heavy ones...After a few weeks she said that she was entirely free of backaches and other uncomfortable feelings..." Her clothes weighed one-fourth what they had before, and the differences in weight gave more freedom of movement, and oppressive heat about the loins was avoided.[14]

Remedies for snake bites were numerous and diverse: gunpowder and vinegar, tanglefoot oil, tobacco juice, brandy and salt, bark from a black oak tree, the tail of a dead snake, and large amounts of whiskey.

Most successful physicians on the frontier were quite aware of the power of advertising. They posted detailed signs outside their offices and placed card notices in newspapers. The aforementioned Edward Willis, the doctor at Placerville who dueled his rival and eliminated him, had this sign painted:

SURGERY. Dr. Edward Willis, M.R.C.S.
Surgery and Physic in All Branches.
Sets Bones, Draws Teeth Painlessly, Bleeds.
Advice Gratis.

In April 1859, A.F. Peck, M.D. placed a notice in the *Rocky Mountain News* stating that he could be found in his office at all times "when not professionally engaged or digging gold." In the June 9, 1878, issue of the *Arizona Citizen*, W.H. Bluett, Physician and Surgeon, Picket Post, Arizona Territory, announced himself as being prepared "to attend all ailments that Picket Post flesh is heir to, or any flesh for that matter."

Doctors in frontier settlements usually adopted the rough mannerisms of their patients, particularly in mining and military locations where males far outnumbered females. And if a well-educated and experienced physician settled in communities evenly balanced by the sexes, he was often regarded as indispensable, a lord of sorts who could get away with almost anything.

In John J. Fox's memoir of the 1880s, he tells of an English doctor who came to Carbon, Wyoming, to practice among the coal miners. He charged each miner fifty cents a month, guaranteeing them medical attention without further fees. The doctor's recreation was poker and he sometimes played through the night. One morning, not long after he had dropped off to sleep, he was awakened by a banging at his door. Two miners came in, one holding up an injured hand, still bleeding from being caught on a rusty nail in a mining handcart.

The doctor looked at the hand, and was so angry at being awakened for what he considered an insignificant wound that he punched the miner in the jaw and knocked him down. "There now!" he cried. "If you ever come and wake me up in the middle of the night again for a scratch like that, I'll kill you. Put some more turpentine on it and come back at ten o'clock."

He had to treat the miners rough, the Englishman told Fox. "Once let those miners think you're soft and they'd be bothering you for attention all the time on the slightest pretext. What do the blighters expect for fifty cents a month—a hospital cot?"[15]

In Denver during the 1870s, Dr. F.J. Bancroft developed a practice among ranchers who lived along the Kansas Pacific Railroad east of town. He was a very large man, weighing about three hundred pounds, and was known by sight to almost everyone in the area. One day after attending a ranch patient, he walked to the railroad track and flagged down a Denver-bound passenger train. It stopped with a screeching of brakes and hissing of steam, and Dr. Bancroft heaved his bulky body and medicine bag aboard.

He was greeted by two irate trainmen who were new to that railroad division—the conductor and brakeman.

"What do you mean flagging this train down?" the conductor demanded. "What's the emergency?"

"No emergency," the doctor replied. "I just want to get back to Denver in time for supper."

"That's against the rules," the brakeman shouted.

"Well, I read those rules," Bancroft declared. "And they say this train can be flagged in case of emergency or for a large party. Don't you think I'm a large party?"

For a moment the trainmen looked at the hefty doctor blocking the aisle, and then they could not help breaking into laughter. Dr.

Bancroft got his ride and was in Denver by suppertime.[16]

Although most doctors behaved as they pleased, there was one on the Arkansas frontier whose wife refused to let him go on calls in the countryside unless she accompanied him. When they reached a patient's house after a long buggy ride, the wife expected to have a place prepared for her to rest. It became customary among families served by that doctor to prepare a bed for his wife. Not until she was placed comfortably in the bed was the doctor at liberty to examine the patient he had been summoned to minister to.[17]

Pseudo-doctors became a problem and an embarrassment to bona fide medical men along the unregulated frontier. As early as 1835, a group of physicians in Texas circulated a petition decrying the prevalence of medical charlatans, implying that more Texans died under their hands than from the attacks of hostile Indians.

"We had at any time rather see a company of armed Mexicans in battle array," the petition stated, "than a squad of these grave gentry, parading with Pandora's boxes in the shape of pill bags ...dealing damnation round the land by various infernal compounds of mercury, lead, ratsbane, etc...Some of these impostors have acquired the honorable and distinguished title of doctor merely by the simple process of migration and distinguished by that vast fund of medical knowledge acquired in a livery stable, cook shop, or tan vat."[18]

Such protests had little effect, however, and quacks continued to flourish. Patent medicines, for instance, composed mostly of alcohol and whatever bitter herbs were handy and cheap, were peddled under hundreds of flashy brand names. As soon as electric batteries became readily available, spurious practitioners claimed that electric currents would cure all known ailments. Chairs were fitted with "Galvanic Faradic Batteries" so that patients could sit in comfort while electrical charges titillated their bodies and made them feel hale and hearty.

As it was practiced in the opposing armies of the Civil War, medicine probably reached its low point, particularly in the western theater of that conflict. Soldiers' letters reflected its crudities and absurdities with considerable black humor. "The doctors is out of medicine," wrote a Texas soldier. "If they had a waggon load, it wouldn't do any good, for they are so lazy they wont get up when they are setting down to give a sick man a dose of medicine...Frank Thompson is ded. He had the flux & the doctor gave him so much morphine, the boys says they killed him."[19]

On the march somewhere in the West, another soldier noted the death of a comrade. "It was believed that Doctor Sanderson's medicine killed him; he gives calomel and the sick are almost physicked to death."

Much more popular than doctors were the itinerant pitchmen who peddled medicines along with entertainment in the form of medicine shows, sometimes called liniment shows. These exhibitions roamed from town to town, and not until the frontier closed did their numbers begin to decline. A few endured well past the first World War. When the wagon, or wagons, rolled into a town all other forms of recreation ceased. The pool halls, saloons, lodge meeting houses, even the early silent movie theaters closed on the evenings that medicine show performers were beguiling the citizenry and selling them countless bottles of phony tonics. The standard price ranged from two bits to a dollar a bottle; the contents cost the bottler no more than two cents.

A medicine show could consist of one wagon, two wagons, or a small caravan that included a sizable canvas tent. The one-wagon show was the most common, the vehicle being about the size of a Conestoga or prairie schooner freight wagon, but built high and squared off at the ends. It had to be spacious enough to house three or four people, carry stores of alcohol, glycerin, opium, licorice, cinchona, and a considerable supply of bottles. Some vehicles carried a knockdown stage; in others the rear door was installed so that it would drop down and form a platform, or stage.

The sides of the wagon were painted in gaudy colors, with the name of the show in large block letters. As most shows bore Indian names, a crude drawing of a feather-bonneted warrior or medicine man added excitement to the display. For some reason the more popular secret Indian herb remedies seemed to come from the Kickapoo, Osage, and Cherokee tribes.

The products of the Kickapoo Medicine Company, the Ton-

Ki-Ki-Medicine Show, the Hamlin Wizard Oil Company, and Pawnee Bill's Indian Remedies Show became so highly regarded by consumers of tonics and liniments that each company had to send several units out simultaneously to entertain and heal the folk in small towns of the West.

The most important member of a medicine show was the pitchman, also know as spieler, caller, or talker. He was usually the owner. He gave himself the title of doctor or professor, and fancied long-tailed coats and tall silk hats. He might actually be a former physician, or perhaps a defrocked clergyman who possessed a booming persuasive voice that could bring tears to the eyes of his listeners when he related tales of dying youths saved at the last moment by his magical nostrums.

"Come closer, ladies and gentlemen," the spiel usually began. "Gather round. We have no seats to offer you, but you will be so excited and astounded by what you will see here tonight...absolutely free to all, that you will be glad to stand up."

Accompanying the spieler were two or perhaps three others—a female who could sing and dance and play a musical instrument, a sturdy quick-footed male who could perform feats of strength, eat fire, spin trick ropes, or play straight man to the jokes of the spieler. His other duties included passing bottles of medicine out to the members of the crowd, collecting the money, and quelling disturbances. As many of these shows were family affairs, there might be a youngster or two available to help with the chores, distribute the bottles, and even do a bit of clowning.

The main objective of course was to sell the tonics, bitters, liniments, salves and curative soaps. With their high percentage of alcohol, the liquid remedies were especially popular in areas that had come under sway of the temperance movement and prohibitionists. "It would take nearly nine bottles of beer," a newspaper reporter noted, "to put as much alcohol into a thirsty man's stomach as the temperance advocate can get by drinking one bottle of Hostetter's Stomach Bitters."[20]

In the early days of the medicine shows, the spielers usually opened their recitations with strong attacks upon the local physicians, impugning their competence, and charging that the cause of so much illness in the community was lack of access to the magical herbal remedies available only from the medicine show. The doctors retaliated by trying to persuade the local political forces to drive the shows out of town. As the years passed, however, the physicians and the showmen made a peace for their mutual benefit. As soon as the spieler saw his sales dropping he would pack up and move on to the next town, leaving behind on the shelves of the local doctors a good supply of his particular elixir of life.

The local physicians may have had little confidence in the healing powers of the bottled herbs, alcohol, and opium, but they knew their patients would soon be eager to pay for fresh bottles—at least until an even more miraculous potable came to town.

Greasepaint in the Wilderness

THEATER CAME TO THE FRONTIER almost as soon as cabins were built in clusters to form communities, and like some of the pioneers, the first performers traveled westward on riverboats. As early as 1835, a theatrical company managed by Samuel Drake was traveling on a flatboat along the Ohio, stopping at every village that was of sufficient size to make a performance pay.

Accommodations were crude, but the Drake company of eight artistes usually managed to find bed and board in farmhouses and rough taverns. At a river settlement where they stopped late one day, there was only a single room available for the night. It contained two beds and a floor pallet, not enough for the entire company, but offering more comfortable lodgings for the older members than the hard boards of the flatboat.

While the actors went to secure their baggage, a pair of odorous mule drovers seized the room and refused to leave, claiming right of prior occupancy. Accustomed to extemporaneous solutions to unexpected dilemmas, both on and off the stage, the Drakes sized up the simple-minded drovers and decided to play the ghost scene from *Hamlet* for their benefit. Instead of the armor costume they used in the play, they decided that something white would be more suitable for the drovers. Sam Drake chose a white canvas dress that they sometimes used in a *Don Juan* pantomime, and asked an actor named Hull to play the part of the ghost.

"The appearance was extravagant, and ridiculous in this instance, but it answered the purpose intended," one of the performers, Noah Ludlow, later recalled. "His face was to be whitened with chalk and flour, and marked with burnt cork, in order to make it look cadaverous and corpse-like." About ten o'clock the actor Hull as the ghost was standing just outside the room's open window, while Sam Drake and his son began delivering the lines from *Hamlet* leading up to the appearance of the ghost.

Hull could see that one of the mule drovers had shed his boots and trousers and evidently was already asleep. Sitting on the other bed, smoking a pipe and removing his boots, was his companion. With a theatrical glide, Hull stepped through the window into the room—moaning, and beckoning to the pipe smoker, while Drake senior was intoning: "Angels and ministers of grace defend us! Be thou a spirit of health or goblin damned?"

"My God! What is that?" the man cried out. He turned to his sleeping companion, shook him awake, and shouted in his ear: "Hans! Hans! God in Heaven! Wake up!"

When the sleeping drover opened his eyes, Hull in his white makeup and ghostly costume stood over him. Both drovers began howling, and both were shaking with fear. Grabbing his boots and trousers, the rudely awakened Hans led his companion in a hasty flight back to their mules, abandoning the room to the resourceful actors.[1]

The first company of players to visit Fort Scott, Kansas, came down from Leavenworth in 1862, only to find that the schoolhouse they had expected to use for a theater had been converted into a military hospital. Civil War battles had occurred recently along the Missouri border. Undaunted, the troupers cleaned out an old ice house, knocked some benches together, installed a drop curtain and placed candles inside halves of tin cans for footlight. The performances apparently were well received by audiences of convalescent soldiers and local citizens, but according to one report were of such a nature that women were not admitted.[2]

In California during gold-rush days, Dame Shirley, the doctor's wife at Rich Bar, was admitted to a naughty varieties entertainment, but complained that she was in danger of being swept away by a flood of tobacco juice. "Luckily the floor was uneven and it lay around in puddles, which with care one could avoid."

The first performers on the frontier usually traveled alone or in pairs (the Drake company of eight was unusual) and offered feats of strength, magic, or marksmanship. Frequently they were accompanied by one or two circus animals seldom seen in the West.

Sometimes these animals were fakes, as was the case of the "gowrow" brought into the Ozarks by a clever showman. The gowrow was advertised as a fabulous monster and was exhibited in a tent that bore a lurid painting of the animal in the act of devouring a family of mountaineers.

When a crowd gathered around the tent, the showman began selling admission tickets. He asked the ticket buyers to form a line in front of the entrance flap, which he kept closed. After a considerable number of tickets was sold, the showman's partners inside the tent set up a fearsome racket—bloodcurdling roars and cries, clanking chains, the firing of several gunshots.

At the proper moment, the man inside would stagger out in full view of the prospective audience, his clothes torn to shreds, blood running down his face. "Run for your lives," he would yell. "The gowrow has broken loose!" Then the back part of the tent would collapse, with more thunderous roars and rattling chains. The spectators always reacted by running away in panic, without stopping to get their money back.[3]

Another typical frontier performer was the sharpshooter. Occasionally a woman would take the role, and was usually expert enough and confident enough in her skill to add a bit of income by challenging local marksmen to compete. John J. Fox told of a woman who came to Carbon, Wyoming, in the 1880s for an exhibition in the earthen-floored log "opera house." She shot out the flame of a candle, smashed a potato swinging on a string, extinguished the candle behind it, and astonished the miners with difficult angle shots. For a thrilling climax she persuaded a member of the audience to step up on the stage and let her shoot a potato from his head.[4]

In the early days of San Francisco, the inhabitants craved entertainment so desperately that they would pay large sums for almost any kind of performance. According to a correspondent for a New Orleans newspaper in 1849, a tiny circus visiting San Franciso collected three thousand dollars in one evening. He went on to write somewhat disparagingly of the presence of two or three sets of "serenaders" earning small fortunes in the city's establishments "who nightly lament of the absence of Miss Neal, mourn over the fate of Rosa Lee, inform the public that they have just arrived from

Alabama, or request, in the most earnest manner, to be carried back to 'Old Virginny.'"[5]

Small circuses, similar to the one in San Francisco, traveled everywhere along the frontier, sometimes by boat, sometimes overland in wagons. Friedrich Gerstäcker told of a Frenchman bringing a cougar, a chimpanzee, and several monkeys into the canebrakes of Arkansas. The backwoodsmen, having never seen a chimpanzee, decided it was a wild man. They seized the animal, put it on trial, sentenced it to death, and hanged it to a tree limb.

By the 1870s the circuses were much larger, some traveling in railroad cars. Unfortunately for the smaller frontier towns, only inferior shows put in appearances, and they were usually accompanied by thieves, pickpockets, and other disreputable camp followers. Local newspapers often condemned these circuses as humbugs, and advised their readers not to put themselves at the mercy of fakirs, money-snatchers and cheats. "Remember that every dollar you contribute to these humbugs is that much money taken out of the country," warned the *Fayetteville* (Arkansas) *Democrat*, "and what are you benefitted. We think the sooner these humbugs are put down, the better it will be for the country."[6]

Such exhortations evidently had little effect upon the border folk seeking merriment. "The Big Circus and Menagerie has come and gone," lamented one editor in 1875. "The people ditto. By thousands they went to see the show. Purse strings lost their grip. With depleted pockets the masses have returned home. Half of them are figuring every night until low twelve, trying to ascertain how much wiser they are, & see if their increased wisdom is proportioned to their expenditures. The other half have already given up the problem, as too deep for them to solve and may now be seen near the twilight hour, as the dusky shade of evening veils the surrounding landscape in the somber hued mantle, emblematic of death and the grave, sitting out on the wood pile wishing they 'hadn't went.'"[7]

Perhaps some of the dross had been removed by 1880; at least a reporter for a Fort Smith newspaper described a visiting circus as "simply grand and glorious" with a more than adequate menagerie. "A circus day in a border town like Fort Smith is one long to be remembered. Here the rural lads and lassies come into town in droves to see the elephant and feast on ginger bread and bologna. They came from fifty miles from surrounding counties and the Indian Territory to witness the tarnationist biggest show that has exhibited at Fort Smith—since the last one...I had a good time finding the seat I had engaged, but I crowded in on the end of one of them and decided to set there if I did look like a young rooster on a rickety hen roost. After getting well balanced on about two inches of the seat, I took in the entire canvass at a glance as it were. It was one mass of suffocation, fun and sweat. Positively, I don't think I ever saw so large an attendance at a prayer meeting, and I've been to lots of them."[8]

As for the early stage shows, they certainly had their critics, too, and the targeted actors lived precariously even behind the footlights. Cowboys arriving in Dodge City and other railheads after a long trail drive liked to unwind in a theater by firing revolvers into the ceiling. Sometimes they brought their lariats, and indicated approval or disapproval by lassoing the performers. On one occasion a cowboy roped an actress he admired, and pulled her off the stage into his lap, bringing on a mild shootout amongst the audience.

During a presentation of *Uncle Tom's Cabin* at the Bird Cage Theater in Tombstone, Arizona, in 1882, a cowboy became quite wrought up over the plight of Eliza being pursued across the ice by a bloodhound. He drew his pistol and shot the dog dead. Of course the curtain had to be brought down on the scene, and this so infuriated the audience that they attacked the perpetrator. Only the interference of the sheriff saved the cowboy from a severe beating.

The strains of such carryings-on undoubtedly affected the behavior of actors unaccustomed to such treatment. A dramatic company traveling in Kansas in 1870 fell to quarreling among themselves, and on the night they were to present *Lady of Lyons*, Mr. Burr, the leading man, and Mr. Frye, another principal member of the cast, refused to go on stage unless certain demands were met by the management. "Mr. Frye became so demonstrative," reported the *Fort Scott Daily Monitor* of February 15, "as to make his arrest by the police necessary during the performance."

Unexpected interruptions of action on the stage were so common that actors learned to take them in stride, although there was one incident that could have happened only in San Francisco. To report the arrival of ships through the Golden Gate, the ingenious citizens had built a signal device on Telegraph Hill to indicate the type of ship approaching—a contraption with slatted arms that could be raised at different angles. Arms at right angles signaled a sidewheel steamer. One evening at the American Theater, an actor playing in *The Hunchback* walked to the center of the stage, raised his arms at right angles to his body, and cried: "What means this, my lord?"

A young spectator in the gallery immediately responded: "Sidewheel steamer!" A prolonged outburst of laughter from the knowledgeable audience stopped the puzzled actors for several moments.[9]

Some daring companies presented full-length dramas under canvas in the turbulent railroad construction camps. One evening an actor who played the role of Joe Morgan in *Ten Nights in a Bar Room* was just completing a gripping scene where in a state of drunkenness he knocks down his own child with a tumbler full of whiskey. Suddenly there was a crash of glass out in the audience. Impelled by the reality of the scene, an Irish track layer had jumped up, pulled a whiskey bottle from his pocket and was dashing it to pieces against the back of a seat. "I'll never taste another damn drop," he shouted, "as long as I live."

One actor who was trouping throughout the West during the late 1870s apparently learned to enjoy the boisterous treatment received from his audiences. He was Eddie Foy, and his relations with the cowboys of Dodge City started off badly. The morning after Foy made some disparaging jokes about them from the stage of the Comique Theater, a group of cowboys confronted him on Front Street. They lassoed Foy, put him on a horse's back and led him down to the local "hanging tree" near the Arkansas River. There they strung the rope around his neck and asked him what last words he would like to say. Foy kept his cool and replied that he could say them better at the bar in the Long Branch Saloon. The cowboys liked his spirit, and for many weeks afterward they packed the Comique Theater, laughing at the comedian's jokes about them and begging for encores of Foy's specialty, "Kalamazoo in Michigan."[10]

The tendency of frontier audiences to relate personally to the magic of theater, especially in matters they were familiar with, continued into early days of the silent movies. When Emerson Hough's *The Covered Wagon* was being shown in Colorado theaters, one of Jim Bridger's aging former associates, Hiram Vasquez, went to see the film. He was fascinated by the scenes around Fort Bridger, but when the actor playing Bridger appeared in a drunken sequence, Vasquez jumped up and shouted at the screen: "That's a damn lie! Jim Bridger never took a drink of liquor in his life!" Vasquez then stalked angrily from the theater.[11]

During boom times in Leadville, Colorado, "wine theaters" became the rage. Admission was free, and the entertainment was usually upstairs above a well-stocked bar. Boxes curtained for privacy faced a stage where skits were performed continuously and repetitively. Male visitors were expected to patronize the bar liberally, and girls in scanty costumes were sent to sit in their laps and persuade them to buy wines or other alcoholic drinks. One guest who refused to buy more than two beers was tossed down the stairs. For his recalcitrance, he suffered a broken leg and a bruised and battered face.

One-man shows in the form of humorous readings, anecdotes, and character delineations were popular with performers because they required little in the way of baggage or stage furniture. It was possible for a one-man show to penetrate into remote and thinly settled regions where it was economically prohibitive for a full dramatic company.

Charles Farrar Browne as Artemus Ward was a pioneer in the field, his style being a forerunner of Mark Twain's famed humorous lectures. According to the editor of a Leavenworth, Kansas, newspaper in 1864, Ward had a "commanding form, and would make a good figure to hang old clothes on for a sign to some second-hand clothing store. His hair is the color of dirty molasses candy and his eyes are blue, gray, sorrel or black, we don't know which, but they have color, and we are credibly informed that his sight is excellent. His nose and moustache are his most prominent and handsome features. The first is indescribable. The moustache is very near the color of his hair—has a little dirtier look, and stands out as if it had always had its own way."[12]

Artemus Ward would go anywhere he could find an audience. He stopped at the Nevada mining camp, Big Creek, population three hundred, and drew a house of three hundred. "He converted a barroom into a theater, with lights furnished by candles stuck in the posts and a wood fire burning at one end of the bar," wrote his manager Edward Hingston, "while at the other end of the bar the keeper of it, with his shirt sleeves rolled up is busy selling beer and slicing loaves. Whenever Artemus pauses, and the audience applaud, the bartender yells out, 'Bully, boys, bully,' and once, over-excited, he exclaims: 'That's Artemus Ward from New England. Listen to him! Ain't he sweet, ain't he hell!'"[13]

At Carson City, Nevada, Hingston found the theater to be but a slight improvement over the barroom at Big Creek. The auditorium consisted of a pit with raised seats, the entrance being through a shabby drinking establishment, where miners were gambling, smoking and drinking. "They are roughly clad, and wear large slouching wide-awake hats. Beside the door leading from the bar into the theater proper is a painted notice:

NO WASHYBUMS ADMITTED HERE

On inquiry I found that the notice is intended to warn those who have spent all their money in the drinking saloon that they cannot go into the theatre without making additional payment."[14]

During a tour through Missouri and Kansas in 1864, Ward drew packed houses. "A large and delighted audience gathered together by the magic of his name," reported the *Atchison* (Kansas) *Champion* on March 17, "cheerfully paid their half dollars, laughed and disappeared. The 'lecture' defies criticism, being unique in every particular, as well as some others. Personally, Artemus is a boon companion, with an unconquerable aversion to whisky, and given to the mild nourishment of cigars. He wears a large amount of good clothes, has a pug nose, and combs his moustache over his forefinger."

In St. Joseph, Missouri, the *Morning Herald* said that five hundred people "were convulsed with laughter during the delivery of the lecture...Ordinary mortals quiver, shake, roar, boil over, and collapse when listening to his racy, side-splitting lectures."[15]

At the time of Ward's 1864 frontier tour, the finest theater in the West was at Salt Lake City. It was tastefully decorated in gold and white, and could seat three thousand people. It was one of the few places where the famous humorist failed to fill the house, but he was amused by the Mormons' barter system, which extended even to theater admissions. In an article for a contemporary magazine he described in his usual hyperbolic style his receipts for the evening:

"Three cows, one with horns, and two without, but not a stump-tail—fourteen pigs, alive and grunting; seventeen hams, sugar cured; three babes in arms, two cutting their teeth...no end of old hats, ladies' hoops, corsets...also a second-hand coffin, three barrels of turnips and a peck of coals...a footless pair of stockings without the legs, and a pair of embroidered garters."[16]

During the decade following the Civil War, cities large and small in the West built theaters to rival the one in Salt Lake City. Even such roisterous frontier towns as Cheyenne, Wyoming, had two—McDaniel's Theater and an Opera House, the latter boasting a band of eight pieces and a resident troupe of twenty-five performers.

During her railroad tour of the West in 1877, Miriam Follin Leslie, wife of the publisher of *Frank Leslie's Illustrated Newspaper*, paid a visit to McDaniel's Theater:

"Passing through a bar gorgeous with frescoed views of Vesuvius and the Bay of Naples, and remarkable for its cleanliness, we found ourselves in the parquette, so to speak, of the theater—a large room fitted up with chairs and tables, for the use of convivial parties, and served by pretty waiter girls. The stage was narrow, the drop-curtain exceedingly gorgeous, and statues of the Venus de Medici, and another undressed lady of colossal proportions, posed strikingly at either wing. At each side of the hall are tiers of boxes, so called, reached by long narrow flights of stairs from the parquette; these boxes are closed in, and have each a window, through which the inmates must project head and shoulders if curious to witness the performance on the stage; but, as they contain tables and chairs, it is possible that a glass of wine or lager and social intercourse may be more the object than spectacular entertainment."[17]

From Cheyenne, Miriam Leslie journeyed on to Salt Lake City where she visited the theater that Artemus Ward had lectured in thirteen years earlier. The interior had been redecorated in pink and gray, and the building's capaciousness was a surprise to Mrs. Leslie. She compared it to the Fifth Avenue Theater in New York. "We did not see the rocking chair in which Mr. Young [Brigham Young, Mormon leader] is fond of sitting in one of the aisles to witness the performance, but two of the four proscenium boxes, we were informed belonged to him, and some members of his family are generally to be seen there, as he is a zealous patron of the drama, and encourages a large attendance. We went behind the scenes, and found the green room spacious and comfortable, furnished with piano, sofa, chairs, and a long mirror; the dressing rooms commodious, and the 'star' chamber luxuriously furnished."[18]

Albert Richardson, the newspaper correspondent, also visited the Salt Lake theater and observed that professional actors from the East were usually supported by local amateurs. "Whatever they lack in art they make up in freshness and freedom from the mannerisms, especially the stilted and unnatural reading of old actors." He saw Julia Dean Cooper, playing in *East Lynne*, bring the audience to sobs, "and tears even streamed from the eyes of Brigham who sat in his private box." *Camille* produced even more tears, and one old lady left her seat to rush upon the stage with a glass of water for the dying girl. Another declared in a voice audible throughout the house: "It is a shame for President Young to let that poor lady play when she has such a terrible cough."[19]

In San Francisco, the Chinese Theater drew the attention of travelers because of its novelty. "A long, low room, all the walls garnished, or rather daubed," said J.H. Beadle of the *Cincinnati Commercial*, "with gorgeous Chinese scenes, all without perspective, and lighted by a variety of colored lanterns—the whole crowded with Celestials, and noisome with the smoky fumes of some weed I can't recognize, it is not particularly inviting…Yet here we sit an hour mostly studying the audience, but occasionally turning an eye on the monotonous play. From the lively pantomime and the explanations of our guide, I make out that it represents some marvelous incidents in the career of Rip Sah, or some other old humbug, whose name and monarchy were great in China about sixty thousand years since...

"The musicians sit upon the stage directly behind the actors, who enter and retire always by the wings; and the dying groans of Rip Sah, who expires in a fit just after having triumphed over all his enemies and behead fifty thousand prisoners, are drowned by the monotonous droning of something like a tin drum and two three-stringed instruments, about as musical as a hog with his nose under a gate, and not half as expressive."[20]

Miriam Leslie also visited the Chinese Theater. "Actresses are unknown," she said, "the female parts being filled by men coarsely painted and tawdrily dressed. Nearly all the performance is in pantomime, and when speech is considered advisable it is uttered in a high, harsh falsetto, entirely unlike the human voice...There was no scenery of any kind, but at either wing a red-curtained doorway through which exits and entrances are made quite without disguise or ceremony; even when a death is represented, the actor, after going through the contortions and struggles of the last agony, gets up and quietly walks off through one of these doorways, nodding and smiling to his fellow actors or the musicians. The latter sit in a row at the back of the stage, between the two doors, pounding away industriously at the gong cymbals, or scraping the little Chinese fiddles. They seem to have no method in their madness, but just bang away independently—each man making as much noise as possible..."

In describing the play, Miriam Leslie appears to have been as baffled as J.H. Beadle. "Then these grotesque and phantom-like figures began a series of the strangest evolutions, marching in and out, around each other, backward and forward, all making the same ferocious and monotonous gestures, to the accompaniment of that frightful discord of barbaric sound, until it all seemed more like a feverish dream, the fancy of a lunatic, or the vision of an opium eater than an actual stage peopled with human beings. Each warrior as he entered threw one leg in the air and spun around upon the other; this represented the act of dismounting from his horse; and regardless of the fate of the imaginary charger he plunged at once into the battle...

"Finally the scene culminated in the performances of a half-naked man, with his nose painted of a glaring white, who did everything but turn himself inside out; he tied his legs around his neck, jumped on his elbows, stood on the crown of his head with his arms folded, and propelled himself around the stage on acute angles of his frame without the aid of either legs or arms, until there was absolutely no contortion of the muscles left for him to achieve, and then he left off! Our party, the only Americans in the house, gave him a round of applause, at which the silent Celestials turned and grinned at us in wonder and derision, and we got up and went out. They never applaud or disapprove of anything, but sit stolidly and smoke throughout the performance, the women in the gallery also indulging in this luxury, and patronizing the vender of sugar-cane and sweet-meats who walks about with a basket of these delicacies on his head, but does not break the sombre silence by crying his wares."[21]

A more popular playhouse in San Francisco was closed down in 1852, and the owner arrested on grounds of indecency. According to the *Alta California*, the impresario entertained his customers with a music box and a magic lantern. "His pictures represent members of the human family in the Texas costume. Whilst the exhibition is going on, he grinds Yankee Doodle out of the box and charges two rials a sight. He was discharged and the indecent pictures ordered to be destroyed."[22]

In the booming mining towns inland, theaters were slow to meet the demands of a prosperous clientele hungry for music and drama. Albert Richardson, visiting a performance in Virginia City, Montana, was disappointed when he went to see *Lady of Lyons*. "The drop-curtain was of cambric; the stage, as large as a very small bedroom; five tallow candles served for footlights; and the orchestra consisted of four performers. Many spectators wore revolvers, but the rough crowd was wholly decorous, in deference to the half-dozen wives and sisters present."[23]

A Denver theatergoer was even more disparaging, describing "a shabby curtain rising on a shabby stage where the shabby artists were arranged in a row of shabby chairs."[24] An English visitor, after attending a play in Denver, was as critical of the audience as he was of the play. If a performance was that bad in England, he said to a local friend, the spectators would protest audibly instead of sitting quietly and respectfully. The friend explained that because of Denver's shady past, the play-going citizens like to be bored because they were under the impression that respectable people are always bored, and that being bored meant they were respectable.

In Colorado, however, the situation changed remarkably for the better in 1879 when the eccentric and occasionally very rich Horace Tabor built a magnificent opera house in Leadville. Opulence was the word for the Leadville playhouse, with its expensive frescoes, comfortable seats imported from the East, elaborate scenery, and bright gaslights. The plays brought in from New York did not always please the local audiences, however, and a writer for one of the Leadville newspapers called the miners "ignorant dolts" for their behavior during performances. They shouted insulting remarks at the actors, laughed in the wrong places, and talked loudly among themselves. A production of *Othello* drew a full house its first night, an almost empty house the second night. For some reason, the most popular play presented in Leadville—some fifteen years after the Civil War—was *Uncle Tom's Cabin*, which ran for weeks. One critic insisted that the stars of the drama were the bloodhounds, "the largest and fiercest ever brought upon the stage, but not allowed to hurt the audience."[25]

In 1881, when he decided to build his Grand Opera House in Denver, Horace Tabor spent weeks touring the East in order to examine theaters there, and he dispatched his architect to Europe to continue comparisons. Finally he decided to combine features of London's Covent Garden with those of the Academy of Music in Paris. He imported marble from Italy, cherry wood from Japan, and fabrics from France. The curtain alone cost a fortune; a painting across its wide breadth depicted the ruins of ancient Rome. Eugene Field of the *Denver Tribune* described the Grand as "modified Egyptian Moresque." It was the only theater west of Chicago with hot running water in the dressing rooms.

On opening night Tabor entered the glittering lobby with his manager to greet the people of Denver. Noticing a portrait hanging in a prominent spot, he asked: "Who's that?"

"That's Shakespeare," replied the manager.

"Who is Shakespeare?"

"Why the greatest writer of plays who ever lived."

"Well, what the hell has he ever done for Colorado!" shouted Tabor. "Take it down and put my picture up there!"[26]

In the latter half of the nineteenth century, newspaper editors and reporters on the frontier used stage shows and actors as sources of comedy to amuse their readers. Mark Twain was an early practitioner, one of his first efforts being made when he was nineteen and reviewed *The Merchant of Venice* for a Muscatine (Iowa) newspaper. He said he had always thought the play was a comedy until the actors made a farce of it. "The prompters found it hard to get the actors on the stage, and when they did get them on, it was harder still to get them off. 'Jessica' was always 'thar' when she wasn't wanted, and never could turn up when her services were required."[27]

Eight years later, in 1863, Mark Twain was writing for the Virginia City *Territorial Enterprise*. During a visit to San Francisco, he went to see Adah Isaacs Menken in *Mazeppa*—an actress and a play that captivated masculine audiences in the West. "They said she was dressed from head to foot in flesh-colored tights," Twain wrote, "but I had no opera glass, and I couldn't see it, to use the language of the inelegant rabble. She appeared to me to have but one garment on—a thin tight linen one, of unimportant dimensions. I forget the name of the article, but it is indispensable to infants of tender age—I suppose any young mother can tell you what it is, if you have the courage to ask the question...

"Here every tongue sings the praises of her matchless grace, her supple gestures, her charming attitudes. Well, possibly, these tongues are right. In the first act, she rushes on the stage, and goes cavorting around after 'Oliska'; she bends herself back like a bow; she pitches head-foremost at the atmosphere like a dancing-jack; her every move is as quick as thought; in a word, without any apparent reason for it, she carries on like a lunatic from the beginning of the act to the end of it. At other times she 'whallops' herself down on the stage and rolls over as does the sportive pack-mule after his burden is removed. If this be grace, then the Menken is eminently graceful...”[28]

Soon after Twain returned to Virginia City, Adah Menken brought *Mazeppa* there, and he had other opportunities to view her celebrated undressed ride up a runway between cardboard representations of mountain crags. He evidently became quite enamored of “The Frenzy of Frisco,” and wrote a glowing review of her Virginia City performance that was reprinted in newspapers across the country. When he called upon her at her hotel, he found her seated at a table sipping champagne and feeding her pet lap dog sugar cubes dipped in brandy. He was so charmed by the actress that he showed her some of his writings, including a conudrum about her lovely hands, and asked for her criticism.

Twain of course was only one of hundreds of males in Virginia City who were infatuated by Adah Menken. A group of miners presented her with a bar of bullion worth two thousand dollars, and fifty shares of mining stock, which she later sold for a thousand dollars a share. The town named a street and a mine in her honor. One night in the Sazerac Saloon she announced that she could box as well as any man (one of her husbands had been a prizefighter) and volunteered to put on the gloves with anyone willing. A rash miner stepped forward, and according to legend she knocked him out in the second round.

Not all the frontier critics admired Adah Menken, however, one writer declaring that her exhibitions were immodest and “unfit for the public eye, degrading to the drama whose temples they defile; and a libel upon woman, whose sex is hereby depraved and whose chastity is corrupted.”

Mazeppa was so popular in the West, however, that even the William Chapman family troupe, who usually presented wholesome entertainment, added it to their repertory. Caroline Chapman, who knew Mark Twain, wrote him a letter in December 1865 describing the wintertime rigors of the dramatic arts in Helena, Montana. Twain used some of this in a piece for the San Francisco *Golden Era:*

“The idea of a jolly, motherly old lady stripping to her shirt and riding a fiery untamed Montana jackass up flights of stairs and kicking up and cavorting around the stage on him with the quick-silver frozen in the thermometers and the audience taking brandy punches out of their pockets and biting them, same as people eat peanuts in civilized lands! Why, there is no end to the old woman's energy. She'll go through with Mazeppa with flying colors even if she has to do it with icicles a yard long hanging to her jackass's tail."[29]

Early in 1867 Twain was in New York, reviewing *The Black Crook* for his San Francisco readers. After seeing "seventy beauties arranged in dazzling half-costumes, and displaying all possible compromise between nakedness and decency," he pondered the eventual effects of this trend upon serious drama. "Edwin Booth," he predicted, "will have to make a little change by-and-by and peel some women."[30]

One of Adah Menken's rivals in the West was Lola Montez, whose chief claim to fame was her Tarantula, or Spider Dance. In a later time she would have been a premiere burlesque queen. The Spider Dance was variously described by newspaper writers of San Francisco and the mining towns of California. From their testimony it appears that Lola began the dance by pretending to find a spider on her clothes, and then kicking her legs and wiggling her body in efforts to shake it off. More and more spiders swarmed upon her, and she kicked higher and higher in all directions. "First it was this leg and then it was the other," said one observer, "and her petticoats were precious short, on purpose, to give her a fair chance." The spiders were ingenious contraptions made of rubber, cork, and whalebone. Behind the footlights they were quite fearsome creatures.

Lola Montez was her own press agent, deliberately creating an aura of seductive scandal around her persona. She told inquisitive news writers that she was an illegitimate daughter of Lord Byron, and offstage she wore Byronic shirts and jackets. She also claimed to have been mistress in turn to Alexandre Dumas, Franz Liszt, and King Ludwig of Bavaria, who made her a countess. She strolled the streets of San Francisco with two greyhounds on a leash and an enormous parrot upon her shoulder.

In the 1870s, Kansas newspapers carried on a constant derisive bedevilment of thespians, poking fun at the *soubrettes, danseuses,* and *cantatrices*—favorite critical terms for the lively young actresses, dancers, and singers. An anonymous drama critic for the *Fort Scott Daily Monitor* was no Mark Twain, but he must have stirred considerable merriment among his readers with his comments on traveling players.

"Mrs. Pontifex did not know her part, and the prompting was unartistically done," he wrote. "Miss Mortimer swung out too much voice, forgetting the size of the hall, but modulated it with exceeding tact, and was throughout graceful, *piquante,* and versatile. Not the least interesting part of her performance was the by-play with the foot, hurt by the rough stage, and the deft way she went through the narrow crack left for an exit, or doubled herself up in a corner, when unable to get out."

Of the same actress, the critic had this to say about her performance in another play: "Her fainting was very artistic, so was the last hook on her dress."

When *East Lynne* came to town, the cast was alternately praised and scolded. "It was played with much ability—too much in fact. There is no use in putting a whole audience in tears; an actor ought to play kind of easy when he sees a prominent citizen stepping down for his handkerchief with his eyes shut, he ought to 'weaken' on the pathos…"

After seeing productions of *The Hunchback* and *The Marble Heart,* the writer chided two of the actresses in the company. Miss Gray was "too lachrymose," and Miss Tiffany "too fearfully gushing for Southern Kansas."[31]

At Atchison during that same decade, editor Ed Howe of the *Globe* made merry with the great Sarah Bernhardt, playing in *Camille.* "She is distressingly ugly," he said, "and her smile is painful, because it displays a big mouth and a prominent row of butter teeth…Her dress was of white and costly stuff, and cut so low in front that we expected every moment that she would step one of her legs through it…

"We waited patiently for the embrace for which she is said to be the champion of two countries. It came in the third act, and Armand was the recipient. He parted with her, and started to go out, but she followed, and finally embraced him by shambling up, breaking in two at the middle, and throwing her tendrils around her."[32]

In Laramie, Wyoming, Bill Nye had his fun with *The Bohemian Girl*. "The plot of the play seems to be that Arline, a nice little chunk of a girl, is stolen by a band of gypsies owned and operated by Devilshoof, who looks some like Othello and some like Sitting Bull. Arline grows up among the gypsies and falls in love with Thaddeus...

"After a while the Gypsy Queen, who is jealous of Arline, puts up a job on her to get her arrested, and she was brought up before her father, who is the Justice of the Peace for that precinct and he gives her $25 and trimmings, or 30 days in the Bastille. By and by, however, he catches sight of her arm and recognizes her by a large red Goddess of Liberty tattooed on it, and he remits the fine and charges the costs up to the county...

"There is a good deal of singing in this opera...Emma Abbot certainly warbles first rate...But Brignoli is no singer according to my aesthetic tastes. He sings like a man who hasn't taken out his second papers yet and his stomach is too large. It gets in the way and Arline has to go around it and lean up on his flank when she wants to put her head on his breast."

After attending a performance of another production starring Hazel Kirke, Nye commented on the actions of a male member of the audience who was seated in the dress circle. "When Pitticus made a good hit or Hazel struck a moist lead, and everybody wept softly on the carpet, this man furnished a war-whoop that not only annoyed the audience, but seemed also to break up the actors a little. Later, he got more quiet, and at last went to sleep and slid out of his chair on the floor...

"Another point while we are discussing the performance of Hazel Kirke. There were some present on Monday night, sitting back in the third balcony, who need a theatrical guide to aid them in discovering which are the places to weep and which to gurgle.

"It was a little embarrassing to Miss Ellsler to make a grand dramatic hit that was supposed to yank loose a freshet of woe, to be greeted with a snort of demoniac laughter from the rear of the grand opera house.

"It seemed to unnerve and surprise her, but she kept her balance and her head."[33]

Even the traveling correspondents from the East used colorful stories of stage entertainers to add merriment to their dispatches from the West. In 1878, a writer for the *New York Tribune* told of Lurline Monte Verdi, "with her dark eyes and tresses, who on her arrival in Deadwood stood upon a board and was borne through the town on the shoulders of four strapping miners and who now deals '21' and dances a jig with a far-off look in her left eye."[34]

Monte Verdi used various names, including Belle Siddons and Mme. Vestal, but apparently she was Monte Veri when she began her journey from Denver, where she had a four-horse omnibus remodeled into a boudoir. Accompanied by several of her "attendant sporting men" and wagons loaded with gambling furniture, she traveled in style to the Black Hills. At Deadwood she found that operating a gambling parlor and restaurant was more profitable than singing in a theater. She also won considerable local fame by using her knowledge of doctoring—learned from one of her husbands, an army surgeon—to repair the wounds of injured gunmen, some of whom were outlaws.

A wide variety of theatrical entertainment came and went across the West during the years following the Civil War. If the local "opera house" was temporarily dark, there might be a medicine show out on the streets, or a circus in a vacant lot. Traveling stereoptican shows were especially popular, and were usually presented in a schoolhouse or church. By using a pellet of lime with gas, the operator created a light brilliant enough to project views from glass slides upon a large screen. The stereoptican consisted of two projectors which made it possible to dissolve one view into another while showing them in sequence, giving an allusion of motion. The more enterprising operators hand-painted some of their slides.

And if none of these diversions was available, there was always a visiting lecturer to provide entertainment, or stimulate interest in the finer things of life.

On the frontier itself was born a new form of action drama—the Wild West Show. It began with a crude sort of rodeo in the roundup camps of cowboys, blended with the outdoor medicine shows, and then crossed with Buffalo Bill Cody's stage shows. In 1881, Texas Charlie Bigelow added cowboys and Indians to his Kickapoo Indian Medicine Company, and sent several units out from his home state to ride, shoot, and sell nostrums.

A few years earlier Buffalo Bill had persuaded Wild Bill Hickok, Texas Jack Omohundro, and several Pawnee Indians to join him in a traveling stage show, *The Scouts of the Prairie*. Wild Bill was bored by the sham fights with the Indians in the confined spaces of theater stages. To amuse himself he began firing blanks so close to the Pawnees' legs that they felt the burn of the fire. After they complained several time to Cody, he ordered Hickok to stop his pranks. Wild Bill replied that he was homesick for the Plains, anyhow, and left the show.

Had Hickok continued a few more seasons at stage acting, he would not have met his doom at Deadwood, South Dakota, but probably would have become a glittering star of the outdoor Wild West Show that Buffalo Bill later organized at North Platte, Nebraska, in 1883. The dashing Pony Express riders, mock Indian attacks on speeding stage coaches, the roping, riding, and shooting, and the spectacle of massed horsemen, buffalo, and longhorns brought excitement and merriment not only to frontier towns, but to the East, and eventually the world.

Cowboys at Play

COWBOYS WERE AT WORK on the very first American frontiers of colonial days, driving cattle up and down the Atlantic coast. They were called drovers, however, and looked more like farmers than the romantic horsemen of the Old West—nor did they make as much merriment as did their successors beyond the Mississippi. Like the accoutrements, tools, dress, and customs of Western ranching and trail driving, the name *cowboy* came from Mexico—*vaquero*, literally "cow herder." During the early days in the Southwest, the word "cowboy" had an outlaw connotation, and this view persisted into the trail-driving days when cattle by the thousands were driven overland from Texas to railroad shipping towns in the North. Many early cowboys were former Confederate soldiers, and many of the entrepreneurs and lawmen waiting for them in the Kansas shipping towns were Yankees.

Cowboy life was adventurous, but it was probably the most arduous occupation in the West. A cowboy worked under blazing skies, in drenching rains, and raging blizzards. His hours were long, his duties perilous, his food very poor, his pay negligible. Much of the time he was bored and lonely. The length of his working career was about the same as that of the average professional football player today—seven or eight years. To endure his hard life, the frontier cowboy found it necessary to manufacture a bit of merriment now and then; pranks and comic show were a great antidote to his dreary routines. His favorite targets were tenderfeet, especially the British newcomers to ranch life. But if he could not find a tenderfoot, he turned to one of his fellows.

Typical was the cowboy treatment of a cattle buyer who drove his wagon into a cow camp while wearing a high silk hat. As most of the boys were still out rounding up the cattle, the buyer found a resting place, laid his hat aside, and went to sleep. When the cowboys came in, the first object they noted was the high silk hat.

"What is it?" one said.

"It's a bear," another said.

"It's the venomous kypoote," another said. "It's one of those things that flee up and down the creek and hollow 'walo wahoo' in the night time."

One called out: "Boys, it's a shame to stand peaceably by and see a good man devoured by that varmint."

By this time the cattle buyer was wide awake, and he was startled when one of the cowboys drew his pistol and shouted a warning: "Look out there, mister, that thing will bite you!"

The cattle buyer sprang to his feet and jumped away, not stopping to get his hat. As soon as he was clear of the target, several cowboys fired bullets into the silk hat until they shot off the crown.

An observer reported later: "Our good-natured old friend, after recovering from his scare, took a hearty laugh over the little jamboree and called the boys all 'round his wagon and drew out a jug of sixteen-shooting liquor—then they celebrated the death of the terrible varmint.

"One of the boys loaned the jolly old boy his hat, and he wore it until he could get one from town, when they all chipped in and bought one of the best to be had, a regular cow-man's hat...Besides, they offered to pay for his, which he positively refused to let them do. But one thing is certain, he hadn't been in that outfit three days until every man on the ranch, even the cook, would have fought his battles for him, if occasion had presented itself."[1]

A cowboy who was a smart aleck or was delinquent in his duties was quite likely to become a victim of his fellow workers. John Callison related the story of a malingering cowboy known as Big Jim. "He was not lazy, but he just had a way of letting the other boys do the work. We decided at a council of war that we would break Jim of the habit of laying down under the chuck wagon every time it was in camp. One hot day he took off his boots and sox and rolled up his pants and drawers, so his feet would cool off while the cook was getting dinner. Then we all got busy...

"While some of the boys were out after a tarantula, the bite of which is said to be sure death, I was making medicine to cure Jim. When the boys got back to camp with a big tarantula, they killed him and laid him down close to Jim's leg. Then they got a pin and fastened it in the end of a stick and everything was ready, Dad Williams gave Jim two or three in the calf of his leg with that pin. That brought Jim up in a hurry. Some of the boys put their foot on that tarantula and mashed it, and we made him believe that he had been bitten by that tarantula. As Jim and I were good friends, he came to me to be doctored. I told Jim that it was a bad case, and he wanted me to do something to save him. The first thing I gave him was a pint of bear's oil that one of the boys had...Then I gave him a package of soda, then a half teacup full of vinegar, then a quart of water that I had been soaking a ten-cent cut of tobacco in. By that time Jim was about as sick a boy as ever lived to tell about being bitten by a tarantula. About that time his brother got back from a road ranch with a two-gallon jug of whiskey. I gave him a little whiskey to bring him back. The rest of the gang drank the whiskey at Jim's expense. Jim always believed that he was sure bit, and he thought I was a wonderful doctor to save him, away out in the prairie, miles away from a sure-enough doctor."[2]

Another example of cowboy mischief and generosity was the treatment of a simple-minded ne'er-do-well from the Brazos country of Texas. He joined a cattle drive to Kansas, and his gullibility provided considerable merriment for his fellows. By the time the herd was driven into Dodge City, the cowboys were a scrubby lot—dust-covered and travel-worn—but none was as bedraggled as the young man from the Brazos. He had not started with proper clothing in the first place and from the beginning was an outsider among the wranglers. He was now a very tattered cowboy—with holes in his clothing at elbows and knees, and with sockless toes sticking out of his cracked boots. The boys made it up among themselves to do something about his case.

As soon as they were paid off, they surrounded their victim. They jerked off his ragged hat and trampled it in the dust. They pulled off his boots and knifed them into strips; they ripped off his shirt and trousers and shredded them. Having no underwear, the boy from the Brazos was now naked as a newborn. Although he kicked wildly and shouted his limited number of profane insults repeatedly, the cowboys hoisted him upon their shoulders and paraded him in broad daylight down Front Street and into a clothing store. Every man contributed a share to buy him a complete outfit, and then they arranged a bath, a shave, and a haircut. By this time the formerly tattered cowboy knew he had been accepted by the outfit. He led the boys into the Long Branch Saloon and spent most of his meager pay on drinks around.

In the Medicine Bow, Wyoming, cattle country of *The Virginian*, community dances seem to have been the scenes of many cowboy pranks like those related by Owen Wister. At a dance in the Elk Mountain schoolhouse, nineteen-year-old John Fox, conniving with the boys of his outfit, attended in the guise of a girl. From a lady storekeeper he borrowed a very large corset, a pair of striped stockings, a white underskirt trimmed with lace, a Dolly Varden hat that tied under his chin with ribbon, and a turkey-red Mother Hubbard dress.

Fox declined to go all the way, however; beneath the long skirt he wore his English riding breeches. But he did agree to ride side-saddle to the schoolhouse. "I went in on the arm of Dexter Jones and was introduced to some people I did not know as Miss Ferguson from Scotland. I endeavored to be very gracious, not to say condescending, and really succeeded in taking in one or two people for a few minutes...

"One young lady, the daughter of a large stock rancher, had just returned from an Eastern 'Finishing School' where culture was dispensed; and as Dexter said, she 'put on more airs than a studhorse' to show her aloofness. When I was presented she looked at me coldly but curiously and gave a stiff little salutation—not even a simper. I do not know if she was waiting for somebody that failed to show up, but she refused all offers of partners for the Lancers...

"Just as we finished the first figure of Lancers, that wretched piece of string that secured my white lace-trimmed underskirt broke and down the silly thing came in billowy folds around my feet. Now it is probable that if I had been a woman, such a thing might in those days, have been very embarrassing indeed—quite a catastrophe, but to me it meant nothing at all. I simply stepped out of the mess, rolled it up and deposited it on a vacant chair beside Miss X, the finished one.

"She drew up her skirts in horror and disdain, moving her chair well away from the accursed thing...I left the room, reached my overalls and blue shirt from the back of the saddle and changed back to a man again.

"On re-entering the room I was re-introduced to Miss X, who was not only most gracious to me, but actually thawed out and became human with the bunch. That eastern silver plating was very thin. She was born on a cattle ranch the very year that Wyoming became a territory and had been raised on horseback. Even an eastern 'Young Ladies Seminary' could not piffle that off."[3]

Cattlemen were also ingenious with their trickery, sometimes being downright dishonest. One of their stratagems was borrowed from Civil War days when they deceived the enemy into believing they had double or triple their actual cavalry strength by marching the same horsemen two or three times past a given point. During a tour of west Texas, Richard Harding Davis learned that three Englishmen had recently been there to buy three thousand steers apiece, but later discovered the nine thousand they counted and paid for had been driven three times around a small mountain and past their counting station. Each of them had actually purchased one thousand cattle at triple the going price.

The cowboy's ingenuity in avoiding unnecessary complications was legendary. A brush popper from New Mexico rode a magnificent stallion into Tombstone, Arizona, during its lawless days. Dismounting at the famed O.K. Corral, he passed the word that he was broke and was willing to sell the horse for half its worth. He soon found a purchaser, who paid in full, and then asked: "What about the bill of sale?"

"Oh," replied the cowboy, "don't worry about the horse's title. It's perfectly good as long as you go west with him. But don't take him east; it's not so good in that direction."[4]

A bunch of resourceful cowboys driving a herd across Colorado to the Platte River noticed that one of the cows had recently calved and had a full bag of milk. As they were fed up with using water to wash down their cheese-and-cracker rations, they roped the cow. But when they started to milk her, they could not find a container in the outfit. Not to be outdone, one of the more inventive of the boys unpacked his slicker, spread out its waterproof folds, and milked into it. They then gathered round, broke their crackers into the milk, and added a pint of whiskey. "Oh, what a mess," one of them later recorded, "but we all enjoyed it nevertheless."[5]

Cowboys working out on the range evidently preferred to eat beef belonging to a ranch other than their own (something like the grass being greener on the other side of the fence). Shanghai Pierce, a colorful cattleman of the trail-driving period, was out scouting for strays one day when he came upon a neighboring outfit dining on beef from a steer whose hide was hanging in plain view. The brand on the hide was a big D— Shanghai Pierce's brand.

Shanghai's face bore an expression of reproach, but he said mildly: "The day is coming when every outfit's going to have to eat its own beef."

"Well, now," replied the neighboring foreman cheerfully. "Mebbe so, mebbe so. In the meantime this here's mighty good meat. Sit down, Shang, and have chuck with us. I've allus found D beef sweeter than any other." Shanghai sat down and joined in the feast of meat which he had furnished without his consent.[6]

During a cattle drive north from Texas, the point riders came upon a fat black yearling that although branded appeared to be a stray. Its brand was unknown to any of the cowboys. With the trail boss's permission they roped the animal, and at evening camp they butchered it for dinner. The cook asked for the hide, saying he needed a belly for the chuckwagon. He pegged it out on the grass to dry.

A few minutes later, the yearling's owner rode into camp. His manner was imperious. He spoke in a thick accent, was brusque in his actions, and was decidedly unfriendly. He dismounted, and without asking permission went over to the drying hide, unpegged it, turned it over, and found his brand. Muttering threats about bringing the sheriff to arrest the malefactors, he mounted and rode off at a gallop toward the nearest town.

As soon as he was out of sight, the trail boss told his men to cut a black yearling out of their herd, butcher it, and peg the hide out exactly where the other one was. He ordered the cook to cut the other hide into small pieces and burn it as quickly as possible. These tasks were scarcely completed when the foreigner came riding back with the sheriff and a deputy.

"Who's in charge of these cattle?" the sheriff asked.

"I am," replied the trail boss.

"Consider yourself under arrest!"

"For what?"

"For stealing this man's yearling!" said the sheriff.

"He's a liar," the trail boss declared. "We killed that one out of our herd."

"I'll show you!" cried the foreigner. Dismounting, he tore the hide loose from its pegs, and flipped it over. There on the hair side as plain as a hat was the herd's road brand.

"You certainly are mistaken," said the sheriff to the complainant. "Everybody in the country knows that road brand."

At this, the trail boss gave the foreigner a cattleman's proper chewing out, half of which the stung outlander probably did not understand. The man knew he had been outfoxed, but he could not prove it. He climbed into his saddle and galloped away in a fury. The trail boss then invited the sheriff to dinner and fed him on beef from the foreigner's yearling.[7]

The ability of cowboys to make do with whatever materials were at hand is legendary. For example, one winter a certain rancher decided to string several miles of barbed wire around his land. He sent his boys out to round up some fence poles and start stapling on the wire. Poles were scarce in that area, and when a couple of punchers came upon a slope covered with frozen rattlesnakes, they decided to drive them in the ground and use them for fence poles. After attaching the barbed wire, they returned to the bunkhouse bragging about their cleverness. Next day, however, the foreman fired both of them. During the night a warm wind thawed out the snakes and they crawled off with a long stretch of expensive barbed wire.

Hasty expedience sometimes brought on embarrassing situations, as was the case of a chuckwagon cook, related by Ab Evans:

"I never will forget what happened to the fellow that was cooking for Ben Mattox when he was running that big outfit down in the Wichitas. They came into Quanah with a herd to ship and camped the last night out in the edge of the 'Nestermints' and the milk pen calves ate the cook's clothes up while he was taking a bath in Riley Wheat's tank. The only surplus clothes in the outfit was a pair of chaps that one of the boys had in the wagon." *(Chaparejos,* or chaps, as anyone knows who is familiar with cowboy gear, cover only the front of the wearer's legs, a sort of apron or armor, but they have no seat or other rear covering.)

"This coosie [cook] climbed into them and got his breakfast and dinner OK and then pulled into town and camped at the railroad tank near the stock pens and got his fire to going and his supper started. He hadn't more than got started good when Mrs. Mattox and a surrey full of women folks drove up to see Ben and eat supper at the wagon. You can imagine how that poor boy felt cookin' a meal of victuals, tending his fires and all without turning his back on them women folks."[8]

A giant among cattlemen was Charles Goodnight, who started developing the enormous JA Ranch in the Palo Duro canyon of west Texas. In his later years, Goodnight recalled the days when the Palo Duro was filled with one hundred thousand cattle. "To care for them over such an extensive range," Goodnight said, "we employed a little army of men called 'cowboys.'" Before that he had called them "boys," but by the late 1870s they were becoming known as "cowboys" all across the West. Although a strict disciplinarian—Goodnight permitted no gambling, drinking or fighting—he had a high regard for the men who worked for him. When they were away for several weeks, driving herds or line riding, he paid interest on any pay that was past due them. When they got into trouble that was not of their making, he was always there to defend them.

Because of his reputation for being rough as a cob, some cowboys had no desire to work for Goodnight. Others eagerly sought employment with him, but Goodnight was slow to hire a stranger, as cowboy Dave McCormick discovered. When McCormick arrived at the ranch, he found the cattleman planting fruit trees near the ranch house—not the sort of work that appealed to a cowboy. McCormick politely asked for a job punching cattle, but Goodnight just kept on digging.

"Directly I picked up a shovel and went to digging, too," McCormick said later. "After a while old Dudley the cook hollered and said dinner was ready. I tell you it wasn't near as ready as I was! Well, Goodnight asked me to come on in and eat so we went in and washed up and ate dinner. Mrs. Goodnight was a mighty fine woman and…she saw to it that I had plenty to eat that day and she was so nice to me I forgot that Mr. Goodnight hadn't been very cordial.

"After we got through eating, we went back to the orchard and I went to digging again. We never had hardly anything to say to each other and he never paid me any mind again. I guess he decided that I had come to stay. Well, it kept on like that. He never did hire me but he put me on the payroll."[9]

Black cowboys were more numerous in frontier days than the popular literature of the time reveals. One of the legendary ones in Texas was Matt Hooks, known to all his friends as Bones. After establishing a reputation as a champion horse breaker, Bones took a job as Pullman porter on the Santa Fe Railroad out of Amarillo.

Rumors of an unbreakable horse at Pampa came to Bones's attention, and every time the train stopped at that town, east of Amarillo, he would hear more stories of how the best riders in the West had come there and paid their entrance fees only to be defeated by the horse. The purse had risen to $250, but still nobody could break the bronco.

One day some cattlemen that Bones knew from his cowboy days boarded the train. They were full of talk about the outlaw horse. One of them was a rancher that Bones had once worked for, and he told the man he would like to break the wild bronco.

"We think a lot of you, Bones," the rancher said. "We don't want to see a good porter get hurt."

"But I can ride that bronc. Just get the two hundred fifty dollars and have the horse down at the train at Pampa and I'll ride it while the train is in the station. If I don't you can give my money to the Sunday school and hang me."

A date was set, the rancher promising to make the necessary arrangements. On the morning of that day, Bones appeared at the train in Amarillo wearing his Stetson and cowboy boots. The conductor refused to let Bones aboard, and demanded an explanation as to why he was wearing a cowboy outfit. Bones told him he was going to ride the outlaw horse at Pampa.

"What'll happen if you break a leg?" asked the conductor. "What'll the Santa Fe officials say if I let my porter ride a bronc while he's on duty?"

They decided to go down to the locomotive and talk it over with the engineer. "How long will it take, Bones?" asked the engineer.

"Five minutes."

"Well, we can make that time up," the engineer said to the conductor. "I'm willing to let him try."

As the passenger train rolled on toward Pampa, news spread through the cars that Bones was going to try breaking the wild bronco. Numerous bets were made. At the Pampa stop, all the passengers unloaded to see the contest. Bones's rancher friend had been unable to come, but he had telegraphed instructions, and the horse was there. The $250 purse was handed to the nervous conductor, who looked unhappy about the whole affair.

Blindfolded and tightly reined, the horse was brought forward. With one swift motion Bones snatched off the blindfold and leaped into the saddle. In less than the five minutes allowed, the black rider stayed in the saddle until the outlaw stopped pitching. Then he quietly dismounted.

The whistle on the locomotive blew a little salute, and the passengers began reloading. On his way back to the Pullman car, Bones stopped briefly at the telegraph window in the Pampa station and sent a message to his rancher friend: "Outlaw rode. Got money. Gone east. Bones."[10]

When Hernando Cortés introduced Spanish cattle to America in the sixteenth century, he branded them with three crosses to prove ownership. The custom of branding continued into the open-range days of the nineteenth century—and to our own times. A goodly lot of frontier humor went into devising much of this heraldry of the cattlemen. Some famous brands that can be visualized from their names were the Frying Pan, Ox Yoke, Turkey Track, Hog Eye,

Buzzard on a Rail, Scissors, Andiron, Stirrup, and Dinner Bell. Pancho Villa fittingly chose a Death's Head. After winning a big pot in a poker game with four sixes, Burk Burnett used them for his brand—6666.

Smart ranchers tried to design brands so distinctive that rustlers could not alter them and claim the cattle as their own. A certain cattleman whose initials were IC used them to brand his livestock. Rustlers stole several of his cows and added a U to the brand—ICU. When the owner managed to recover the stolen cattle he added a 2 to the brand—ICU2.

Another range legend concerns a rancher's daughter named Lillybelle, whose beauty created intense rivalry among all the cowboys for miles around. One ingenious puncher roped a maverick steer, branded its rump LIL and presented it to the young lady. She was so pleased that the boy's numerous rivals began rounding up unbranded strays, branding them LIL, and making gifts of them to the lucky Miss Lillybelle. She soon had a sizable herd.

While her army of suitors waited impatiently for her to choose one of them, she was visited by a handsome tenderfoot from the East. She chose the tenderfoot, and with her herd of LIL cattle they began ranching and lived happily ever after.[11]

When the cowboys from the vast and lonely ranges brought cattle into one of the larger frontier towns such as Denver, Cheyenne, or Kansas City, they were like visitors from another planet. They found themselves in environments totally unfamiliar. The buildings, food, customs, and commercial amusements had to be dealt with, which they did in their own merry ways.

In the early 1880s roller skating rinks made their first appearance in New Mexico. "I'm more used to riding on horseback," a cowboy said after his initial experience on roller skates, "but last night I thought I'd try them little wagons. I got one with a double cinch, and another to match it, and as soon as I straddled the layout I could feel 'em begin to bow their backs, and was wishing I had a buck rein, because I was expecting them to stiffen their knees and go to bucking every minute, but they didn't. I walked 'em over to the other end of the corral to gentle 'em a little, and directly they started off at an easy canter, and were coming around back right through the herd; and there was a dude there with a stiff hat who was trying to cut out a Polled Angus heifer, in a blue dress, and I fouled and roped both my hind legs with a hoop skirt, and it had me stretched out for branding quicker'n a spring calf can bawl with its mouth open and its lungs stretched."[12]

After spending most of their working years sleeping in crude bunkhouses or in blankets on the ground, cowboys visiting a big cattle town often had trouble with the modernities in hotels. An Englishman traveling through Texas reported seeing this sign in a San Antonio hotel:

GENTLEMEN ARE REQUESTED TO
REMOVE THEIR SPURS BEFORE RETIRING[13]

A Texas boy checking into the Windsor in Denver was informed that the only room available had a folding bed. He replied cheerily that he could handle that. Next morning he left without comment, but when the chambermaid entered the vacated room she found the bottom drawer of the bureau pulled out as far as it would come. In it were all the scatter rugs in the room, with a towel spread over one end for a pillow, as though the cowboy had tried to sleep there. On the bureau top was a note: "Gol' darn your folding beds. Why don't you make 'em longer and put more kivers onto em? Mebbe you expect a man to stand up and sleep in your durned old cubberd." The darned old cupboard of course was the folding bed.[14]

Two drunken cowboys visiting Denver chanced to enter John Elitch's fancy restaurant that had been created to meet the demands of the newly rich mining nabobs. Elitch imported French chefs and waiters and printed his menus in French. Unable to read the menus, the visiting cowboys handed them back to the waiter, who told them politely that the restaurant could serve them anything they wanted.

"Bring us a rattlesnake steak," one of them said.

"Pardon, messieurs," the waiter replied.

"Rattlesnake steak," shouted the other cowboy. "That's what we feed on where we come from. Good, strong, fried rattlesnake."

The perplexed waiter took the problem to the chef, who called the manager. A decision was made to prepare two orders of eel, a gourmet dish of the times. When the waiter brought out the eel, sautéed and basted with sherry, the cowboys stared at it in disbelief, until their eyes turned glassy from queasiness. As one, they kicked back their chairs and with hands at their mouths, raced out of the restaurant.[15]

Limburger cheese was a popular subject for cowboy merriment, a typical incident being reported in a New Mexico newspaper. Two weary range riders entered a restaurant and ordered steaks. While they were waiting, one who had imbibed too freely fell asleep in his chair. Obtaining a piece of limburger cheese, the other cowboy carefully smeared it across his companion's full moustache.

When the waiter brought the steaks, he awakened the one who was sleeping. The cowboy yawned, blinked his eyes, and picked up his fork. Then he began sniffing the air. He raised the steak, smelled it, and dropped it back on his plate. He called the waiter. "Here, you," he said. "Take this piece of dead cow out of town and bury it—it's rotten—and then you waltz up here with a piece of cow that didn't die a natural death and is well cooked—do you hear me?"

The waiter bowed, examined the steak, and declared nothing was wrong with it.

"I tell you it stinks," yelled the cowboy. "It's rotten."

Standing his ground, the waiter replied that it made no difference whether the cowboy ate the steak or not; it must be paid for.

The cowboy arose, angrily knocked over his chair and moved away from the steak to the counter. He paid the waiter hastily, complaining once more that the steak was rotten. "It stinks," he shouted. "You stink. The house stinks. Let me have some fresh air." He fled into the street and drew a long breath. But it was no use. Turning to his companion with a look of dismay, he exclaimed, "Jim, this whole gosh darned town is spoilt, it stinks. You can cut the stink with a knife. Let's pull for the ranch, Jim, 'fore we smother," and the boys mounted and rode off.[16]

Being in the business, so to speak, cowboys were more choosy than most about the steaks served to them in restaurants. A New Mexico newspaper related the experience of Red Pugh, a local cowboy who traveled to Britain with Buffalo Bill's Wild West Show. He went into a restaurant and ordered a rare steak. "The waiter brought him one so rare that it jerked around on the plate. Red drew his gun and fired three or four shots through the steak, 'to kill it,' as he explained, when everyone in the establishment joined in a general stampede. After killing the steak, Red sat down to eat his meat, but he was interrupted in a few minutes by the arrival of about fifty police, who told him that it was against the laws of Her Majesty Queen Vic...He was arrested and fined."[17]

Relations between cowboys and the soiled doves in trail-town dance halls often led to merriment, occasionally tinged with violence. A chivalrous cowboy was so outraged when he saw a bully boy drive his fist into the face of a calico queen in a Cheyenne whorehouse that he interfered and struck the offender with his six-shooter. The blow caused the gun to fire, and when the man fell to the floor, the cowboy fled, believing he had killed the man. When a doctor was called to the scene, he found the victim free of bullet holes, but suffering pain from three scalp wounds made by the barrel of the cowboy's revolver. "The cowboy," reported a local newspaper, "was not found and probably never will be."

The anonymous reporter for the Cheyenne *Democratic Leader* who found much to be amused about on his beat during the 1870s and 1880s witnessed a jolly meeting between several cowboys and two dance-hall girls at nearby Pine Bluffs. "Both wore yellow hair and store complexions. The garments which they wore weren't very costly but were rather variegated and colors bordering on crimson predominated. Each had on a Leghorn hat, which was only less elevated than a steeple, and wore bangle bracelets and jewelry till you couldn't rest. The jewelry was of that character which is euphoneously termed 'snide,' but it shone like a tin pan on a milk house.

"There were many cowboys in the vicinity, and finally one bolder than the rest advanced toward the pair of females. He was received with ostentatious manifestations of kindness. One of the women addressed him as 'Pete' and he called her 'Maude.' They seemed to be overjoyed to see each other. Other cowboys soon appeared, and, without the formality of introduction, immediately became intimately friendly. Then followed beer. This was succeeded by quite a lot of beer. Then came beer.

"From some standpoints the platform levee of the women

might be considered a vivid and even lurid success. For eight mortal hours the pale air was laden with disjointed chunks of revelry. It was a scene of the wildest and most extravagant carousel set down in the quiet midst of the bleak prairie, and one which would give life and reality to an early-day border romance."[18]

Occasionally a cowboy would find a wife in the ranching country. One pair honeymooned in a city where such wild tales of white slavery and kidnapping abounded that the girl was fearful of being left alone. When the cowboy left the hotel room on an errand, he locked his bride inside, taking the key with him.

While making his rounds the cowboy met some of his friends who invited him to join them in a poker game. The play became so exciting that he forgot about leaving his bride locked in the hotel room. Many hours later, when he suddenly remembered her, he jumped to his feet. "If there's anything left of me in fifteen minutes, boys," he cried, "I'll be back. But I done left Eda May locked up in a room for twenty-four hours, an' I ain't neither fed nor watered her."[19]

Cowgirls had sly ways of showing approval and disapproval of cowboy suitors. A story that appeared in print in the *Black Hills Pioneer* and was reprinted during 1882 in various frontier newspapers told about a Deadwood, South Dakota, girl who was embroidering a dress with cattle brands. The brands she chose were those of various ranchers and cowboys among her many admirers. "The dress referred to is not only receiving the brands of many of our thoughtless young stockmen," reported the *Pioneer*, "but the initials of their names as well. An artistic seamstress in Fountain City is doing the embroidery, under a contract of $200. Some of the investors in the dress will no doubt be heartily ashamed of their foolish investment before they die, if not sooner. The brands and initials of her particular favorites cover the side of her neck and bosom, and the brands, etc. of those occupying but an indifferent corner in her affections are attached to the bottom of her skirt, and some are located so as to be frequently sat down upon. After reading the explanation her admirers will be enabled to discover at a glance their standing in the girl's sinful love, whenever she appears in her novel frock."[20]

The wildness of cowboys has been exaggerated. No doubt they cut loose occasionally in the trail towns, particularly after their long drives, and when some of the towns grew more sedate, the authorities were less tolerant of their merry antics. Even the broad-minded writer for the *Cheyenne Daily Leader* thought it unwise for visiting cowboys to buck their broncos in the busier streets, and wondered if the riders could keep their seats if their horses ran up a telegraph pole to the crossbars.

Fred Harvey, who built a chain of restaurants along the Santa Fe Railroad before dining cars were introduced, had a set-to with a group of boisterous cowboys in his establishment at Las Vegas, New Mexico. Fresh off the range, they rode their ponies into Harvey's luxurious lobby and shot some of the whiskey bottles off the bar. They then demanded that drinks be served. "Fred Harvey came forward, and with all the dignity of a clergyman, told the ruffians that his house was built for the entertainment of ladies and gentlemen, and he would have to ask them to leave immediately. They tiptoed to the door, leading their horses, then disappeared in the distance and never came back."[21]

Visiting cowboys riding to the saloon in Carbon, Wyoming, liked to take potshots at signs displayed on the outside walls of the little railroad depot. So many stray bullets whizzed around the person of the station master inside that the holders of that position resigned one after the other. Finally the district superintendent of the railroad ordered the station hoisted upon a flat car and moved outside the town limits and the line of fire.

James Clyman, the old Mountain Man, was not impressed by the cowboys he saw in California, categorizing them as "indolent, doing nothing but ride after herds or from place to place without any apparent object." But then he went on to say that it was impossible to hurry any person in California "where time is no object and every man must have his own time to sleep and move about business as though he was pained to move or even breathe."[22]

Lady Rose Pender, an Englishwoman traveling through Montana in 1883, just plain disliked cowboys, but she also disapproved of almost everything else she encountered on the frontier. She described the average cowboy as "a strange creature, unlike any other of his fellow men, and all he does must be done with swagger and noise…I did not like the cowboys; they impressed me as brutal and cowardly, besides being utterly devoid of manners or good feeling."[23]

One of Lady Pender's countrymen, Edward Money, who tried ranching in Colorado for a short time, was annoyed by the constant spitting of his tobacco-chewing cowboys. "True, they are good shots," he said, "and can generally make sure to three square inches of the spot they aim at; still when you are surrounded by shooters…you feel nervous."[24]

Bill Nye, the Laramie, Wyoming, newspaper humorist, had little use for cowboys, terming them "dry land pirates…under the black flag." Nye considered the image to be a myth, a romantic dream. The cowboy, he wrote, was "generally a youth who thinks he will not earn his twenty-five dollars per month if he does not yell and whoop and shoot, and scare little girls into St. Vitus's dance. I've known more cowboys to injure themselves with their own revolvers than to injure anyone else. This is evidently because they are more familiar with the hoe than they are with the Smith & Wesson."[25]

Ardent reformers in the towns were always lying in wait for visiting cowboys, determined to show them the errors of their sinful ways. A temperance movement sister confronted a puncher who had just taken a swig from a bottle. "What will the Lord think," she asked him, "when you arrive in Heaven with whiskey on your breath?"

"Lady," he replied, "when I get up to the Lord, I'm a-goin' to leave my breath down here."[26]

Even the labor union organizers went after the range riders. William (Big Bill) Haywood, who later founded the International Workers of the World, invited all the cowboys in Denver to a dinner meeting in a hotel ballroom. Haywood's success in organizing Rocky Mountain miners led him to believe that he could do the same with workers for the cattle barons. Perhaps it was the champagne flowing freely that brought out the mischief in the boys. In the midst of the orations, they charged Haywood with being a skeleton at the feast, and laughed when he told them they were downtrodden slaves. "Go and form a union of gunslinging outlaws," they shouted, and Haywood departed with dire warnings of their future fates.

Or perhaps it was not the champagne. Cowboys of the nineteenth century chose their way of life in order to escape controls. They took orders only from the ranch foremen and trail bosses, who were recognized necessities like the captains of ships.

The cowboys' attitude is illustrated by an incident observed one day in the early 1880s by Clarice Richards at Westcliffe, Colorado. In those times Westcliffe was the rail destination for Britons coming to visit their countrymen's ranches in the valley east of the Sangre de Cristo Mountains. Two cowboys, a veteran named Jim and a rookie named Pete, were watching an incoming train stopping at the Westcliffe station.

As soon as the baggage car door was opened, the trainmen began unloading suitcases, hat boxes, writing cases, duffle bags, and other impedimenta. "What the hell?" Pete asked in astonishment.

"Oh, just some of them Lords comin'," Jim answered. "When they goes visitin' they most generally brings everything with them out of the castle but the cook stove. I reckon them that stays behind's got to have that or they'd take it, too. I've been seein' 'em come to the valley for ten years and kinda wondered what they'd do if the whole family left their range at once; seems like one Lord's got to have so much room. Looks like these two's going to stay a while."

Pete seemed wholly absorbed in his contemplation of the two Englishmen who had stepped off the train and were looking about expectantly. One of them saw the cowpunchers and called impatiently: "Here, you."

"Is that there Lord tryin' to attract my attention?" Jim asked with a drawl that Pete recognized as a danger signal.

"He does seem kinda set on speakin' to you; better go and see what he wants," and Pete grinned as Jim rose and sauntered over to the new arrivals. The one who had called spoke again: "Here, you, take hold of the end of that box."

Jim's eyes hardened but his voice was gentle. He gave the man one steady look, then shifted his quid into the other cheek. "Sorry," he said unconcernedly, "but I'm punchin' cows for the King of England and he don't like me to do no odd jobs on the side."[27]

CHAPTER FIFTEEN

Soldier High Jinks

THE SO-CALLED "INDIAN-FIGHTING ARMY" in the West was completely composed of volunteers, and as one of the enlisted men said in summing up his experiences, they were "a tough bunch in those days." Immigrants from numerous countries, ex-Confederate officers, alcoholics, fugitives from the law, and ne'er-do-wells from distinguished families made up its cosmopolitan ranks. In many regiments class barriers between officers and enlisted men were sometimes nonexistent, many of the junior officers having moved up through the ranks. Yet discipline was rigorous, court-martials frequent, punishments severe. The principal reason given by the soldiers for subjecting themselves to military control for three years at thirteen dollars a month was economic. They needed the pay, which with free food, shelter, and clothing was considerably better than they could get as civilian laborers. Nevertheless one of every three men deserted before ending their terms of enlistment.

Like the cowboys, the soldiers of the frontier engaged in pranks and practical jokes to relieve the harshness of their lives. They drank more alcohol, fought more fistfights, and spent more time in forced confinement than did their contemporaries of the open range.

Considerable rivalry existed between the infantry and the calvary, the latter being the glamor arm of the military, although cavalrymen spent a lot of extra drudge time taking care of horses. On record is an incident in which several sportive cavalrymen from Custer's famed Seventh Regiment stole the uniform blouses of infantrymen stationed at the same fort and wore them while committing mild thievery and other depredations, thus escaping blame for their shenanigans. This was meant as a practical joke, but the innocent infantrymen suffered the inevitable punishment.

The most loosely organized army—and possibly the most

democratic—that was fielded by the United States in the nineteenth century were the voluntary units assembled to march hundreds of miles across the Southwest in 1846. In the contemporary climate of Manifest Destiny, their reason for being was to wrest California from Mexico. They were mostly adventurous young men, and had little use for the spit and polish of military discipline. Desertions and mutinies were frequent, sometimes in wholesale lots as Lieutenant John M. Hollingsworth noted in a diary entry for October 28, 1846:

"Mutiny is among us. The men of Company D were ordered to bathe, which they refused to do. Capt. Negly seemed determined to be obeyed. Capt. Shannon detailed some men from Co I, to carry the order in to execution, by some mistake all the men were composed of new recruits. They mutined also, and they were sent to the guard house with the rest of the mutineers. The guard house is full. When will this end."[1]

Strong drink may not have led to the mutiny of the anti-bath soldiers, but it kept a considerable number of men busy pursuing drunken comrades who were frequently absent without leave. In one of his letters from Fort Randall, Dakota Territory, in 1875, Sergeant John Cox related his difficulties in finding and arresting such delinquents:

"I soon picked up a few stragglers. Presently I saw a soldier come out of a saloon and I called to him to stop. He was probably the same man who got the first sergeant in trouble. He started to run and I after him. I had been a sprinter in my day; besides, I was sober. I gained on him rapidly as we dodged and squirmed through the crowds of excited people. Suddenly he dashed through a door. I followed without hesitation and found myself in a gambling den in full swing. Gamblers sitting at tables were taken by surprise; they sat motionless. As I entered the room I caught a glimpse of the blue coat disappearing through a side door. I made for it. Passing through I found myself in a finely furnished living room, with an irate woman standing before me. Curtly she asked me what I wanted.

"'I want that soldier that just entered by the way I came,' I said firmly.

"'There's no soldier here, and you go out by the way you came,' she ordered in true military fashion. I had come to the Territory to fight Indians and not to oppose women. I therefore bowed myself out, although I have always been confident that the lady hid my soldier. As I passed out through the gambling den the men were still sitting motionless at the tables."[2]

Keeping peace among soldiers and civilians was frequently a problem for local authorities, especially in saloons. A traveler bound for Montana gold mines in 1866 found himself in the midst of just such a row at the Fort Kearney, Nebraska, stage station. "Whiskey was the prime cause of all the difficulty," he noted. "The result was that all the citizens came out badly beat and cut up and some nearly 'kilt' while the soldiers came out of the battle with but one or two wounded and that slightly. My observation and experience tells me to not interfere with soldiers under any circumstances, and more especially when they are under the influence of liquor."[3]

Officers of the frontier army also had a weakness for firewater, and were involved in as many merry drinking escapades as the enlisted men. Their attitude is indicated by a post commander's sardonic reaction when his requisition for supplies from a distant commissary depot resulted in the arrival of six wagons of whiskey and one wagon of provisions. He dispatched a telegram to headquarters: "What the hell shall we do with all these provisions?"

And there was the case of the frantic sergeant at a California fort who was desperately trying to find the officer of the guard to request his aid in locking up a defiant drunken soldier. Eventually the sergeant discovered that the officer himself was under arrest in the guard house "for getting drunk and raising the devil generally."

Little mercy was shown to any soldier caught stealing whiskey from medical supplies, even though he may have taken the wrong bottle as did a man in the Second Colorado Infantry in 1863. By mistake he took a bottle of kerosene, drank it down, and fell violently ill. "He was placed in the ambulance, the end gate turned down that his head could reach over. As he lay there vomiting he was the picture of forlorn misery, many jokes were passed at his expense. Lieutenant Gooding created a laugh by saying: "Boys, don't let the fluid waste, we will put a wick in his mouth tonight and use him for a lamp."[4]

Locking up a soldier for drunkenness could bring on perilous developments, as Lieutenant John Hollingsworth discovered while he was based at Los Angeles in 1847. One day when Hollingsworth was on duty as officer of the guard, a Private Van Beck was brought to the guardhouse in such an acute state of inebriation that the lieutenant was obliged to put him in confinement.

"He has a wife here, and she was furious at hearing of it," Hollingsworth later noted in his journal. "She has always done my washing, and we were on the best of terms. As soon as she heard of the arrest, she started for the guard house with a pot of hot coffee determined to throw it in my face, but meeting Lt. Bonnycastle, she told him what she was going to do. He begged her not to do it, for said he, 'Madame, Lieut. Hollingsworth is a very diffident young man, and you will frighten him to death.' She then went to the Col. and told him, of her resolution. He advised her not and told her to take care what she did. She said Col. I thought you were more of a gentleman than to permit Lt. Hollingsworth to put my husband under arrest. She then came to the Guard house and commenced abusing me at a high rate asked me if I thought she had nothing to do but to bring her husbands breakfast up there and said she had left all my clothes hanging on the line and that she prayed to God that they might all be stolen. I was all smiles and bows, told her that I regretted very much my having given her the smallest trouble that I was sorry that I had been obliged to punish her better half and begged her not to let any one steal my clothes. She did not throw the coffee in my face but gave it to her husband to drink. It was well she did so for had she done other wise I should have put *her* in one of the dark cells of the guard house! It created a great laugh at the mess table, at my expense."[5]

Legend has it that frontier soldiers were masters of magnificent oaths, second only to the bullwhackers who found their use necessary in persuading their oxen to move freight wagons across the West. To document this we must depend upon hearsay evidence largely, because in those Victorian times not many of the stronger-flavored expressions were written down, except occasionally with only the words' beginning letters followed by dashes or dots.

A few officers refused to use profanity, but most of these abstainers were of dubious character. For example, the notorious

Colonel John M. Chivington, who saw nothing wrong in slaughtering Indian women and children at Sand Creek, Colorado, would not soil his lips with dirty words. Whenever this part-time Methodist parson had difficulty getting his soldiers aligned for inspection, he would call for Major Hal Sayr to come forward and use his foul vocabulary to get the regiment into line.

Irish soldiers, who made up a considerable part of the frontier army, were the real masters of the vernacular of that time, pronounced, according to Captain John Bourke, "in a brogue rich as cream." One of Bourke's favorites was Captain Gerald Russell, a man who had been promoted from the ranks, a man who when off duty loved to go on hellbenders that sometimes wound up with him berating his dog for being drunk.

Bourke preserved an example of Irish army speech, as spoken by Jerry Russell. It was delivered to a detachment of raw recruits who had just arrived at Fort Selden, New Mexico Territory, in the autumn of 1869. They were drawn up in two ranks in open order facing the captain.

"Young Min! I conghratulate yiz on bein assigned to moi thrupe, becos previously to dis toime, I vinture to say that moi thrup has had more villins, loyars, teeves, schoundhrils and, I moight say, dam murdhrers than enny udder thrupe in de United States Ormy. I want yiz to pay sthrict attintion to jooty—and not become dhrunken vagabonds, wandhrin all over the face of Gods Chreashun, spindin ivry cint ov yur pay with low bum-mers. Avoide all timptashuns, loikewoise all discipashuns, so that in toime yez kin become non-commissioned offizurs; yez'll foind yer captin a very laynent man and very much given to laynency, fur oi niver duz toi no man up bee der tumbs unless he duz bee late for a roll-call. Sorjint, dismiss de detachment."[6]

The loose discipline among volunteer troops in the Southwest was noted in December 1846 by a German immigrant who had joined an Illinois regiment attached to General John E. Wool's command. According to Augustus F. Ehringer, General Wool was heartily disliked by the soldiers because of his autocratic manner and harsh treatment of them:

"The Arkansas Volunteer cavalry which General Wool calls

Colonel [Archibald] Yell's Mounted Devils, if provoked by him, would at the first opportunity blow out his life. Recently an Arkansas volunteer passing the General's tent, stopped and out of curiosity looked in. It displeased the General, and he told him to leave; as he did not leave immediately he told his orderly to point his gun at him. The Arkansas soldier pointed his gun at General Wool and said, 'Old Horse, damn your soul, if you give such orders I will shoot you for certain.' General Wool withdrew quickly. Another Arkansas soldier who met the general wearing civilian clothes in his tent, asked him, 'Stranger, have you seen my bay horse this morning?' although he knew it was General Wool. Another time General Wool sent his orderly to the Arkansas camp with the request not to make too much noise. The Arkansans replied, 'Tell Johnny Wool to kiss our ———.'"[7]

Colonel Philip St. George Cooke—who commanded the Mormon Battalion attached to General Stephen W. Kearney's Army of the West—also had some odd relations and confrontations with his volunteer troops. A member of the battalion, Henry W. Bigler, recorded an incident of December 20, 1846, while he was serving as Colonel Cooke's orderly:

"On going to his marquee to report myself I found him feeding his mule some wheat he had brought from Tucson. There was another mule determined to share with the Colonel's. He had driven it away several times but as soon as his back was turned the mule would march boldly up for another morsel of wheat until at last the Colonel turned around and said, 'Orderly, is your gun loaded?' I replied, 'No, sir,' he then said, 'Load your gun and I will shoot that G. D. mule,' and walked into his tent. I knew it was not one of Uncle Sam's for it did not have the U.S. on it and therefore it must be a private mule belonging to some of our men. All of a sudden a thought came into my mind not to cause the mule to be killed and I took from my cartridge box a cartridge, clapped it in my mouth and with my teeth tore off the bullet and put the ball in my pocket and emptied the powder into my musket and rammed the paper on top of it. Pretty soon out came the Colonel walking up to me, seized my gun and ran up within ten feet of the mule, standing broadside and fired. The moment he saw the mule was not hurt he dropped the musket and with an oath said, 'You did not load the gun right.' His bugler and others who saw the trick nearly split their sides with laughter, the Colonel walked into his tent and I have wondered how it was he did not punish me for disobeying his order."[8]

A few days later, after an arduous march, Bigler noted Colonel Cooke's anger when some of his troops climbed a mountain near the evening camp and amused themselves by rolling large boulders down the slope, "making a noise like peals of thunder, fairly shaking the earth like an earthquake, while others in camp sang songs, fiddled and danced." All these outbursts of energy led Cooke to swear "that he did not see how it was when the men could barely keep up with the command but when they got into camp, by G. D. the fiddle was going and the men dancing."[9]

(After reaching California and receiving his discharge, Henry Bigler found employment with John Sutter, and was one of the men present at Sutter's Mill the day gold was discovered in the millrace, setting off the great gold rush of 1848–49. Philip St. George Cooke eventually became a Union cavalry general in the Civil War, and was the father-in-law of Jeb Stuart, a cavalry general on the opposite side.)

From the enlisted men's viewpoints, some frontier officers deserved all the disrespect they received. Braxton Bragg, who later became one of the Confederacy's most inept generals, was so detested by his artillerymen during the invasion of Mexico that they talked of blowing him up in his tent—or in modern military parlance, fragging him while he slept.

During military operations in Utah in 1859, Lieutenant Colonel Charles F. Smith, commanding at Camp Floyd, won no friends among his men when he ordered the regiment out for a grand parade on a threatening midwinter day. The February temperature was frigid, the western sky heavy with dark clouds of an approaching blizzard, an icy wind beginning to rise.

The formation, which extended for more than two hundred yards, was struck by a sudden blast, and only the most resolute of the soldiers refrained from turning in their places to avoid the biting cold. Although the snow was advancing in a thick white wall, Lieutenant Colonel Smith ordered the troops to pass in review.

"Wheeling for the march past," Captain Albert Tracy recorded in his journal, "we caught the whole, and word of command, sound of bugle, or bray of the band were with the uproar of the storm, soon muffled well nigh from hearing...only the habit of the men kept them in line or step. Guidons, or even the line of the companies at front, were scarcely discernible...and we only guessed at the points of wheeling, following as we might in the track of our predecessors, for the guidons were alike invisible. Coming round the point of the reviewing officer—we distinguished through the cloud, dim objects, gray and ghostlike, believed to be Smith and his staff, and at these we saluted, agreeable to the regulation, with our sabres—doing the best we might...in the instruments of the bands, the horns and ophicleides at their broader ends looking like ice cream heaped up in a narrow glass. Our felt hats, with broad or looped up brims, and plumes of ostrich were simply a mess, and shocking to behold. It may be said to have been rather a crest-fallen appearing body of men that moved afterwards for dismissal upon their company grounds. Smith himself is said to have at last relented, and the distribution by his order of one gill per man, perhaps did much to salve over the wounded dignity and morale of the morning."[10]

Outrageous, eccentric, and callous punishments of individual soldiers certainly must have wounded the "dignity and morale" of entire units. At Camp Sheridan in western Nebraska, a bugler was ordered to sound "First Call" in a certain key. When he failed to do so, he was court-martialed for disobeying an order. Another bugler in New Mexico, instructed to sound reveille as soon as the morning star appeared, blew a blast when he saw the evening star, and roused the company at midnight. His punishment was also severe. At Fort Robinson, Nebraska, a cavalry trooper was sentenced to a year at hard labor for emulating the cowboys and riding his horse into a saloon in the neighboring town of Crawford.

Some commanding officers assigned undignified and un-military tasks to enlisted men and junior officers, undoubtedly creating resentment that was silent in the presence of the commanders but quite vocal among their sympathetic peers. General Eugene A. Carr, for example, assigned his orderly the task of caring for a pair of greyhounds in addition to his regular duties. On one of Carr's scouting expeditions against Tall Bull's Cheyennes, he took the greyhounds along for amusement. Soon after leaving Fort Mc-Pherson they were in antelope country, and Carr asked Captain Luther North and his scout, Buffalo Bill Cody, to find an antelope and drive it up within sight of the greyhounds. When Cody questioned the ability of dogs to catch antelope, Carr tartly assured him that his greyhounds could catch anything.

After a great deal of time and trouble, Cody and North managed to turn one of the swift-footed animals to within two hundred yards of the greyhounds, the orderly, and General Carr. Everyone was ordered to keep out of sight in ravines and behind ridges, and then at Carr's signal the orderly released the dogs and they began racing toward the lone antelope. But when the antelope sighted the greyhounds, its curiosity was aroused and instead of fleeing, it ran toward them. The dogs had closed to within a hundred feet when some of the excited soldiers showed themselves, frightening the antelope into turning and running the other way.

Carr was angry, but he shouted that his greyhounds would yet catch the antelope. The entire party mounted up and galloped in pursuit to witness the kills. "The antelope soon went out of sight over a hill about a mile away," Captain North later recalled, "with the dogs about two or three hundred yards behind, and when they reached the top of the hill they stopped for a minute and looked, then turned and came trotting back."

"No one had said a word up to this time, when Cody spoke. 'General,' he said, 'if anything the antelope is a little bit ahead.'

"Everybody laughed, I think, but the General...and I never saw him take the dogs out again on that expedition."

According to North, the orderly was still required to tend the dogs—in a military manner, of course—while the cavalry column continued its search for Tall Bull's Cheyennes.[11]

The renowned George Armstrong Custer was another general who kept a number of enlisted men busy caring for his dogs and other pets. Custer supposedly was accompanied by a dog when he arrived at West Point in 1857 to enter the Military Academy, but he had to take care of that one himself. While serving in Texas after the Civil War, he began collecting hounds in earnest. When he and his wife returned from Texas to her home in Michigan, he had his men load several of his canine pack aboard a boat at Galveston and attend to their wants all the way across the Gulf of Mexico to New Orleans.

Reassigned to Fort Riley, Kansas, Custer added a young female wolf to his retinue, ordering a sergeant to look after her. The unfortunate noncom bore the brunt of the abuse from the officers' wives whose tablecloths and sheets were pulled off the drying lines and chewed into rags by the pet animal. During one of Custer's expeditions, on which he was accompanied by his dogs and the wolf, the latter came in heat, attracting so many male wolves that the enlisted man's field tent was entirely surrounded and overrun.

Among frontier military officers of high rank, Custer had the best relations with the press, welcoming journalists to his camps and encouraging them to accompany him on expeditions. He was ahead of his peers in manipulating newsmen to his advantage, creating an image of a daring, dashing, handsome cavalier whose picture appeared frequently in the national weeklies. This may partly explain why, after the debacle at the Little Bighorn, so much press coverage was devoted to him and the event.

Sherman, Sheridan, and other officers who far outranked Custer, and who soldiered much longer in the West than he, were distrustful of newspaper reporters. They lived mainly on their Civil War glories, and missed out on the Wild West lionization that only the press could give them. An example was a report that appeared in the *Las Vegas* (New Mexico) *Gazette*, March 28, 1883:

"General Phil Sheridan and staff passed through the city yesterday in an elegant private coach bound for Washington.

"The party is in excellent spirits as the following will show.

"Reporter—hat in hand and smiling blandly—'General, I am a member of the great daily press. I have been deputized by the owners of the *Las Vegas Gazette* to propound to you a few interrogations. Where are you going, General? Where have you been traveling to, and what is your program in the future?'

"General Sheridan replied thusly: 'It is none of your G— D—— business, sir.'"[12]

Like all armies, the frontier units of the United States suffered from acute shortages and foul-ups, and the officers and men poured out endless complaints, both oral and written. Sometimes they endured in silence, as did members of the Colorado Volunteers at Fort Garland in the winter of 1862, when uniforms were so scarce that Company A was issued only one old gray overcoat.

"At one corner of the garrison, where a guard had to walk his beat, it was extremely cold," Ellen Williams later recalled, "a draft cutting through all the time, consequently the old gray coat was called into requisition, to the infinite disgust of the major, who turned to the orderly, Pat Ford, asking him if the same man was always on guard, and received for answer, 'No, be jabers, but the same coat kivers the whole company now.'"[13]

A favorite outlet for soldiers who wished to air their complaints was the *Army and Navy Journal*. During the years immediately following the Civil War, its letters columns were filled with criticisms and denunciations from posts in the western Territories. In many cases soldiers sent letters as warnings to their peers in the States; in others they were amusing revelations of military life in the American West.

From the frontier in 1867, a captain addressed himself mainly to recruiting officers back in the East, urging them to stop enlisting men unable to speak English and sending these recruits to the West. "I have lately had an addition to recruits in my company, and when I wish to instruct them, I find myself obliged to speak French, German, and even Arabic, for I have a Persian. Now, Mr. Editor, I was born in America, and though able to speak French and German sufficiently to get along with most of my recruits, I confess that my Arab rather got me, and now my poor Arabian friend is to be tried by a General Court-Martial for quitting his post, as a sentinel, and my Frenchman likewise for other violations of the Articles of War, and probably to suffer punishment."[14]

Another officer, stationed at Fort McPherson in Nebraska, wrote of the "lamentable ignorance in the East of the vast extent of the country known as the 'frontier,'" and of the requirements of those whose military profession sent them to the West for duty.

"I had a second lieutenant report to me not long since without even a uniform," he continued, "and when I asked him what he proposed to do and how he expected to dress, he said that an old officer (he must have been *very* old) in Washington told him that officers never wore anything out here except common soldiers' clothes, and he was surprised to find that such was not the case."

Possibly the green second lieutenant had been misled not only by the *very* old officer in Washington, but by seeing pictures of George Custer in the illustrated weeklies. Custer led his frontier contemporaries in devising picturesque frontier uniforms, the details of which were exaggerated by artists who had never been in the West.

Whatever the reason for the lieutenant's reporting for duty without a uniform, the anonymous letter writer at Fort McPherson firmly advised all officers transferred to the West to bring a trunk filled with uniforms, as well as a roll of bedding, camp chairs, and a mess chest, and to leave his measurements with a tailor and boot-maker in the East. Army officers are supposed to be gentlemen, he pointed out, and not "a set of frontier ranchmen, who sleep on the ground and eat fried bacon with their fingers."[15]

Of all the joys of army life, nothing brought on more merriment than being mustered out, especially at the end of a long dreary conflict such as the Civil War. It mattered not whether they were victors or vanquished, they celebrated. In Marshall, Texas, a force of Confederate artillerymen, learning that the war was over, collected all the government-issue harness and cooking utensils and sold them at bargain rates to civilians in town and around the countryside. On their last day in Marshall they lined up their twenty-four cannons and shelled woods and fields with considerable enjoyment. They then laid a dozen or so shells in a row on the ground, sprinkled gunpowder between them, lighted a fuse, and withdrew to observe the explosion. The detonation was thunderous, and bits of metal flew in all directions. Miraculously, no one was seriously injured. Next morning they spiked the cannons and departed.

Among the few allurements of military service in the Old West were the wonders that men on expeditions were likely to encounter in that pristine land. "A region in which the wildest romance was strangely mingled with the most startling reality," was the way John Ross Browne put it. As an agent of the U.S. Government during the Civil War, Browne traveled about the Southwest with a small command of California Volunteers in 1863 and 1864. One of his examples of "wildest romance" was the military company's encounter with "the fast woman" at Cocospera Mission just south of the Arizona Territory border.

"All along the road," Browne said, "we hear vague rumors of the adventures and exploits of this remarkable woman, who seemed to be ubiquitous, and to possess at least a dozen different names. Even the Mexicans, when they spoke of her, did so with a smile and shrug of the shoulders as to say she was 'some,' even in that country."

Cocospera was a desolate place. Lieutenant Arnold, who commanded the thirty soldiers, ordered them to make camp while Browne and another civilian official went to find the "unprotected American female." They found her sitting on a pile of adobe bricks, "humming over a lively strain some popular ditty of the times." She was a good-looking, sunburnt, freckle-faced young woman who greeted them with a lively enthusiasm.

Browne described the meeting: "She immediately arose and grasped me by the hand; I was just the man she was looking for. By the way, hadn't she seen me in Frisco? My countenance was familiar. Didn't I keep bar on Dupont Street? No? Well, by jingo! that was funny. She was very glad we had come, anyhow; shook me by the hand again very cordially; had been expecting us for several days; wanted to make tracks from Cocospera as soon as possible; was getting tired of the society; good enough people in their way, but had no snap about them. She liked people with snap. These Mexicans were dead-alive sort of cusses. The men had no grit and the women no jingle. Thought, upon the whole, Cocospera was played out, and would prefer going to Santa Cruz. She claimed to be a native of Georgia, and was strong on Southern rights. Said she had prospected awhile in Australia, and bobbed around Frisco for the last few years. Got tired of civilization, and came down in the streamer to Guyamas last July in company with 'a friend,' who left her at Magdalena. Another 'friend' brought her up here and went 'a prospecting.' She had claims, and expected they would turn out rich; but hang it all, she didn't care a cuss about the mines. The excitement pleased her; it was so jolly to be knockin' around among the Apaches! Wouldn't she like to skelp some of 'em!; you bet, she'd make jerked meat of their ears if she once got a show at 'em! She didn't speak Spanish; had been eight days at this infernal place among a set of scallywags who didn't understand her lingo. Was about ready to change her location; didn't care a flip where it was, so there was fiddles around the premises. Was a photographer by profession; that was played out; dull work; didn't pay. Hadn't any instruments at present, and wouldn't photograph scallywags anyhow. Heigh-ho! Rickety Jo! Great country this!"

That evening this extraordinary female visited the California Volunteers' bivouac. "She stepped with a grand swagger into camp, nodded familiarly to the soldiers, and said, 'Them's the boys I like to see.' For a while she entertained the men by singing a few popular songs.

"Having thus cast a glow of inspiration over the younger members of our command, she suddenly jumped up exclaiming, 'Hurrah, boys! Let's stir up the town! Who's got a fiddle? By jingo, we'll have a fandango!'

"Nobody had a fiddle, but there was a guitar in camp, and it was not long before the fandango was under a full head of steam. Greasers, Yaqui Indians, soldiers, and señoritas were at it full tilt, amid all the noise and din and horrible confusion of a genuine Spanish *baile*. The fast woman jumped and capered and pirouetted in a style that brought down the house; and it was long after midnight when our part of the company began to struggle into camp."

Next morning as the soldiers were preparing to resume march to Santa Cruz and Camp Tubac in Arizona Territory, Lieutenant Arnold and John Ross Browne discussed the problem of what to do about the fast woman. The lieutenant was reluctant to assume any responsibility for her; this expedition was his first real command, and he knew she could cause trouble for him. Yet, as Browne advised him, there was nothing else to be done. They could not leave an American woman, no matter her character, stranded in the midst of Apache country.

They made room for her in the baggage wagon. "All along the road, in the wildest and most dangerous places, she popped her head out at intervals to see how things in general were flourishing; twitted the 'boys' on their styles of riding; sang snatches of opera, and was especially great on ballads for the multitude."

As the march progressed, she began making a play for Lieutenant Arnold. Although she had asked him only for escort to Santa Cruz, she refused to stop there. San Antonio ranch also failed to please her, and Camp Tubac was "too infernally dull for a coyote or a wildcat." She told the lieutenant that she rather enjoyed "sloshing around" and said she would like to accompany his expedition where it might take her.

"It was abundantly evident to us all that she was inspired with a romantic attachment for our gallant Lieutenant. The shafts of Cupid began to shoot from her glittering eyes, and their fatal influence became fearfully perceptible. He grew pale and weary; was fretful and impatient; and seemed like a man burdened with heavy cares. After a week or so it became necessary to send the wagon down to Tucson for a fresh supply of provisions. The Lieutenant brightened up; a happy thought struck him; he would shuffle off this incubus that hung upon him like a millstone. What excuse he made I never could learn, but he packed up our enterprising female, addressed a note to the officer in command at Tucson, stating the causes which had induced him to give her transportation, and sent her to that tropical region, which he thought, would be congenial to her tastes. The last I heard of her she was enjoying the hospitality of our vaquero."[16]

This "wildest romance strangely mingled with the most startling reality," recorded by John Ross Browne, had no finale. Such encounters by soldiers in the West rarely ended with all the loose ends tied up. The men were always marching off somewhere else. Browne did not even record the fast woman's name. Whoever she was, we can be rather certain that for at least a few days in that winter of early 1864, she surely made life merry for the soldiers in the Tucson barracks.

CHAPTER SIXTEEN

The Profane Sentimentalists

FRONTIER MINING WAS MOSTLY gold and silver, with gold being the main prize during the first decade after a carpenter from New Jersey found a pea-sized nugget in the millrace of a sawmill on the American River in California. The date was January 24, 1848, and the carpenter was James Marshall. He was building the sawmill for Captain John Sutter, a Swiss who had obtained a land grant of fifty thousand acres in the Sacramento Valley. Sutter built a fort, named his colony New Helvetia, and lived in the splendor of a baron.

Marshall took the shiny particles found in the millrace down to the fort and showed them to Sutter. Neither man knew how to test for gold, but Sutter owned an encyclopedia and in it he found instructions that they followed until they were certain that what Marshall had found was indeed gold.

Both Marshall and Sutter were made merry by the gold discovery, but their merriment was short-lived. The secret could not be kept, and within six months all of California, and then the nation, was in a state of mad revelry. Blacksmiths, bartenders, bricklayers, bakers, farmers, lawyers, physicians and merchants dropped whatever they were doing and started for the American River. Soldiers deserted, and sailors left their anchored ships. As one observer put it: "All were off for the mines, some on horses, some on carts, and some on crutches, and one went in a litter." By the thousands they sought out the famous finder of gold, James Marshall. Like unrestrained holidaymakers they swarmed over his 640-acre land claim, which lay near Sutter's fort.

They stole Marshall's horses, his food, and even his mining tools. When he tried to drive the invading army away by force, they hired armed guards to keep him off his own property. When he went to court, he found that judge and jury were allied with the trespassers. His own lawyer was paid off by them. Awakening one morning to the realization that he had lost everything (except a bag of rice) he resolved to leave for another prospecting site.

But the fortune seekers kept a close watch on Marshall, believing he possessed magical powers, that he could find gold by divination. A small army frolicked after him, surrounding every place where he stopped to dig or pan, gleefully threatening to hang him unless he found another rich lode for them. Finally he gave up and returned to Coloma, near where he had found the gold that set off the wild rush. For several years he eked out a living by sawing wood, plowing gardens, and working at other odd jobs.

In 1871, Marshall was invited to go on a lecture tour, which restored some of his forgotten fame. Upon his return to California, the legislature granted him a small pension, but two years later they discontinued it because he spent too much of it on wine and whiskey.

The day that James Marshall died in 1885 he became a very important person. The Society of California Pioneers and the Native Sons of the Golden West quarreled so long over where he should be buried that his body had to be packed in ice to preserve it. Eventually they agreed to bury him on a hill overlooking the place where he had discovered gold. The Californians who had been unwilling to sustain James Marshall in the declining years of his life spent thousands of dollars for a monument and appropriated funds for a caretaker to clean bird droppings from his statue and keep its surroundings neat for tourists.

Jolly bands of gold seekers also intruded upon the Swiss settler, John Sutter, overrunning his lands and his fort. Some of the men who worked for him joined the mob; others fled. The invaders slaughtered Sutter's livestock, trampled his field crops, and even stole the cannons from his fort. The corrupted local courts declared his land title invalid, and the prospectors joyfully divided New Helvetia into gold claims.

Journeying to the nation's capital, Sutter spent the remainder of his life vainly trying to persuade Congress to return his lost lands. He died in 1880, ignored and forgotten, in a cheap hotel in Washington. Not until historians began proclaiming his importance after the turn of the century did official California take any notice of John Sutter's contribution to the development of the state. As a memorial, they rebuilt his vandalized fort for the benefit of tourists visiting Sacramento.

Most of the discoverers who set off the Old West's numerous gold and silver rushes were eccentrics, nonconformers, possibly lunatics. They were as much obsessed by the hunt as by the prize. Sometimes they made their lucky strikes through serendipity, sometimes by dogged searches over months and years. James Marshall was a loner who truly believed that he could see visions of future events. His associates considered him "peculiar," and although he was almost forty when he sighted the flakes of gold in the millrace, he knew so little about the game that he was not certain of what he had found.

Henry Thomas Paige Comstock did not discover the Comstock Lode which bore his name and created the legendary Virginia City in Nevada. In the spring of 1859, a pair of impecunious Irishmen, Peter O'Riley and Pat McLaughlin, were digging a small reservoir to collect water for rocker mining. They were working in Six Mile Canyon near Gold Hill. One day O'Riley and McLaughlin decided to wash some of the gravel they were digging. They found large amounts of gold, but were annoyed by the presence of a blue-black clay which kept getting in their way.

Late in the afternoon of that day, Henry Comstock rode into the area on a mustang so small that the rider's feet dragged on the ground. The prospectors hailed him as "Old Pancake," a nickname he had acquired because pancakes were his preferred diet. Comstock rode closer to the rocker trough, but they made no effort to conceal the "color" they had found.

Dan De Quille later described the incident: "When the gold caught his eye, he was off the back of his pony in an instant. He was soon down in the thick of it all—'hefting' and running his fingers through the gold and picking into and probing the mass of strange-looking 'stuff' exposed.

"Conceiving at once that a wonderful discovery of some kind had been made, 'Old Pancake' straightened himself up, as he arose from a critical examination of the black mass in the cut wherein he had observed the glittering spangles of gold, and coolly proceeded to inform the astonished miners that they were working on ground that belonged to him."[1]

Comstock apparently maneuvered a spur-of-the-moment confidence game, although he later declared that he made the discovery himself, in a gopher hole. To avoid conflict he invited the Irishmen to be his partners, and before the inevitable gold rush started they all gained considerable fortunes. The blue-black earth turned out to be loaded with silver, so that they and Virginia City were enriched doubly.

According to H.T.P. Comstock himself, Virginia City received its name from a fellow prospector named James "Old Virginny" Finney. "Old Virginia and the other boys got on a drunk one night there," Comstock said afterward, "and old Virginia fell down and broke his bottle, and when he got up he said he baptized that ground Virginia —hence Virginia City—and that is the way it got its name. At that time there were a few tents, a few little huts, and a grog shop; that was all there was. I was camped under a cedar-tree at that time—I and my party."[2]

A few weeks later Virginia City was swirling with boisterous activity. "Entering the main street," said John Ross Browne, "you pass on the upper side huge piles of earth and ore, hoisted out of the shafts or run out of tunnels, and cast over the 'dumps.' The hillsides, for a distance of more than a mile, are perfectly honey-combed. Steam-engines are puffing off their steam; smoke-stacks are blackening the air with their thick volumes of smoke; quartz-batteries are battering; hammers are hammering; subterranean blasts are bursting up the earth; picks and crow-bars are picking and crashing into the precious rocks; shanties are springing up, and carpenters are sawing and ripping and nailing; storekeepers are rolling their merchandise in and out along the wayside; fruit vendors are peddling their fruits, wagoners are tumbling out and piling in their freights of dry goods and ore; saloons are glittering with their gaudy bars and fancy glasses and many-colored liquors, and thirsty men are swilling the burning poison; auctioneers, surrounded by eager and gaping crowds of speculators, are shouting off the stocks of delinquent stockholders; organ-grinders are grinding their organs and torturing consumptive monkeys, hurdy-gurdy girls are singing bacchanalian songs in bacchanalian dens..."

Browne was amused by the "flaming" advertising handbills posted along streets and hillsides:

LOOK HERE!
For fifty cents you can get
a good square meal at the
HOWLING WILDERNESS SALOON

NOW OR NEVER!
Cheapest coats in the world!
PANTS GIVEN AWAY!!! WALK IN GENTS

"All is life, excitement, avarice, lust, deviltry, and enterprise. A strange city truly, abounding in strange exhibitions and startling combinations of the human passions. Where upon earth is there such another place?"

Virginia City's streets, Browne added, were "paved with a conglomerate of dust, mud, splintered planks, old boots, clippings of tinware, and playing cards. It is especially prolific in the matter of cards. Mules are said to fatten on them during seasons of scarcity when the straw gives out."[3]

Meanwhile H.T.P. Comstock was thriving in the city he thought of as his own. He was not an avaricious man. He had moved in on O'Riley and McLaughlin's claims mainly for the merriment of it, to see that it was properly developed and that all of his friends got a share. His friends and acquaintances in fact believed him to be simple-minded, "a little cracked in the upper story"—a man flighty in his imaginings.

"Although Comstock had a passion for possessing rich mines," Dan De Quille said, "and appeared to have a great greediness for gold, yet no sooner was it in his possession than he was ready to give it to the first man, woman, or child who asked for it, or to recklessly squander it in all directions. Anything that he saw and took a fancy to he bought, no matter what the price might be, so long as he had the money. The article to which he had taken a momentary fancy once purchased, he presented it to the first person who appeared to admire it, whether that person was white, red, or black."[4]

Old Pancake Comstock's only known venture into matrimony was a comedy of errors, frustrations and deceptions, according to De Quille. It began with the arrival of a Mormon gold seeker from Salt Lake City, "a little sore-eyed fellow named Carter," who brought a woman into Virginia City aboard a dilapidated wagon. Carter drove right up to Comstock's place in search of work. The moment that Old Pancake set eyes on the woman, he was smitten. "His soul went out toward her as she sat there in the end of the little canvas-covered wagon, mournfully gazing out from the depths of her calico sunbonnet." Mainly because he liked the looks of her, Comstock gave Carter a job in his Ophir mine.

The pair from Utah continued using the wagon as living quarters, and Old Pancake began spending most of his daylight hours there, keeping the woman company while her husband was at work. One day they were seen sitting together on the wagon tongue; the woman was lovingly combing Comstock's hair. Next morning they disappeared from Virginia City.

Comstock took her to the Washoe Valley, where a preacher friend married them, and then off to Carson City they went for a honeymoon. The delights of marriage had scarcely begun when Carter suddenly appeared, demanding the return of his woman. Old Pancake held his ground; after all he was the grand mogul of the Comstock Lode. Shouts and expletives and threats shortly gave way to negotiation, with Comstock giving Carter a horse, a revolver, and sixty dollars in cash. For these, Carter gave Comstock a bill of sale for the woman.

Believing that everything was settled satisfactorily to all, Comstock left his wife ensconced temporarily in Carson City while he set out over the Sierras for a hurried business trip to San Francisco. Upon arriving in Sacramento he was handed a telegram from friends in Carson City. His wife, it seemed, had run away with "a seductive youth of the town," and the pair were known to be fleeing to California on the Placerville Road.

Comstock immediately turned back, and with a group of sympathetic friends hastened to Placerville. Sure enough, the runaway pair soon appeared from the east. With his usual aplomb, Comstock separated his wife from the youth, and took her into a hotel room to discuss the problem. Eventually he reappeared to assure his friends that all was well and thank them for their support. As soon as his wife tidied up from her arduous travels, he added, he would bring her out to thank them in person also.

But when Old Pancake returned to the room, his wife had vanished. She had climbed out of a back window and fled again with the seductive youth. Comstock immediately offered a hundred dollars for her return. He went to the Placerville livery stable and hired all the horses, and within a short time virtually every male in the town rode off in the search for the runaways.

Next morning a miner came riding into Placerville, his six-shooter drawn on the pair of lovers, who were walking in front of his horse. Comstock was delighted. He paid the reward, and took his wife to a room in the upper story of the hotel to have another long talk with her. His friends seized the seductive youth, locked him in another room, and drew straws to determine who would stand guard over him.

Soon after dark, the guard decided to join his companions celebrating in the downstairs bar. He told the youth that Comstock's friends were planning to take him out and hang him for making a business of stealing the wife. The only way for him to save his life, the guard said, was to try to escape. "I'm going down to the bar to take a drink, and if I find you here when I come back it will be your own fault."

The seductive youth did not linger, nor was he ever seen in the diggings again.

"By practicing eternal vigilance," wrote De Quille, "Comstock managed to keep his wife that winter, but in the spring, when the snow had gone off and the little wild flowers were beginning to peep up about the rocks and round the roots of the tall pines, she watched her chance and ran away with a long-legged miner who, with his blankets on his back, came strolling that way.

"Mrs. Comstock finally ceased to roam; she came to anchor in a lager-beer cellar in Sacramento."

Not long after that, Old Pancake sold his mining interests in the famed Comstock Lode and opened general merchandise stores in Carson City and Silver City. He was no merchant, however; the stores failed and he lost his fortune. Some of his friends said he gave away too much of his merchandise. Many a time he was seen passing out armfuls of red blankets and brilliantly hued calico to his Piute Indian friends.

A prospector at heart, Comstock drifted north to Montana, searching for another rich strike. But that was not to be. On September 27, 1870, he died by shooting himself in the head with a revolver.

According to Dan De Quille, "it was supposed that he committed the act while laboring under temporary aberration of mind, and this is doubtless the case as his was by no means a sound or well-balanced brain."[5]

As for Comstock's close friends from their days of laughter and carousing, they fared little better. Old Virginny Finney, his pockets filled with money, mounted a horse while drunk and was thrown off and killed. Peter O'Riley died penniless in an insane asylum. Patrick McLaughlin tried to pyramid his fortune into a bigger fortune by buying and selling shares of mining stock. He lost everything and ended his days in poverty as a mining camp cook.

After the merriment died, Virginia City became a ghost town.

"Pike's Peak is in everybody's mouth and thought, and Pike's Peak figures in a million dreams," the St. Louis *Missouri Republican* declared on March 10, 1859. "Every clothing store is a depot for outfits for Pike's Peak. There are Pike's Peak hats, and Pike's Peak guns, Pike's Peak boots, Pike's Peak shovels, and Pike's Peak goodness-knows-what-all, designed expressly for the use of emigrants and miners...We presume there are, or will be, Pike's Peak pills, manufactured with exclusive reference to the diseases of Cherry Valley, and sold in conjunction with Pike's Peak guide books; or Pike's Peak schnapps to give tone to the stomachs of overtasked gold differs; or Pike's Peak goggles to keep the gold dust out of the eyes of the fortune hunters; or Pike's Peak steelyards (drawing fifty pounds) with which to weigh the massive chunks of gold quarried out of Mother Earth's prolific bowels."

A few months later an Iowa newspaper editor, undoubtedly writing with tongue in cheek, told of a man just returned from Pikes

Peak. The gold on the mountain was so plentiful, he said, that it could be mined with wooden sleds shooting down the slopes. The gold would curl up on the front of the sleds, like shavings, and could be gathered in as the sleds descended.

Pikes Peak of course was only the landmark, not the source of the gold associated with that strike. Three brothers named Russell and several Cherokees who had learned to mine gold in Georgia found small amounts in Denver City's Cherry Creek, and many other prospectors were panning along the South Platte and on the Cache la Poudre. When winter came at the end of 1858, several of these gold-hunters returned to border towns along the Missouri River to buy supplies for another season of searching. They paid for their goods with gold dust, and rumors immediately began to spread of another strike like the one in California a decade earlier.

The Pikes Peak rush in Colorado, and the Virginia City rush in Nevada, took place at the same time, but the former was not favored with the force of a picturesque Henry Comstock. Many anonymous miners were involved. The man who set off the Pikes Peak rush was a dilettante prospector and part-time guidebook writer from Pacific City, Iowa, named D.C. Oakes.

Oakes published his *History of the Gold Discoveries on the South Platte River* just as rumors of the mythical big strike began circulating through the East. It sold as fast as copies could be printed. Readers of that day were inclined to believe anything they read in print, and Oakes was a born promoter. He had been to Denver City but exaggerated the ease with which gold could be found there. As soon as his small book began selling, imitations quickly followed, some of them containing notable fictions: the sands in every Rocky Mountain stream were pure gold; nuggets were as plentiful as pebbles; a few days of easy labor would provide a vast fortune to any man who came there. Oakes's less excessive guide was the first one published, however, and his name was indelibly linked with the Pikes Peak rush. Colorado Territory being much closer to the nation's populated states than Virginia City, a massive stampede toward Pikes Peak quickly began.

Across the Plains rolled stagecoaches, wagons, and carts. Mixed among them were men, women, and a few small children traveling on horseback or on foot. Someone painted lettering on a canvas-topped wagon: PIKE'S PEAK OR BUST! In the fashion of Americans, the phrase was copied upon thousands of vehicles. The words became a slogan. Most of these unskilled argonauts carried copies of Oakes's or some other fraudulent guide. Fifty thousand, a hundred thousand—no one knows how many human beings crowded into the area around Denver City. Food supplies were soon exhausted; shelter was nonexistent; few had brought sufficient supplies. If there were merchants among them, they had come to find gold, not to sell groceries, clothing, and tools.

Thousands were soon hungry, in rags, without shoes. And nowhere along the creeks or the Platte were any rich discoveries of gold being made. Twenty cents a day was the average yield, one experienced observer estimated, and another visitor denounced the Pikes Peak gold rush as a stupendous humbug. The mob's discontent quickly turned to anger. Starvation became widespread, and many began leaving, turning their wagons and carts eastward toward home. Those who still had PIKE'S PEAK OR BUST! emblazoned upon their canvas-topped vehicles drew a line through the words and added BUSTED, BY GOD! or some other phrases more profane.

During the midst of this panic rush in reverse, D.C. Oakes the guidebook author had left Iowa and was heading in the opposite direction with sawmill machinery that he intended to put to profitable use in Denver City. According to a story that may be apocryphal, a man returning with a group of disillusioned pilgrims recognized Oakes. The malcontents seized him and threatened to hang him for writing one of the books that had brought them so much misery. Reason eventually prevailed, however, along with a bit of grim humor. Instead of putting Oakes to death, they built him a tombstone of buffalo bones and a piece of board, and let him go. On the board they inscribed his epitaph in axle grease:

Here Lie the Bones of D.C. Oakes
Killed for Starting the Pike's Peak Hoax.

As it turned out, there was gold in Colorado, and plenty of it, but not where Oakes had said it would be. Those who endured simply moved westward into the mountains from Denver and mined many a fortune. John Gregory, one of the prospectors from Georgia, made a rich strike near what was to become Central City. Soon afterward, Horace Greeley visited Gregory Gulch and set off a rush with dispatches to his *New York Tribune*. Abe Lee, another Georgian, made the first gold discovery in Leadville's California Gulch. He squandered his first fortune, found another, and then lost it. Abe spent his last days driving a water wagon to lay the dust upon the streets of Leadville, the city his gold discovery had created.

Silver became big in Colorado mining somewhat later than it did in Nevada. Fifteen years after Lee's and Gregory's strikes, William Stevens found rich silver veins in the very same places where gold had been discovered and then worked out, the claims left abandoned. As had happened at Virginia City, the silver ore was viewed as a nuisance by the early gold miners.

Soon after "Uncle Billy" Stevens's silver strike, he was assailed by a horde of lawyers employed by alleged owners of the abandoned claims he was working. The lawyers took seven million dollars from Uncle Billy, and in disgust he turned his explorations southward into virgin territory.

"If I ever locate another mine," he said, "I'll stand over it with a shotgun, and shoot every damn man who comes on it. It is cheaper and safer to defend yourself against murder than to defend your property in the courts." In 1879, Uncle Billy discovered promising ore about halfway between Leadville and Colorado Springs. Although winter was coming on, he was eager to get the mining under way before others swarmed in to clutter up the place with claims. He hired about 150 miners and led them on a seven-day trek from Colorado Springs through deep snow. On the site, he had already stocked a company store, but he had not bothered to bring money to pay the miners. When they mutinied, he agreed to give them generous credit for supplies, an offer that failed to satisfy them.

Deciding to enjoy a bit of black humor at Uncle Billy's expense, the miners accused him of being broke and trapping them into working for nothing. Stevens swore that he had money in a bank in Leadville and would pay them in the spring, but they refused to listen to him. They brought up a rope as though to hang him from a tree. At the last moment, however, the ringleaders announced that they would make him a prisoner and sent a party of men over to Leadville to make certain the bank was holding enough money in Stevens's name to make a payroll. If there was not enough money, then they would hang him.

And so for almost a month, while awaiting the party's return, the miners stopped work while Uncle Billy was kept locked in a cabin on a diet of bread and water. At last, after traversing sixty miles of snow-packed mountains and passes, the men returned. Their first announcement was that they had experienced a fine old time in Leadville's bars and dance halls. But what had they learned about Uncle Billy's bank account? One hundred and fifty thousand dollars, they replied, as good as gold. The miners cheered, released Uncle Billy, apologized to him with high-flown speeches, and went merrily back to work.[6]

The second Virginia City, the one in Montana, came into being during the Civil War, and the gold rush there was started by miners loyal to the Confederacy as well as some who supported the Union. Both governments were in dire need of gold to finance their war efforts, and miners were encouraged to go to Montana and dig. The miners themselves preferred prospecting over risking their lives in battle. They could also enjoy a more lighthearted life, and there was always the possibility they could gain a fortune with no pangs of guilt.

Credit for the first big strike belongs to Bill Fairweather, leader of a party of six young gold hunters. They encamped beside a lake at the foot of Bald Mountain the afternoon of May 26, 1863. Fairweather and Henry Edgar took their pans and a pick and shovel into a gulch while the others explored in the opposite direction. Fairweather dug up some dirt and dropped it into Edgar's pan.

Edgar recorded the incident in his journal. "I went down the creek to wash it," he wrote. "While I was washing the dirt, Fairweather scratched around in the bedrock with his butcher knife and called: 'I've found a scad!'

"I had the pan about half washed down, and I replied: 'If you have one I have a thousand.' And so I had."

When the other four prospectors joined them, they refused to believe what they saw in the pans, and accused Fairweather and Edgar of "salting" the dirt. Next day they staked off claims, and in a few hours easily took out enough gold to buy all the supplies they needed at the Bannack trading post.

"What shall we call the gulch?" Edgar asked.

"You name it," one of the prospectors said.

"So I called it Alder Gulch on account of the heavy clump of alders along the creek."

When they went into Bannack, they tried to keep the discovery a secret, but that was impossible. Within ten days a stampede was on, and a tent and shanty town quickly sprang up. The Confederates wanted to call it Varina in honor of Jefferson Davis's wife, but they were overruled by a local judge who named it Virginia City.

During the following few months, ten thousand would-be millionaires swarmed into the new town of Virginia City, Montana, and millions of dollars in gold were taken from Alder Gulch. All this wealth had to be transported out of the territory over lonely roads and trails to ultimate destinations in the Union and Confederacy. It soon attracted bands of road agents, notably Henry Plummer and his murderous outlaws.

Bill Fairweather, for one, evidently did not ship very much of his gold out of Virginia City. This young man who had led his five companions to the riches of Alder Gulch delighted in finding gold, but cared little about keeping it. His greatest joy was to trot his horse along the streets of Virginia City, tossing little buckskin bags of gold dust to scrambling gangs of children. Dead at thirty-nine, Fairweather ended up as a tourist attraction—among the hanged road agents in the town's Boothill Cemetery, his grave overlooking the gulch where the gold was discovered.[7]

"I am restless here in Oregon," Edward Schieffelen wrote a friend in 1870, "and wish to go somewhere that has wealth for the digging of it. I can't say that I care to be rich—it isn't that. If I had a fortune, I suppose I'd not keep it long, for, now I think of it, I can't see why I should. But I like the excitement of being right up against the earth, trying to coax her gold away to scatter it."[8]

Born in Pittsburgh, Pennsylvania, in 1848, Schieffelen traveled with his parents to Oregon while he was still a youngster. Shortly after writing the letter in 1870 he left home to embark on a quest for riches in the earth that lasted for seven years. Late in 1876 he attached himself to a column of cavalry marching to establish a new post in the Apache country of Arizona Territory—Fort Huachuca.

Using the fort as his base, Schieffelen began searching for signs of gold and silver between the San Pedro River and the Dragoon Mountains. His only companion was a burro that had cost him seven dollars. Occasionally he would return to the fort where the officers would express surprise at his still being alive in Chiricahua Apache country.

"Have you found anything?" they would ask, and he would reply in the negative, adding that he was certain he would eventually find something.

"You'll find your tombstone," one of the officers said.

And so when Schieffelen did discover his first promising ore, he named the location Tombstone. It was early autumn of 1877, and by that time he was out of food, money, and clothes. His shirt and pants were in tatters, his beard matted, his long hair tangled over his shoulders.

Schieffelen took his silver ore samples to the northern part of the territory where his brother Albert was working with an assayer, Richard Gird. After testing the samples, the three men returned to the Tombstone area, and a few weeks later Ed dug into a rich lode. "You're a lucky cuss," said his brother Albert, and Lucky Cuss became the name of the mine.

While the Schieffelen brothers and Dick Gird continued to open other mines—the Tough Nut, the Owl's Nest, the West Side—a town called Tombstone began rising in that desert land. The boom times came more slowly to Tombstone than to other mining towns of the West, and the three men who had started the show stayed around to enjoy the merriment. Ed built an opera house, the grandest theater between El Paso and San Francisco. Someone else built the Bird Cage, which featured ladies in pink tights, jig dancers, and early burlesque. Dick Gird put up the money for a newspaper, and he may have named it—the *Tombstone Epitaph*.

The happy trio began selling their many properties and

departed Tombstone as millionaires before the violent times of the Earp brothers, Old Man Clanton, Johnny Ringo, Doc Holliday, and the O.K. Corral. Al Schieffelen died young of tuberculosis, but Ed went on a tour of the nation, seeing the sights and staying in the best hotels. In San Francisco he met and married a local belle and tried enjoying life in high society. Although then in his late forties, Ed kept getting an urge for "the excitement of being right up against the earth, trying to coax her gold away to scatter it."

He went to Alaska for a while and then back to Oregon to search around in some of the diggings where he had had no luck before. On May 14, 1896, a neighboring prospector found him dead at his cabin, probably from a heart attack. In his last will and testament, Schieffelen left instructions for his burial "in the dress of a prospector, my old pick and canteen with me, on top of the granite hills about three miles westering from the city of Tombstone, Arizona..." Like James Marshall in California and Bill Fairweather in Montana, Edward Schieffelen was laid to rest so that his spirit could overlook the place where he had lived the merriest day of his life.[9]

George Armstrong Custer was not a gold hunter, but he must be given much of the credit, or blame, for the discovery of gold in the Black Hills. In July 1874, Custer led a considerable force of cavalry and infantry, with a brass band, three Gatling guns, a cannon, and more than a hundred supply wagons into the Black Hills. This action was a violation of a six-year-old treaty that forbade non-Indians to enter the sacred hills without permission of the tribes.

Custer did not bother to ask permission. The expedition was one of those merry military outings of the frontier—with tented camps, champagne suppers served on clothed tables, drinking parties and band concerts in the evenings, and wild game hunts and gold prospecting during the days. On August 3, he sent a report out by a dispatch carrier, announcing that gold had been discovered. Horatio Ross and William McKay were the diggers, but Custer signed the message and won the glory.

Back east a few days later newspaper headlines spread the word: GOLD! STIRRING NEWS FROM THE BLACK HILLS. Within weeks hordes of miners swarmed into the Indians' *Paha Sapa*, as they called their sacred hills. The treaty was now shattered forever, and the succession of events that followed during the next two years led directly to the Little Bighorn where Custer met his doom.

Deadwood, South Dakota, was the roisterous mining town created by gold miners of the Black Hills during the late 1870s. Its wildness and its fame embraced two characters who were not miners but who became almost mythical—Calamity Jane and Wild Bill Hickok.

A correspondent for the *Denver Tribune* found that most of the inhabitants of Deadwood came from other mining towns. The best miners, he observed, were from California. Those from Virginia City, Nevada, demanded the most money for their claims. Those who spent the most time in saloons were from Colorado. The weakest-kneed were "from down east."

He went on to bemoan the lack of old-time prospectors. "I see no Starbottles nor John Oakhursts here...The miner of today is a bitter disappointment to Bret Harte's readers...One sees no eight-foot neck chain nesting against coarse woolen shirts, no three-ounce nugget breastpins, no betting of oyster cans of gold on the sex of a horse three blocks away. It is true the miner of today loves whiskey, cards and women; but as compared with the forty-niner of California or the fifty-niner of Colorado, he is a hollow mockery, and a fraud."[10]

The Denver newspaper correspondent's recollection of Bret Harte's John Oakhurst and Colonel Starbottle as miners was in error. Although to millions of American readers of those times, Harte's Oakhurst was the prototype for California mining camp heroes, he was a full-time gambler who probably never soiled his card-dealing hands at panning gold. Colonel Starbottle was a speechmaker who officiated at functions such as duels.

Bret Harte visited the mining camps and may have done a bit of gold hunting himself, but like Oakhurst, he was a dude. He fancied elegant frock coats, waistcoats, and cravats instead of the red shirts and rough boots of the miners. But he did originate many of the characters that have become stereotypes in the popular image of the Far West. His miners were hard-drinking, hard-fighting, sentimental brutes, who could weep over the plight of a dying prostitute's baby and then burst into the vilest profanity. John Ross Browne observed that many of the miners in Virginia City, Nevada, did nothing night and day "but drink fiery liquids and indulge in profane language."

During a tour through the Montana mining towns in 1867, Alexander McClure corroborated Bret Harte's depictions of miners redeemed from uncouth creatures swilling and whoring to oversentimental toilers with melting hearts, all teary-eyed over the sight of a tiny girl child. "As a rule they are good citizens," McClure said, "but they don't cramp themselves with the religious ideas of the Puritans…Such a thing as a sermon I have neither heard nor heard of since I have been in Union City. Occasionally a stray shepherd comes along to look after his lost sheep wandering through the mountains, but as a rule the shepherd gets lost among the sheep, and seems to prefer glittering nuggets of gold from the gulches and mines to the promised glittering stars in his future crown for the salvation of souls."[11]

Mark Twain tried twice to be a miner, and he wrote more about the sweat and pain and physical exhaustion than did his contemporary, Bret Harte. In *Roughing It*, he told how he and his partner put in hours setting powder charges to blast rocks out of a claim near Virginia City, Nevada. After risking their lives for a week, they had a hole twelve feet deep with no sign of "color." They then tried tunneling for a week with no better results. "I resigned," Twain said, and for a while he tested his luck at trading claims with other prospectors. During the tumult of swapping mine footages and trading stock, he and his partner forgot to put picks and spades to use at securing their interest in a mine that became a bonanza. Losing their part-ownership lost them a fortune. "I can always have it to say," Twain declared, "that I was absolutely and unquestionably worth a million dollars, once, for ten days."

Another go at mining also proved unrewarding. Digging down about eight feet, Twain kept trying to shovel rocks out of the shaft. After several shovelsful fell back on his head and down his neck he decided he'd had enough of mining. "I never said a word, but climbed out and walked home. I inwardly resolved that I would starve before I would make a target of myself and shoot rubbish at it with a long-handled shovel."

Shortly afterward the owner of the Virginia City *Territorial Enterprise* offered Twain a job as city editor. Writing about mines and miners proved to be more gainful for him than digging and blasting and panning. Yet afterward he looked back on the youthful experience with remembered pleasure: "We were stark mad with excitement—drunk with happiness—smothered under mountains of prospective wealth—arrogantly compassionate toward the plodding millions who knew not our marvellous canyon—but our credit was not good at the grocer's."[12]

Sage Hens, Fillies, and Calico Queens

WOMEN AND HORSES, so the old saying goes, had a hard time of it on the western frontier. Wives and daughters often found themselves doing what was then known as "women's work" as well as tasks that back in the settled areas of the nation were usually performed by males. Circumstances forced many frontier women to become resourceful, tough, and independent. With an independence virtually unknown in the East, women of the West puzzled and disturbed male observers who tried to ease their own anxieties by poking fun at them.

Martha Cannary, better known as Calamity Jane, is a case in point. During her early teens she moved with her family from Missouri to Montana where she learned to handle horses and shoot straight. By the time she was twenty, she was working as a teamster and probably as camp follower to the U. S. Army, traveling through Wyoming, Kansas, and the Black Hills. She sometimes wore men's clothing and preferred the company of men. Local journalists and correspondents for eastern newspapers found her irresistible as a source of copy.

"That notorious female, Calamity Jane," the *Cheyenne Daily Leader* noted on June 20, 1876, "greatly rejoiced over her release from durance vile, procured a horse and buggy from Jas. Abney's stable, ostensibly to drive to Fort Russell and back [a total distance of six miles]. By the time she had reached the fort, however, indulgence in frequent and liberal potations completely befogged her not very clear brain, and she drove right by the place, never drawing rein until she reached Chug, 50 miles distant. Continuing to imbibe bug-juice at close intervals and in large quantities throughout the night, she waked up the next morning with a vague idea that Fort Russell had been removed, but still being bent on finding it, she drove on, finally sighting Fort Laramie, 70 miles distant. She turned her horse out to grass, ran the buggy into a corral, and began enjoying life in camp after her usual fashion."

Another woman similar in character to Calamity Jane, but not well known outside Wyoming and the Black Hills country, was "Mam" Shephard, a survivor of a gang of Louisiana outlaws. Mrs. Shephard fled to Wyoming in the 1870s and built a roadhouse near Raw Hide Butte between Fort Laramie and Lusk on the Cheyenne–Black Hills stage route.

Mam Shephard like to wear red pantalettes tied around her ankles, and they fluttered gaily when she rode her horse at a brisk pace. This sight amused the cowboys in the area, reminding them of "a feather-legged chicken in a high wind." One of them called her "Mother Feather Legs," and the sobriquet was quickly established.

With wagon and stagecoach traffic steadily increasing over the route to Deadwood and the Black Hills gold mines, Mother Feather Legs was soon operating a profitable business. She kept a good supply of whiskey, imported a pair of professional gamblers to fleece the passersby, and maintained a sort of "bank" where she kept deposits of money and stolen jewelry for outlaws.

The last of these services probably led to her sudden demise. One day in 1879, a neighbor found Mother Feather Leg's body lying in the mud beside a spring near the roadhouse. She had been shot to death. More than a thousand dollars was missing from her "bank." The cowboys and journalists who had viewed her as a subject for buffoonery and a source of humorous copy mourned her passing.[1]

While George W. Featherstonhaugh was traveling through the frontier Ozarks in 1834, he found wry amusement in observing the toughness of women caught in the harsh environment. "Mr. Barkman we did not see, but I shall certainly not forget his lady soon, as I have never seen any one, as far as manners and exterior went, with less pretensions to be classed with the feminine gender...She chewed tobacco, she smoked a pipe, she drank whiskey, and cursed and swore as heartily as any backwoodsman, all at the same time; doing quite as much vulgarity as four male blackguards could do...She must have been a person of surprising powers in her youth, for I was informed that she was now comparatively refined to what she had been before her marriage; at that period, so full of interest to a lover, she was commonly known by the name of 'She B'ar.'"[2]

Whether by necessity or by inclination a number of young frontier women joined the ranks of the "soiled doves." Some lived as well or better than their respectable sisters, but their experiences were as varied as the title of Anne M. Butler's serious study of the subject, *Daughters of Joy, Sisters of Misery.*

That they sometimes added humor to the lives of hard working males was attested to in contemporary diaries and letters. "Misses Lilly and Maud, two scarlet ladies," logger Ormond Twiford noted, "who stay at our hotel, came into my room this evening where I sat reading, and putting on my pistols and belts played 'cowboys.' They looked romantic thus accoutered."[3]

Western miners, who usually lived in all-male areas, were quite willing to sacrifice their comforts to assure a plentiful supply of prostitutes when money was available to pay for their services. "There was a regular red-light district," a miner at Copperfield, Utah, recorded, "but on paydays 250 prostitutes came into town and the men gave up their rooms to accommodate them during their stay."

In the nearby mining town of Bingham, the editor of the *Press–Bulletin* was fascinated by an episode that involved a Japanese, a Greek, and a prostitute. "A queenly maiden from Missouri," he wrote, "known to her friends in this section as Billie, crushingly beautiful, worked in a house in Copperfield for two years. Japanese Yoko accused Billie of taking a hundred dollars. Billie denied 'cabbaging' the money, but beat it out of the neighborhood to Salt Lake with the Greek. They were found at the Newhouse Hotel. In Billie's muff officers found 1,400 dollars and a thousand dollars in diamonds."[4]

That frontier women adjusted to the facts of life while still quite young is indicated by an anecdote told in various versions late in the nineteenth century. One morning a stranger knocked on a settler's farmhouse door. It was opened by the settler's daughter of about sixteen. "I'd like to speak to your father," the stranger said.

"Pa is way back the other side of the field," the young girl replied. "But I take care of his business accounts, and I can tell you about most things. If you want to breed a mare, our stud fee is ten dollars. If it's a cow our bull is fifteen dollars. If it's pigs, the boar's fee is also fifteen dollars."

"No, no, miss, it's nothing like that," the visitor said. "What I came for is about your brother, Jake. He's courting my daughter, you see, and I thought maybe your father and I should talk—"

The girl interrupted brightly: "You're quite right, mister, you better go across the field and talk to my Pa. I don't know what fee he charges for Jake."

If the occasion demanded, pioneer women could command strong tongues. A couple of ladies met on a street in Cheyenne after not seeing each other for several years. One said: "My, I hardly recognized you, Annie, you look so much older." Annie replied: "I wouldn't have known you, either, Emma, excepting for your hat and dress." •

One of the first young women to become a newspaper reporter in the West, Minnie Hall Krauser of Colorado, was typical of the resourceful invaders of professions previously monopolized by males. Ms. Krauser was assigned a beat that took her into some of the more unsavory areas of Denver. Automobiles and telephones were not available in those times, but bicycles were, and she obtained one to use in covering her territory. Late one night a hoodlum knocked her off the bicycle and robbed her, but she managed to climb back on the machine and escape virtually unharmed.

"I applied at police headquarters the next day for permission to carry a gun. It was granted, so I got a detective to select a small automatic for me and I wore it on a belt under my jacket. Almost on my first trip, I rode into a trench dug for water pipes. It was a dark night—no lantern to give warning, and the bicycle and I landed in the bottom of the trench. The gun went off, and I laid very still, wondering if I was shot. Deciding I was all right, I tried to untangle myself from the bicycle and screamed for help. Some man assisted me out of the hole and I gave him the gun right there. Ever after I depended on luck and the Lord for protection."[5]

Shortages of women in the early days of gold-rush California naturally made them more desirable than in more normally apportioned areas. If a rumor spread that a woman had arrived in any mining camp, men would travel for miles just to take a look at a female form and hear a female voice. When Louisa Clappe joined her physician husband at Rich Bar, she was mystified and then amused by the excitement she caused among the miners. A young prospector from Georgia dashed into Dr. Clappe's office, eager to speak to the first woman he had seen in two years. "In the elation of his heart at the joyful event," she wrote, "he rushed out and invested capital in some excellent champagne, which I, on Willie's principle of 'doing in Turkey as the Turkies do,' assisted the company in drinking to the honor of my own arrival."[6]

Caroline Leighton related similar experiences on her journey through California. "At every stopping place the men made little fires in their frying pans, and set them around me, to keep off the mosquitos, while I took my meal. As the columns of smoke rose about me I felt like a heathen goddess to whom incense was being offered."[7]

A clever young man from Illinois, yearning for the female companionship he had left at home, revealed his feelings in a letter by playing on the word *state.* Writing of his weariness with a life in which there was no female society or influence, he declared his determination to emigrate to a *state* where he "could enjoy more of the Sweets and feel more of the influence of female society than in any other in the Union…Tell the girls to look sharp, the boys are all bound for the *state* above mentioned, via Matrimony…As for Charley Wells, he tells me he is going to take a squaw out of spite because the girls back home in Illinois are all marrying old widowers."[8]

The shortage of women was always keenly felt at dances, which were among the most popular of social gatherings. At a soldiers' ball at Fort Vancouver, Oregon Territory, just before Christmas 1850, a young officer complained that there were only seven women present, five of them being wives, and only two single girls. In a rather wistful manner he noted their endurance through the lively cotillions and then their times of departure. "After supper one lady left; at ten, two left. At one o'clock one left, leaving but three. At two, another left, leaving but two ladies in the hall. Misses Melleck stopped at three, all hands returned home."[9]

Because they were so few in numbers at parties and dances, the women who attended were always under constant scrutiny. "If the girls feel a tick biting them at a party," reported one observant male, "and even if they are on the floor dancing, they immediately stop and unpin, and scratch themselves till they find it; it would do your heart good to see how expert the dear little affectionate good-for-nothing creatures are at catching ticks."[10]

Editors of local newspapers had an advantage over their fellows in their ability to advertise at no cost, and anonymously if they so chose, for prospective wives who might read their papers. In 1875 William J. Berry, editor of the *Yuma* (Arizona) *Sentinel* displayed this advertisement:

> WANTED: A nice, plump, healthy good-natured, good-looking domestic and affectionate lady to correspond with. Object—matrimony. She must be between 22 and 35 years of age. She must be a believer in God and immortality, but no sectarian. She must not be a gadabout or given to scandal, but must be one who will be a help-mate and companion, and who will endeavor to make home happy. Such a lady can find a correspondent by addressing the editor of this paper. Photographs exchanged!
>
> If anybody don't like our way of going about this interesting business, we don't care. It's none of their funeral.[11]

The results of editor Berry's advertisement are not known, but his blunt style could have been improved by a printer who worked for another newspaper. In a letter to his brother in Boston, Hiram Whittington wrote: "Miss Leana has been here about three months going to school. She is between 16 and 17, ordinary height and quite delicate...auburn hair, black eyes, Grecian nose, and a mouth so sweet that one would almost forfeit heaven to kiss it; besides the prettiest hand that ever made an apple dumpling or boxed a forward lover's ear...She has inward, mental charm that might entice a hermit from his cell, or tempt an angel from his high estate...her heart knows no guile; deceipt has no place there; misplaced affections have not yet soured her temper."[12]

The charming Leana had numerous choices among the over-supply of males, however, and Whittington lost her to someone else. Like many other young men on the frontier, he had to return home—to Boston—to find a wife.

Rejected lovers in that time of surplus males were often the butt of heartless jokers such as the editor of the Manzano (New Mexico) *Gringo and Greaser,* who printed an item poking fun at Señor Dolores Sedillo. "He fell in love with a piece of Las Vegas calico that is visiting here, but his love was spurned. He then skedaddled, taking with him a mule. The mule died on the plains and left him on foot. The last seen of him, he was making a jackass of himself, being saddled up and trying to ride himself out of the country. A busted heart will raise hell with any man."[13]

Times change, however, and by the turn of the century a surplus of females in such places as the old westward staging areas of Missouri led caustic editors to poke fun at unmarried women. "A new organization called the 'Old Maids' Mutual Aid' is in process of organization," reported the *Sarcoxie Record* of November 4, 1903, "and will probably be launched in this city before the first of January. Next year will be a Leap Year and the society proposes to take advantage of the opportunity thus offered to ladies, who, having arrived at years of discretion are unmated and unloved.

"The object of the society will be to protect its members and advance their matrimonial interests. Meetings will be guarded by the usual lodge restrictions and no one will be admitted who is not an Old Maid in good standing.

"A large membership is secured already and new recruits will easily be found because every day some blossoming tulip is withered by the frost of time, relegated to the ancient and venerable class and thus becomes eligible to membership in this society.

"The *Record* was privileged with an interview from one of the leading organizers of the society and was informed that the motto of the society will be 'Anybody, Lord.'"

About the time that gold was discovered in California and the great overland crossings began, Amelia Jenks Bloomer introduced "flowing trowsers" for women. Mrs. Bloomer was an advocate of sensible costumes for her sex, and the garment was soon named for her. Women preparing to make the overland trek must have viewed bloomers as a godsend, although at first only the more daring wore them. After observing several westward-bound bloomer wearers passing through Utah, Brigham Young recommended the costume for Mormon women making the crossing to Salt Lake City. Most men, however, viewed the costume as an object for laughter.

David Spain, who left South Bend, Indiana, bound for the Pike's Peak gold rush in the spring of 1859, encountered his first bloomer girls at Iowa City. "Saw a couple ladies dressed in Bloomer Costume," he noted in his diary. "Followed them three squares for a fair sight." Spain evidently considered his experience more titillating than funny. Several days later he retold the incident in a letter to South Bend: "We met a couple of 'upper ten' ladies of Iowa City dressed out and out Bloomer style, black cassimere pants and black cloth coats, high heel boots, finished off with a low crown black hat—I think Duey and I followed them about three squares before our curiosity was satisfied."[14]

San Francisco males also found bloomer watching to be a fine sport. "The city was taken quite by surprise yesterday afternoon," reported the *Alta California,* "by observing a woman dressed in a style a little beyond the Bloomer…She really looked magnificent and was followed by a large retinue of men and boys, who appeared to be highly pleased with the style."[15]

Not all bloomer observers, however, were so highly pleased. No doubt the reactions of the beholders depended upon the charm of the wearers. While traveling through the Platte Valley in 1860, Albert Richardson was appalled by a "bloomer" he saw walking and driving a team of oxen. "Her huge dimensions gave her the appearance of an ambulatory cotton bale, or peripatetic hay stack."[16]

Sir Richard Burton was even more acerbic when he encountered one at Horseshoe Station during his tour of the American West in 1860. "The Bloomer was an uncouth being, her hair, cut level with her eyes, depended with the graceful curve of a drake's tail around the flat Turanian countenance, whose only expression was sullen insolence. The body-dress, glazed brown calico, fitted her somewhat like a soldier's tunic, developing haunches which would be admired only in venison…"[17]

A nineteenth-century article of feminine underpinning that the wearers came to detest was the corset, and the women of the West probably did more to free their sex of this abominable shackle than any other group. After all, they had frequent opportunities to view the lissome forms of young Indian women whose bodies were unrestrained by such devices.

In their campaign against the corset, frontier women were aided by the manufacturer of a popular line of patent medicines, The Kickapoo Indian Remedies. A widely circulated pamphlet contained drawings of two female skeletons, one of an Indian woman with a broad rib cage and generous hip bones, the other of "an American lady deformed by corsets." The text beneath the drawings excoriated corsets for squeezing the stomach and bowels into as narrow a compass as possible. "Hence proceeds indigestion, fainting fits, consumption of lungs, and other ailments common to females...Mothers, how is it possible for you to bring into the world healthy children, while suffering from such fearful distortion. Do away with such practices, tight lacing, etc., and you will soon regain your former health. A corset factory would be idle if it depended upon our Indian friends for support."

Some women undoubtedly took advantage of the relative scarcity of their sex, demanding more than some males were willing to put up with. Charles Blair, who traveled with a wagon train to Oregon in 1862 included a warning in a letter to his brother in Ohio: "Tell Thomas if he starts across the Plains he must not get in a company where there is many wimen. If he does they will put him to a tremendous Site of unnecessary trouble. Finely in the end they will pull all the hair out of his head.

"It seems to be a complaint of all the Boys after talking a while about traveling on the Plains. They all Swere they will never Travil in a Train where there is any wimen. I blieve the magority were wimen in our California train. As for my part I had no trouble with them instid of that they were great companey, always jovil and lively when Such a thing was possible."[18]

As soon as those "wimen" in the train reached their destinations they were quickly besieged by hordes of men eager for a sight of the opposite sex. A goodly number of single young women traveled west to become schoolteachers, and pressing demands for them to become wives led to occasional drastic actions by concerned officials. In 1872 a member of the Kansas legislature pledged that he would introduce a law "making it a felony for a young man to marry...a school marm in a county having less than 5,000 population. This is on the grounds of public policy that in the frontier counties it is impossible to educate the young on account of the marriage of teachers."[19]

Other restraints were used to keep young men away from the available single women. In 1870 a Salt Lake City firm issued an edict restricting its male employees from courting more than one evening a week unless they attended church regularly, in which case they could go courting two evenings per week. Any other spare waking moments were supposed to be spent reading good books and "contemplating the Glories and Building up the Kingdom of God."

On August 9, 1872, the editor of the *Fort Scott* (Kansas) *Daily Monitor* published this warning: "Any single young man leaving Fort Scott and going east on a trip who does not file a declaratory statement with the clerk of the District Court, setting forth the nature of his business and the probable length of his absence will be advertised the day after his departure as having gone east to get married."

And when a young woman on the frontier did consent to be wed she usually found very little romance in the proceedings, as indicated by this recorded account of a couple named James and Belle, who rode up on horseback before a justice of the peace who was obsessed with omens and superstitions.

JAMES: Can you marry us?

JUSTICE OF THE PEACE: Well, yes, this is ground hog day, tater planting will be bad; but this is not Friday, and the Almanack says that the sign is in the heart. I have sworn to support the constitution. I guess I can swear you and that gal to support each other. Git down and I'll swear you in. Jine hands. Stranger, do you swear that you believe that the sign is in the heart; that the gal whose hand you are holding, you will support as long as you breathe?

JAMES: Yes, I do.

JUSTICE OF THE PEACE: Gal, do you vow that the sign is in the heart, and that you will let this feller support you as long as you are able?

BELLE: I do.

JUSTICE OF THE PEACE: Now according to the sign of the heart, this is not Friday, and this not being Friday having sworn to support the constitution, I now call you one. Farewell.[20]

Although they were in short supply in many settlements, frontier women still had to contend with the age-old masculine attitude that females were second-class citizens, subject to the whims of the dominant male society. This attitude was magnified in the activities of the star players, the Grand Panjandrums, jack-a-dandies, and lady-killers who formed the male power structure of the times. They were lawmen, gunfighters, trail bosses, wagon train captains, cavalry officers, showmen—the Wild Bills and Buffalo Bills and Indian Fighting Bills. They dressed like swashbucklers and sat in their saddles or strutted around the towns like gods on Olympus. Other males may have envied them, but secretly they laughed at their hollow antics, and so did sensible females who knew intuitively how they treated their women.

Wild Bill Hickok was an example. According to C.F. Gross, who managed the Drovers Cottage in Abilene, Kansas, during the trail driving era, Hickok always had a mistress. "I knew two or three of them," Gross recalled, "one a former mistress of his was an inmate of a cottage in McCoys addition. Bill asked me to go with him to see her to be a witness in an interview. I believe she was a Red Head but am not sure. She came to Abilene to try and make up with Bill. He gave her $25.00, & made her move on. There was Nan Ross but Bill told her he was through with her. She moved on. When Mrs. Lake the widow of 'Old Lake of Circus Fame' came to Abilene she set up her tent just west of the D Cottage on the vacant ground. Bill was on hand to keep order. Bill was a Handsome man as you Know & she fell for him hard, fell all the way clear to the *Basement,* tried her best to get him to marry her & run the circus. She told me all about it. I said why dont you do it—He said 'I know she has a good show, but when she is done in the West, she will go East & I dont want any paper collar on, & its me for the West...'"[21] Hickok eventually did marry Mrs. Lake a few months before going north to the Black Hills where he met his death.

Mark Twain in his Nevada newspaper days viewed women less harshly than Wild Bill, but his machismo sometimes was revealed in his journalism. After failing to gain entrance to a social affair in

Virginia City because he was unaccompanied by a lady, Twain resolved to be properly prepared for the next big event of the season, the Sanitary Ball, by inviting not one, but several to be his companion of the evening.

"We engaged a good many young ladies last Tuesday to go with us," he wrote anonymously in the *Territorial Enterprise,* "thinking that out of the lot we should certainly be able to secure one, at the appointed time, but they all seemed to have got a little angry about something—nobody knows what, for the ways of women are past finding out. They told us we had better go and invite a thousand girls to go to the ball. A thousand. Why, it was absurd. We had no use for a thousand girls. A thous—but these girls were as crazy as loons. In every instance, after they had uttered that pointless suggestion, they marched magnificently out of their parlors—and if you will believe me, not one of them ever recollected to come back again. Why, it was the most unaccountable circumstance we ever heard of. We never enjoyed so much solitude in so many different places, in one evening, before. But patience has its limits, we finally got tired of that arrangement—and at the risk of offending some of those girls, who stalked off to the Sanitary Ball alone—without a virgin, out of the whole litter."[22]

Relations between white males and Indian women on the frontier produced situations that were amusing to contemporary observers, but the humor does not stand the test of time much better than Twain's story about the young ladies he invited to the Virginia City ball. The unions of white males and Indian women were not always entirely voluntary. Some of the big fur companies, such as Hudson's Bay, insisted that their trappers and traders live with Indian women so they would have ties to keep them in the West. If an official based on the frontier went back east on a holiday and married a white girl, the fur companies considered him unfit for further advancement—which proves that there is nothing new in pressures being applied by big corporations upon their employees' private lives.

In most cases Indian women were considered little more than chattel. In 1834, Francis Chardon, a fur trader at Fort Clark on the upper Missouri River, took an Indian wife and noted in his journal:

"Having lived for two months a single life, and could not stand it any longer, I concluded to day to buy myself a Wife, a young Virgin of 15—which cost $150."[23] Another trader paid twice as much, three hundred dollars with fifty dollars down and the remainder due in thirty days. "She is a capital Girl, 16 Years old raised to house Work and Cooking, she is a great Bargain, if Money was to be had in these parts I should not have had her so low."[24]

During his journey west in 1839, Adolph Wislizenus met a trapper who was trying to sell his Ute wife for $250. He claimed he had paid twice that for her, and praised her for her cardinal virtues: "She is young, gentle, easy, and in first rate order."

Although a few matings of white frontiersmen and Indian women resulted in long-time attachments, with children and family life (Jim Bridger was a notable example) most such unions were transitory. Possibly the record number of successive wives was held by a rancher named Fallis near Fort Randall, Dakota Territory. In 1875, when Sergeant John Cox was caught in a blizzard, he took refuge in the rancher's cabin, and noted that he had an Indian wife. For dinner she served coyote meat, dried apples, bad coffee, and worse bread.

"Indian squaws are proverbial bad cooks," Cox wrote. "They seemed to have a particular aversion to using salt in their cooked foods. I said to Fallis, 'Why don't you teach your squaw to use salt?' He answered, 'I can teach her nothing.' Jokingly I replied, 'Well, I would get rid of her then and get me another.' Without hesitation he replied, 'Well, I've had twenty-five different ones and they are all alike.'"[25]

One of the frontier jokes about a lawman named X. Beidler is probably apocryphal, but it illustrated the contemporary viewpoint toward Indian women. While traveling by steamboat up the Missouri River, Beidler was introduced to a white woman on board who expressed surprise when she learned he was married to an Indian. "A native of these great plains," she said. "Where is she now?"

"I sent her to roam," Beidler replied.

"To Rome? To be educated, I suppose, Mr. Beidler. You can't mean Rome, Italy?"

"No, ma'am. To roam on the prairie."[26]

Sometimes prurient attitudes, a kind of voyeurism, was revealed in reports of travelers who encountered handsome Indian women, especially in southern climes where clothing was scant and breasts were uncovered. Lieutenant William H. Emory, a dignified topographical engineer, described an Apache beauty he observed near the Gila River in Arizona, on November 3, 1846:

"She had on a gauze-like dress, trimmed with the richest and most costly Brussels lace, pillaged no doubt from some fandango-going belle of Sonora; she straddled a fine gray horse, and whenever her blanket dropped from her shoulders, her tawny form could be seen through the transparent gauze. After she had sold her mule, she was anxious to sell her horse, and careered about to show his qualities. At one time she charged at full speed up a steep hill. In this, the fastenings of her dress broke, and her bare back was exposed to the crowd, who ungallantly raised a shout of laughter. Nothing daunted, she wheeled short round with surprising dexterity, and seeing the mischief done, coolly slipped the dress from her arms and tucked it beneath her seat and the saddle. In this state of nudity she rode through camp, from fire to fire, until, at last, attaining the object of her ambition, a soldier's red flannel shirt, she made her adieu in the new costume."[27]

Indian males evidently considered most white women unfit for frontier life, and ranked them about on the same scale as white men viewed Indian women. An Army surgeon married to an Indian woman once invited some of his wife's relatives to dinner. During the evening he attempted to explain a bit of Bible history to them, relating how sin and misery came into the world when Eve let a snake talk her into eating forbidden fruit. An old chief listened intently to his host's story about Eve and the snake until the end. Then he declared: "That's just like a white woman. Now if that had been an Indian woman, she would have taken a stick and killed that snake and saved all the trouble."[28]

CHAPTER EIGHTEEN

The Bawdy Natives

ONE OF THE STEREOTYPES of the American frontier is the impassive Indian—taciturn, unsmiling, humorless. From the nineteenth century into the twentieth, illustrators and cartoonists, comedians of stage and films, the litterateurs of our popular culture—all usually depicted American Indians in that way. Male and female, the Indians were shown as monosyllabic blockheads who greeted whites with either "How!" or "Ugh" and were devoid of any capacity for laughter.

So fixed was the image in the minds of immigrants traveling westward, they were startled whenever they encountered an Indian who smiled or laughed. Some made note of this unexpected behavior, as did Edwin Bryant en route to California in 1846: "Emerging from this *canon* we passed over another wide and fertile bottom, at the lower end of which a naked Indian, more bold than his hidden associates, made his appearance from the willows at some distance, and ran towards us with great speed. Approaching us, he extended his arm; and when he came up, shook all of us by the hand with great cordiality. A grin, illustrative of a feeling of much delight, distorted his swarthy countenance…His delight at seeing and saluting us, was apparently so overwhelming, that he could not restrain his emotions, but laughed outright, (an unusual phenomenon for an Indian,) and shouted a gleeful shout.

"We did not suspend our march on his account, but he trotted along by my side for a mile or more, his garrulous tongue rolling out with an oily fluency an eloquence quite as incomprehensible as that of many a member of congress. Three more of his brethren made their appearance from the distant willows, when our good-natured and nearly overjoyed friend left us and joined them."[1]

It would be interesting to know how long this Piute Indian who met Edwin Bryant continued to greet with grins and laughter the legions of white immigrants who passed through his country during the next several years—especially if they cheated him in trades or fired upon him without warning while he was approaching the wagon trains.

In the beginning, the white travelers were viewed by the Indians as curiosities to be examined with dignity. Many Indians were amused by the physical appearance and ineptitude of the intruders, but were too reserved to laugh *at* them, and there were few opportunities provided in which to laugh *with* them. In the later stages of confrontation, the tribes viewed the whites as dangerous invaders. Smiles and laughter do not accompany the emotions of distrust and fear for one's freedom and life.

Frontiersmen who lived with Indians long enough to be accepted into their society soon learned how merry they could be, how earthy was their banter, how raunchy were their jokes. George Belden, who lived with the Sioux during the 1860s, told of spending an evening in a lodge with four or five girls and a couple of young warriors, "and all were laughing and enjoying themselves; some of the girls quizzing the young men as to whom they liked best among the females of the village, and the warriors retorting by joking the girls."[2]

Around strangers, however, Colonel Richard Dodge reported, Indians were grave and dignified, reserved and silent. Dodge, who spent more than thirty years studying several tribes at first hand during the nineteenth century, declared that their stoicism was all a put-on. "In his own camp, away from strangers, the Indian is a noisy, jolly, rollicking, mischief-loving braggadocio, brimful of practical jokes and rough fun of any kind, making the welkin ring with his laughter, and rousing the midnight echoes by song and dance, whoops and yells."

Loud cheering and laughter accompanied Indian ball games, horse races, and gambling sessions. Courtships generated gentle laughter among those who watched the suitors at work. Tales told in the evenings were filled with bawdy double entendres and clever satire, sometimes too subtle for non-Indian listeners. The stoniest-faced human being of any race would have had difficulty keeping laughter from bursting forth while listening to the comic adventures of Coyote or Rabbit or Spider in a trickster story.

Relations between Indians and whites on the frontier often created amusing situations, more often than not at the expense of the Indians. But if no malice was intended, Indians could respond to a good sight gag. In Grantsville, Utah, a town character named Riley Judd liked to greet Indians with dramatic bows worthy of Sir Walter Raleigh. One day an Indian horseman, dressed in his best finery, came riding slowly into town. Judd stepped into the street and gave him a low and sweeping bow, startling the mustang into a double-shuffle buck. Pony and rider were immediately separated. The Indian arose from the street, dusted his buckskins, and expressed himself with quiet humor: "Too much howdyou do, Riley Judd."[3]

While Cornelia Adair, wife of the famous cattleman John Adair, was visiting friends at Sidney, Nebraska, in 1874, a Sioux chief named Two Lance called upon them. From white acquaintances, Two Lance had taken up the habit of chewing tobacco, and soon after he entered the sitting room the "vile juices" began to fill his mouth. "He got up," Mrs. Adair later noted in her diary, "looked all around the room for a 'spittoon' and, not seeing anything that looked like one, and being much to civil to deface Mrs. Morrow's pretty carpet, he at last, in a fit of desperation, held out his own hand and used it as a 'spittoon.' It was rather an extraordinary proceeding, but I positively thought it more gentleman-like than the way our friends on the Mississippi steamboat sent volleys of tobacco juice all day over the beautiful velvet carpets."[4]

At Fort Benton in 1864, a demonstration of a mountain howitzer literally backfired for the commissioners from Washington who wanted to impress a group of Indians with the terrible effectiveness of the weapon. In this case the cannon was mounted on the back of a mule which was led out near the riverbank. A large crowd, half of them Indians, gathered to watch the proceedings.

The commissioners decided to fire the howitzer from the back of the mule at a high bank across the river. "A certain spot was shown to the Indians where the shot was supposed to hit," said Robert Vaughn, one of the spectators. "To strike the spot designated on the clay bank, which loomed up like some old castle, an extra heavy load was put in. Finally the man in charge of the mule stood in front of the quadruped with the rings of the bit in each hand. Now he has the business end of the mule where he wants it; another man was adjusting the cannon and, taking aim, while the third one took a match from his vest pocket, scratched it on the hip of his pants and touched the fuse.

"The hissing sound of the burning fuse made the mule lay down his ears and begin putting a hump in his back; next thing he whirled round and round, in spite of his manager trying to get him back in his first position. By this time everybody was going for dear life, and the mule was making the circle faster than ever, and the gun was liable to go off at any moment. There was a perfect stampede; many went over the bank into the river, others were crawling on their hands and knees, while many laid flat on the ground, broadcloth and buckskin alike—the man held to the bridle and the mule held the fort. Luckily on account of the bend in the mule's back, the shot struck the ground but a short distance from his heels.

"Many of the Indians never moved, thinking that the maneuvers of the mule were a part of the performance."[5]

When a white man or woman was proved right and an Indian wrong, the Indian usually accepted this with good humor. Cephas Washburn, a missionary to the Cherokees in Arkansas, brought from Boston two globes to use in teaching geography. One day the Cherokee chief, Takatoka, visited the schoolhouse, and saw the globes. He went over to the strange objects, put his hands upon them, and asked Washburn what kind of bird laid such large eggs. Washburn explained that they represented the earth, and showed him how the earth revolved. Takatoka protested. The world could not turn over, he said, or all the water would spill out of the rivers and the rocks fall off. One of Washburn's Cherokee students then picked up a bucket of water and swung it around several times, showing the chief that the water did not spill. Takatoka shrugged and smiled and then said: "Washburn is right."

When an explanation for some unfamiliar phenomenon was not readily apparent, an imaginative Indian could usually invent a story that was more entertaining than a factual account. Still told around the Crow Reservation in Montana is Chief Spotted Horse's interpretation of the origin of the monkey.

Not long after the Custer fight at the Little Bighorn River, railroads began pushing through that part of Montana. Work gangs of Irish and Italian immigrants were laying the tracks. One of the Italians had a pet monkey that died. He took the dead animal down near the Little Bighorn and dropped it in the grass.

The next morning a young Crow Indian saw the dead monkey beside a path near the river. At that time, none of the Crows there had ever seen a monkey. The young man called his comrades to come and see what he had found. They were puzzled by this outlandish being with a face that was almost human. It had fingernails instead of claws; it had blue eyes and whiskers and a tail. The young Indians treated the dead monkey as they would have treated a dead person. They did not touch the monkey, but managed to get it onto a blanket, and then carried it back to camp as they would have carried a human being. They took the dead animal to the front of Spotted Horse's tipi, and asked their chief to tell them what it was.

Spotted Horse looked down at the dead animal. He walked around it, studying the almost human face, the blue eyes, the fingernails, and the tail. He remarked on each of these remarkable things.

For a while the chief stood in silence. "I'll tell you what the animal is," he finally said. "It's the product of a mating between a white man and a cat."[6]

In an earlier time than the railroad building era, the Indians probably would have made the monkey into a trickster. Monkeys would have been superb tricksters had they been indigenous to the American frontier, but coyotes, rabbits, spiders, and clever birds like ravens and blue jays took the role for different Indian tribes. Occasionally a sacred being like Old Man of the Blackfoot tribe would perform the part, creating people and then playing tricks upon them. After the Europeans came, White Man became the trickster extraordinaire, sometimes disguised as a spider.

Trickster tales are universal fables in which a character (usually male) sets out to make dupes of others but in the end outsmarts himself. The trickster possesses powers of rapid transformation, from animate to inanimate objects, from huge to minute sizes, taking the shape of a human being, or switching sex from male to female. He is filled with lust, and the male sexual organs play a considerable part in many merry trickster tales.

In his study of Winnebago coyote tales, Paul Radin discovered a trickster whose penis was so long that it had to be carried in a box. During a wrangle with a chipmunk, Coyote chased the animal until it escaped into a hollow tree. Determined to punish the chipmunk, Coyote probed the hollow tree with part of his penis but could not reach the chipmunk. Unwinding more and more of his organ, he still could not feel the animal. Finally, after emptying the box, he gave up and started to withdraw. To his consternation, only a small piece of his penis was left. He had been undone by the chipmunk. The story ends with the observation that the chipmunk had been created for the purpose of gnawing off Coyote's penis so that he would not have to carry it in a box or on his back.[7]

The Arapaho had similar stories. George A. Dorsey and Alfred L. Kroeber collected several for Chicago's Field Columbian Museum, but at the time they were published, in 1903, the lustful sequences were translated into Latin so as to preserve them but not appall readers of that day:

> Nihancan [the Trickster] got to a camp-circle and was heart struck by a chief's daughter, who was very beautiful. The belle wore an elk tooth dress and didn't do any woman's work except quilled work, etc. She was free from dirty work. Nihancan started off and reached a hill, staying on the top of the hill that day until the sun set. *Is nocte ad tabercanulum* (tipi) *se convertit et membro suo dixit: "Age, volo te ad puellem pulchrum quae in principia tabernaculo est ire et in foramen quod inter eins crura est intrare. Cum ad hoc oramen perveneris, transmitte ad me impulsum. Tum ego me propellam, id quod mihi satisfaciet."*
>
> *Itaque membrum virile profectum ad tabernaculum lente serpsit et ad os foraminis pervenit. Nihancan sensit contactum et membrum suum propulsit quod fecit ut puella exclamamans e lecto saltu surgeret. Sanguis e vagina fluit. Pater et mater igni acceso membri caput immensum et membrum ipsum viderunt. Id cultro frustatim deciderunt, dum eius finem venerunt. Membrum ita resectum est ut nihil ex illo tempore noxas fecerit et homines membrum virile valde breve habeant."*[8]

The Arapaho also told a comical erotic tale of a lovers' triangle.

A handsome young man married a beautiful young girl. The husband was a member of the Star Society, and he was jealous of his wife's friendship with an apprentice member who frequently visited their tipi.

One day the head man of the Star Society invited the husband to his tipi for the evening to play a betting game. The invitation was brought at sundown by the apprentice, who again aroused the suspicions of the husband because of the looks exchanged between him and his wife.

As the apprentice was leaving the tipi, he said to the husband: "It is very important that you be there tonight. And bring plenty of goods to bet with. The head man says there will be heavy betting tonight."

"All right," the husband replied. "Tell them I'll be there after I gather some things to make my bets." He then lay down on the bed, planning what he must do. When darkness fell he got up and pulled down a wing fan from the lean-back. Taking a small wing feather from the fan, he split it down the middle, but left both sides attached to the quill. He then took a live coal from the tipi fire, set it on the ground, and dropped incense upon it from his medicine bag until he created a cloud of smoke.

Noticing that his wife was watching him closely, he asked her to go outside for some firewood to make more light in the tipi. She replied that she did not mind staying in the dark during the time he was away at the betting game. He insisted, however, that she get the wood.

While she was outside, he held the split feather over the live coal for a moment, and then carefully concealed it under a blanket at the bottom of the lean-back. After his wife returned he gathered up his betting goods and went to join the players in the head man's tipi.

The game was an exciting one, but the young husband lost steadily and soon had no articles left to bet with. He saw that the Star Society apprentice was still present, watching the play. "Go over to my tipi," he said to him, "and bring some of the arrows from my calf-hide quiver. If my wife is asleep, get them yourself. Bring half the arrows."

He then told the other players that he would continue in the game, and that if he lost he would pay the bets with his arrows. And so the heated game continued while the apprentice went for the arrows.

When the apprentice went into the husband's tipi, he found the wife was still awake. "Your husband sent me after some arrows," he said. "Now we ought to improve the chance before I go back."

"Oh, no!" said the wife. "He might come out after you, and we might get caught. He made threats to punish me if I should make any sign of love to you."

"Well, he told me to come over here," the apprentice replied. "He was in a good humor. They are having a hot game, and he won't leave it until I bring back his arrows."

"Well then, make haste," said the woman, lying back on the bed.

After a little while he tried to get loose from her, but could not. They rolled about and then sat up on the edge of the bed, with her in his lap facing him, but they could not separate themselves.

Back in the head man's tipi, the husband lost two more games, and the Star Society players began complaining because the apprentice had not returned with the arrows to pay off the bets. "You ought to go yourself and get your arrows," one of the men said.

"Oh, no, I can't do it now," the husband replied. "I will play two more games, and if I lose I will attend to the payments of my debts. The apprentice must have gone home and fallen asleep."

After the husband lost another game, he ordered a second apprentice to go and bring the arrows. When this messenger entered the tipi, he saw in the shadows the couple still sitting on the edge of the bed fastened together. He started to put some sticks of wood on the coals so that he could see them better, but the first apprentice spoke up hastily: "Please don't make a light. We are in a shameful fix. Will you go find my older brother and tell him what has happened, and make haste? Will you?"

The second apprentice went to the older brother's tipi. "Your younger brother," he said, "was sent a messenger to bring some arrows for one of the players at the Star Society hand game, and he became involved with the man's wife. Both your brother and the wife are on the bed, fast together, facing each other."

"Is that so? Can it be possible that my young brother is in this fix? I am sorry for him." Without delay the older brother took his best peace-pipe and filled it with tobacco. Then he went over to the tipi and found his younger brother and the woman still sitting locked together.

"We will offer the husband four horses and this peace-pipe," the older brother said.

He hurried over to the head man's tipi where the game was still in progress, and approached the husband. "Take this fine peace-pipe," the older brother said, "and four of my best ponies in payment for my younger brother's deed. And please have mercy on us."

"Don't you see I am busy at this game?" the husband protested angrily. "You are interfering with the play. Can't you wait until the game is over, and then talk to me? We will play four more games, and then I'll see what you want me for. You may hold that pipe a while yet."

And so the play continued until finally the games ended. The husband promised to pay his debts in arrows, and then took the peace-pipe and went with the older brother to the tipi where the apprentice and the wife still sat facing each other in the shadows. The husband put wood on the fire, and as the light flared up he turned and laughed at the guilty pair. "What is the matter with you two?" he said.

At that, the older brother, still fearing the husband's anger, went to him and rubbed down his face, and asked mercy for his younger brother. Without replying, the husband turned to the lean-back and took out the split-wing feather that he had concealed under the blanket. He held the feather up in the firelight and pulled the two halves completely apart. At that instant the apprentice and the wife were able to separate themselves.

"Well, friends," said the husband, "I can't give up my wife; I will keep her. I did this to teach her a lesson. I have no bad feelings against the apprentice." He took up the peace-pipe that the older brother had given him and lighted it. "I am thankful for this pipe and the four ponies you have promised me. Now it is all over with. You brothers go home. I shall live the best I can. For some time I have known of the actions of my wife with the apprentice. Now she has learned a lesson, and will make a good wife hereafter."[9]

The Haida, who lived on the Queen Charlotte Islands off the coast of British Columbia, told stories of the old days against a background of fishing, of whales, and of canoes that were as important to the Haida as horses were to the Plains Indians. A favorite tale was The Man Who Married a Killer-Whale Woman.

A man and his wife lived near Cape St. James, where every day she went to get mussels on the beach. After a while the man became suspicious of his wife's long daily absences. One day he followed her.

When she got near the place where she was going to get mussels she went along singing. She beat upon her mat with her digging stick in lieu of a drum. When she got near the place where the mussels were, a whale jumped ashore sideways just in front of her. Then she went to it, and she lay with it. And the whale went off blowing. He saw it.

Then he knew and he went away. Then he began to sharpen a mussel-shell at some place where she could not see him. It became sharp, and one day, when it was low tide, he sent his wife to get spruce roots for him.

Then he made clothing for himself like his wife's, took the basket, and wore the mat as a blanket. Then he went along the beach...And when he approached the place where his wife was in the habit of getting mussels, he used his mat as a drum. When he sang the same words, the black whale came ashore on its side in front of him. Then he went to it and cut off its penis. Then it got up quickly and went into the water making a noise. Its cries died away into the ocean.

Then he came home and built a fire. And he put stones into the fire. Then he sliced it up, and, when the stones were hot, he steamed it. After it was cooked his wife came home.

Then she asked her husband: "What things are you steaming?"

"I found some thing which had floated ashore. I am steaming them for you. They are cooked. Take the covers off."

Then she took the covers off. Before she had even put the cooked pieces into a tray, she took one off the top and tasted it. After she had taken a bite he said to her: "Is your husband's penis sweet?" She dropped it at once. Immediately she turned toward the door. Right where she sat she shook. Even the ground shook.

And, when his wife started off, he tried to hold her. He could not. Then she went out, and he went out after her. And, after he had followed her closely for a while, she went up in the bed of a creek...All that time he kept looking at her. And, when she got up toward the mountain, she recalled her husband's words.

Now she sat on the top of the mountain, and she again remembered what her husband had said. And, while sitting there, she became ashamed. Then she went away and came to the west coast. And she went out on one side of Elderberry Point. Then she jumped into the water in front of her. The man did not know that he had married a female killer-whale that had been born of a woman, nor that killer-whales are always in love with common whales. Then she settled herself down before him. She became a reef. It is called "Woman." When people get off from a canoe upon it, it shakes with them, they say.[10]

An Arikara tale of a warrior and his wife, an elk, and a bear, is an example of the droll relationships between Indians and the animals they depended upon for subsistence.

A young man who had no ponies to offer the father of his sweetheart persuaded her to run away with him into the wilderness. He killed many deer and elk and they soon had enough skins to make a big tipi, plenty of clothing, and enough dried meat to last a long time.

One day while the young man was out capturing eagles, Bear disguised as a man came to the tipi. He had a robe about his shoulders, bear's claws about his neck, and he smelled so fine that the woman could not help but like him. When Bear started to go, the woman followed him. He led her to his den where there were a dozen or more women that he had taken from their husbands.

When the young man returned to his tipi, he found that his wife was not there. He waited a while and then went in search of her. He ran and walked, and yelled her name, until he was so exhausted that he lay down in the woods.

Elk found him there. The young man told Elk that he had lost his wife, that he thought a great deal of her, and that he was almost dead from searching for her. Elk felt sorry for him and said that Bear must have taken his wife, and he would help get her back. First, the young man had to transform himself into an elk. Then Elk gave him a whistle, and told him that whenever he whistled, female elks would come rushing to him.

"Stay here in the timber," Elk said, "and I will go and watch for Bear to leave his den." After a while Elk returned to tell the young man that Bear had left.

The young man went up close to the cave where the den was and blew the whistle that Elk had given him. As soon as his wife heard the whistle she said: "Women, let us go. That is my husband."

Some of the women were afraid to go, for they feared Bear, but the young man kept on whistling, and when the women heard it again they all followed the young man's wife, who was now outside and rushing to him. The young man embraced his wife and said: "Go and hide while I wait for Bear to return."

Elk came then and said: "Bear is coming back. Fix your bow and arrows so you can shoot him while I put my head down and make a barrier with my horns."

When Bear returned, he attacked Elk, who raised his head and put the whole weight of his horns upon Bear, while the young man shot arrows into him. At last they killed Bear. Elk turned to the young man and said: "I shall now return to my place."

But the young man said: "No, I shall only take my wife; you take the other women. So Elk took the other women, and they all turned into elks. For this reason, when a male elk whistles, all the female elks run to him.[11]

To the Blackfoot, the horse was a much more interesting animal than the elk, and it appeared often as a character in their tall tales. One is a story of a woman who married a horse.

It begins on a day when a Blackfoot camp is moving. A husband went ahead with the scouts, leaving his wife to bring the travois that carried their goods. Along the way, some of the lodge poles came loose, and while she stopped to fix the load, the rest of the people went ahead and disappeared over a hill.

While she was trying the poles, a handsome young man suddenly appeared in the trail ahead of her. She started on, but he stopped her by getting in front of her.

"Why do you stop me?" she said. "I have never had anything to do with you."

"Well," said the young man, "I want you to go with me."

So the woman had to go with him.

When her people went into camp that evening, her husband could not find her. He and several men went back to search for her, but at last they decided she had been lost or captured.

Many moons after this, the Blackfoot were camped near where the woman was lost. When some hunters went out for game, they sighted a large herd of wild horses near a small lake, and in the herd they saw a person. They went back to camp and organized a mounted hunting party. Surrounding the herd, they cut out the horses, and roped the person. It was a woman. She had no clothing, and her body was covered with hair like that of a horse.

She was very wild and struggled in the rope. As the herd of horses ran away, they heard a colt among them neighing as if for its dam. The men took the woman back to the camp, where some of her relatives recognized in her the woman that had been lost for some time before. She was very wild, had lost the power of speech and the knowledge of all human things.

They kept her in the camp a while, but finally her former husband gave up all hopes. "It is of no use to keep her," he said. "The only thing we can do is send her back to the horses." That evening they turned her loose, and she was never seen again.[12]

Indians told some tales on the frontier that eventually made their way into the national culture. The Hopi listened and laughed to a story about Turtle and Coyote that had the same plot but was centuries older then the "tar baby" of Uncle Remus. The Caddo, who almost became an extinct tribe when they were driven out of Texas, knew the story of the tortoise and the hare long before they ever saw or heard of white Europeans. In their version, of course, Coyote instead of Rabbit was the victim:

One time, as Coyote was returning from a long and unsuccessful hunt for game, he passed the home of his old friend Turtle. Being weary and hungry and in no hurry, he decided to stop and make Turtle a visit. Turtle invited him in and offered him something to eat, as Coyote had hoped he would. While Coyote ate, Turtle stretched himself out to rest, saying, "I am tired out. I have just come back from the races."

Coyote asked what races.

"Our people have been having foot races down by the river. Have not you heard of them?"

Coyote smiled at the thought of a slow-moving Turtle racing, and said that he had not heard of the races, and if he had he surely would have been there. "Who won?" he asked.

"I did," said Turtle. "I have never yet been beaten in a race with my people."

Coyote answered, "I have never been beaten either. I wonder how a race between us would come out."

"The way to find out is to have a race," Turtle said.

"I am willing if you are," Coyote answered. "When shall we have it?"

They decided to run the race two days later.

When he arrived home, Coyote sent his son to call all the Coyote people together and announce to them that his father was going to run a race with Turtle, and that he wanted them all to come and bet heavily on the race, for of course he would defeat Turtle.

As soon as Coyote had gone, Turtle sent his son out to announce to the Turtles that his father was going to run a race with Coyote, and that he wanted all of the best runners to come to his lodge. They all came and listened to Turtle's plan to beat Coyote in the race. "We all know that Coyote is a good runner," Turtle said, "but he is also a cheat. He has cheated us in many ways. Let us now cheat him out of this race. Will you help me do it?"

Every one present agreed to help him. Then he continued: "This is my plan. I want each one of you to put a white feather in your hair just like the one I wear, and paint yourselves to look just like me. Then station yourselves at intervals along the course. Coyote will run with his head down, as he always does. One of you will start with him, but when he has left you far behind drop down in the grass. Then the next one will jump up and run. Coyote will look up and see you ahead, then he will run until he passes you. Then the next one will jump up and run, and so on until the last one. I will be the last, and beat him over the goal." The turtles talked over the plan, and then went home to prepare for the race.

Early in the morning of the day of the race, the Turtles stationed themselves along the way in the tall grass, and soon Coyote came. They began to discuss the distance they should run. Turtle wanted to run a long distance, but Coyote did not want to go a very long distance. He thought that he could beat Turtle in a short distance just as easily as in a long distance, and he did not care to tire himself. Turtle insisted, and so Coyote said that he would agree to any distance that he could mention.

Many Coyotes were now arriving, and they began to bet on Coyote.

The two contestants started to run and all the Coyotes began laughing, for Coyote was soon far ahead. To their surprise, however, Turtle quickly resumed the lead. Then Coyote overtook Turtle, and they began laughing again. Soon they heard the Turtles cheering, and to their amazement Turtle was far in the lead. Again Coyote overtook turtle, and again Turtle came up far ahead. The Coyotes cheered one moment and the Turtles the next. Just as Coyote had passed Turtle and was near the goal, Turtle crossed the line, and all the Turtles set up a loud cheer. Coyote ran off in the grass, and is wondering yet how turtle beat him in the race, and all the other Coyotes are angry at him because he lost the race, and caused them to lose many bets.[13]

The merriest Indian tales of frontier days were what are now called shaggy-dog stories. A yarn spinner would begin a simple story, gradually building details and actions until the plot began to ramble, perhaps turning surreal, and then with the story still unfinished the teller might stop abruptly, and ask one of his listeners to tie another one to it.

George B. Grinnell, who lived with the Cheyenne for a time, enjoyed the laughter attending these stories. During pauses between segments, he said, pipes were lighted and smoked while imaginations came into play. When a volunteer resumed the narrative, most likely it would grow more bawdy, more absurd, more anticlimactic. Eventually the hour would grow late, and one of the older listeners would rise and say (as we do now): "This cuts it off!"

Notes

Chapter One. The Chaucerian Way West

1. Austin L. Venable, "Journey of a Mormon from Liverpool to Salt Lake City." *Arkansas History,* Vol. 2, 1943, p. 346.

2. Marian Russell, *Land of Enchantment.* Evanston, Illinois: Branding Iron Press, 1954, p. 17.

3. Ed Donnell, "Letters," edited by Charles J. Wilkerson. *Nebraska History,* Vol. 41, 1960, p. 126.

4. Joseph Camp, "Journal," edited by Truman W. Camp. *Nebraska History,* Vol. 46, 1965, p. 31.

5. Theodore R. Davis, "A Stage Ride in Colorado." *Harper's New Monthly Magazine,* Vol. 35, July 1867, pp. 137–39.

6. Lemuel Clarke McKeeby, "Memoirs." *California History,* Vol. 3, 1924, p. 60.

7. George W. Hardesty, "Diary," edited by Richard H. Louden. *Colorado Magazine,* Vol. 38, 1961, p. 174.

8. Louis L. Simonin, "Colorado in 1867 as Seen by a Frenchman," edited by W. O. Clough. *Colorado Magazine,* Vol. 14, No. 2, 1937, p. 56.

9. *Cheyenne Daily Leader,* May 23, 1883, reprinted in Agnes Wright Spring, *The Cheyenne and Black Hills Stage and Express Routes.* Lincoln: University of Nebraska Press, 1948, pp. 318–19.

10. Mrs. M.B. Hall, "Experiences in Leadville and Independence, 1881–82." *Colorado Magazine,* Vol. 10, No. 2, March 1933, p. 62.

11. Gordon P. Lester, "A Round Trip to the Montana Mines." *Nebraska History.* Vol. 46, 1965, p. 282.

12. Dorsey D. Jones, "He Taught Near Eudora: Arkansas in the Early Sixties." *Arkansas Historical Quarterly,* Vol. 18, 1959, p. 226.

13. St. Louis *Missouri Republican,* April 20 and May 1, 1859.

14. Joseph M. Hanson, *The Conquest of the Missouri.* Chicago: McClurg, 1909.

15. Lester, *op. cit.,* p. 312.

16. Kansas City *Journal of Commerce,* March 13, 1860.

17. Cyrus Woodman, Letter. *Nebraska History,* Vol. 32, 1951, p. 48.

18. St. Louis *Missouri Republican,* Sept. 1858, reprinted in Walker D. Wyman, "Missouri River Steamboatin'." *Nebraska History,* Vol. 27, 1946, p. 95.

19. P.V. Daniel, Letter to his daughter, April 17, 1856. *Arkansas Historical Quarterly,* Vol. I, 1942, p. 161.

20. *Fayetteville Arkansan,* December 15, 1860, reprinted in *Arkansas Historical Quarterly,* Vol. 13, 1954, p. 207.

21. J. Ross Browne, *Adventures in the Apache Country.* New York: Harper and Bros., 1871, p. 364.

22. Albert D. Richardson, *Beyond the Mississippi.* Hartford: American Publishing Company, 1876, p. 282.

23. Harry Ellsworth Cole, *Stagecoach and Tavern Tales of the Old Northwest.* Cleveland: Arthur Clark and Co., 1930, p. 327.

24. Richardson, *op. cit.,* p. 479

25. *Spirit of the Times,* Vol. XVI, August 29, 1846, p. 314.

26. Camp, *op. cit.,* p. 281.

27. Spring, *op. cit.,* p. 178.

28. *Rio Abajo Weekly Press,* June 23, 1863, reprinted in Peter Hertzog, *Frontier Humor.* Santa Fe, New Mexico: Press of the Territorian, 1966, p. 8.

29. *Spirit of the Times,* Vol. XVI, Sept. 5, 1846, p. 331.

30. Simonin, *op. cit.,* p. 61.

31. Sir Richard Burton, *The Look of the West, 1860.* Lincoln: University of Nebraska Press, 1963, p. 247.

32. W.G. Marshall, *Through America, or Nine Months in the United States.* London: Sampson Low, 1881, p. 139.

33. Richardson, *op. cit.,* pp. 281–82.

34. Alexander K. McClure, *Three Thousand Miles Through the Rocky Mountains.* Philadelphia: Lippincott, 1869, pp. 202, 305–06.

35. John G. Bourke, "Bourke on the Southwest II," edited by Lansing B. Bloom. *New Mexico Historical Review,* Vol. 9, 1934, p. 62.

36. McClure, *op. cit.,* p. 116.

37. W.A. Burgess, "Building the Frisco Railroad in Northwest Arkansas." *Arkansas Historical Quarterly,* Vol. 10, 1951, p. 268.

38. Steven Masset, *Drifting About.* New York: Carlton, 1863, p. 255.

39. H.M. McIver, "Water Bound in Arkansas." *Arkansas Historical Quarterly,* Vol. 14, 1955, p. 147.

40. Edwin Bryant, *What I Saw in California.* New York: Appleton, 1848, p. 162.

41. Heinrich Lienhard, "Journal." Utah State Historical Society, *Quarterly,* Vol. 19, 1951, p. 171.

42. Lewis H. Garrard, *Wah-To-Yah and the Taos Trail.* New York: A. S. Barnes and Co., 1890, p. 78–79.

43. Richardson, *op. cit.,* p. 199.

44. McKeeby, *op. cit.,* p. 133.

Chapter Two. Bigwig and Littlewig Sojourners
1. James Parton, *Life of Horace Greeley.* New York, 1855, p. 414.
2. Albert D. Richardson, *Beyond the Mississippi,* Hartford: American Publishing Co., 1867, p. 282.
3. Horace Greeley, *An Overland Journey from New York to San Francisco in the Summer of 1859.* New York, 1860, p. 136.
4. Richardson, *op. cit.,* p. 178.
5. Greeley, *op. cit.,* p. 133
6. *Ibid,* pp. 209–16.
7. *Ibid,* p. 239.
8. Mark Twain, *Roughing It.* New York: Harper and Bros., 1908, pp. 85–88.
9. In addition to the above sources—Parton, Richardson, Greeley, and Twain—more details of Horace Greeley's sojourn in the West can be found in George H. and William Banning, *Six Horses,* New York: The Century Co., 1928, Ben C. Truman, "Knights of the Road," *Overland Monthly,* Vol. XXI, Second Series, 1898, p. 24; and San Jose (California) *Pioneer,* March 24, 1879.
10. Bayard H. Paine, *Pioneers, Indians and Buffaloes.* Curtis, Nebraska: Curtis Enterprise, 1935, p. 157.
11. William W. Tucker, *His Imperial Highness, the Grand Duke Alexis in the United States of America During the Winter of 1871–72.* Cambridge: Riverside Press, 1872, p. 155.
12. Albert Hadley James, "A Royal Buffalo Hunt." Kansas State Historical Society, *Transactions,* Vol. X, 1907–09, pp. 564–73.
13. *Nebraska State Journal,* Feb. 16, 1872, reprinted in Paine, *op. cit.,* p. 176.
14. Chalkley M. Beeson, "A Royal Buffalo Hunt." Kansas State Historical Society, *Transactions,* Vol. 10, 1907–08, pp. 574–580.
15. In addition to the above sources—Paine, Tucker, James, and Beeson—more details of the Grand Duke Alexis's sojourn in the West can be found in David A. Dary's *The Buffalo Book,* New York: Avon Books, 1975; Don Russell, *The Lives and Legends of Buffalo Bill,* University of Oklahoma Press, 1960; and John Burke, *Buffalo Bill, the Noblest Whiteskin,* New York: G.P. Putnam's Sons, 1973.
16. Lloyd Lewis and Henry Justin Smith, *Oscar Wilde Discovers America.* New York: Harcourt, Brace and Co., 1936, p. 332.
17. Oscar Wilde, *Impressions of America,* in *Works,* Vol. 14. New York: Putnam's, 1915, p. 217; Salt Lake City *Tribune,* April 15, 1882.
18. Lewis and Smith, *op. cit.,* pp. 316–18.
19. Joseph G. Brown, "My Recollections of Eugene Field." *Colorado Magazine,* Vol. 4, 1927, pp. 46–47.
20. Lewis and Smith, *op. cit.,* p. 332.
21. Richardson, *op. cit.,* pp. 313–24.
22. J.W. Spear, *Uncle Billy Reminisces.* Phoenix, Arizona: Republic and Gazette, 1940, p. 43.

23. Elizabeth Custer, *Following the Guidon.* New York: Harper and Bros., 1890, p. 122.

24. Sam P. Ridings, *The Chisholm Trail.* Guthrie, Oklahoma: Cooperative Publishing Co., 1936.

25. Philip H. Ault, *The Home Book of Western Humor.* New York: Dodd, Mead and Co., 1967, p. 218.

26. John G. Bourke, "Bourke on the Southwest II," edited by Lansing B. Bloom. *New Mexico Historical Review,* Vol. 9, 1934, p. 61.

27. William A. Baillie–Grohman, *Fifteen Years' Sport and Life in the Hunting Grounds of Western America and British Columbia.* London, 1900, pp. 4–5.

28. John J. Fox, "The Far West in the '80s," edited by T.A. Larson. *Annals of Wyoming,* Vol. XXI, 1949, pp. 7–8.

29. *Lubbock* (Texas) *Avalanche,* September 9, 1909.

30. P.W. Hamer, *Ocean to Ocean,* London, 1871, p. 66.

31. *Omaha Bee,* Sept. 2, 1872.

32. *Ashland* (Nebraska) *Times,* April 12, 1872, reprinted in Richard C. Overton, *Burlington West.* New York: Russell and Russell, 1967, p. 354.

33. C. Reginald Enoch, *Farthest West, Life and Travel in the United States.* New York: D. Appleton and Co., 1910, p. 91.

34. *Ibid,* p. 287.

35. Richard Harding Davis, *The West from a Car Window.* New York: Harper and Bros., 1892, p. 235.

Chapter Three. There's a One-Eyed Man in the Game

1. Richard Erdoes, *Saloons of the Old West.* New York: Knopf, 1979, p. 9.

2. J.E. Durivage, letter of October 31, 1849, published in the New Orleans *Picayune.* Reprinted in John F. McDermott, *Travelers on the Western Frontier.* Urbana: University of Illinois Press, 1970, p. 250.

3. Thomas Kerr, "An Irishman in the Gold Rush." *California History,* Vol. 7, 1928, p. 402.

4. Mark Twain, *Roughing It.* New York: Harper and Bros., 1908, p. 339.

5. Richard Carroll, "The Founding of Salida, Colorado." *Colorado Magazine,* Vol. 11, No. 4, 1934, p. 121.

6. Richard T. Ackley, "Across the Plains in 1858." *Utah State Historical Quarterly,* Vol. 9, 1941, p. 195.

7. George A. Root, "Gunnison in the Early Eighties." *Colorado Magazine,* Vol. 9, No. 6, November 1932, p. 302.

8. *Fort Scott* (Kansas) *Daily Monitor,* April 29, May 5–7, 1870. Reprinted in James C. Malin, "Early Theatre at Fort Scott." *Kansas Historical Quarterly,* Vol. XXIV, 1958, p. 44.

9. J.H. Beadle, *The Undeveloped West.* Philadelphia: National Publishing Company, 1873, pp. 87–95.

10. Edward P. Hingston, *The Genial Showman.* London, 1870, Vol. 2, p. 251.

11. Joseph G. Brown, "My Recollections of Eugene Field." *Colorado Magazine,* Vol. 4, No. 2, 1927, p. 45.

12. Mary C. Ayers, "Howardsville on the San Juan." *Colorado Magazine,* Vol. 28, 1951, p. 252.

13. Stanley Vestal, *Queen of Cowtowns, Dodge City.* New York: Harper and Row, 1952, p. 217.

14. *Dodge City* (Kansas) *Times,* July 21, 1877.

15. James Thomson, "Colorado Diary," edited by K.J. Fielding. *Colorado Magazine,* Vol. 31, 1954, p. 213.

16. Anne Ellis. *The Life of an Ordinary Woman.* Boston: Houghton, Mifflin, 1932, p. 257.

17. Jimmie L. Franklin, "That Noble Experiment, a Note on Prohibition in Oklahoma." *Chronicles of Oklahoma,* Vol. 43, 1965, p. 25.

Chapter Four. Making the Calico Crack

1. Archibald Menzies, "California Journal." *California History,* Vol. 2, 1924, p. 284.

2. Ernest de Massey, "A Frenchman in the Gold Rush." *California History,* Vol. 5, 1926, p. 154.

3. Edwin Bryant, *What I Saw in California.* New York: Appleton, 1848, p. 329.

4. Friedrich Gerstäcker, *Wild Sports in the Far West.* Boston: Crosby, Nichols and Co., 1859, pp. 220–24.

5. James Pike, *The Scout and Ranger.* Cincinnati: J.B. Hawley and Co., 1865, pp. 146–50.

6. Virginia City *Territorial Enterprise,* January 10, 1863. Reprinted in William C. Miller, "Mark Twain at the Sanitary Ball—and Elsewhere." California Historical Society, *Quarterly,* Vol. 36, 1957, pp. 36–38.

7. "A Mexican Fandango," letter signed "Ferris" in *Army and Navy Journal,* Vol. 8, December 24, 1870.

8. John G. Bourke, "Bourke on the Southwest II," edited by Lansing B. Bloom. *New Mexico Historical Review,* Vol. 9, 1934, pp. 76–77.

9. Thomas J. Dimsdale, *The Vigilantes of Montana.* Butte, Montana: W.F. Bartlett, 1915, pp. 9–11.

10. Jess Benton, *Cow by the Tail.* Boston: Houghton, Mifflin, 1943, p. 56.

Chapter Five. Stringing the Greeners

1. Adapted from John F. Lillard, ed., *Poker Stories.* New York: F.P. Harper, 1896.

2. John C. Duval, *The Adventures of Big Foot Wallace.* Macon, 1871, pp. 276–77.

3. Richard Harding Davis, *The West from a Car Window.* New York: Harper and Bros., 1892, p. 232.

4. Albert W. Thomas, "Up the Trail to Montana." *Cattleman,* Vol. 32, Oct. 1945, p. 118.

5. Sir Richard Burton, *The Look of the West, 1860.* Lincoln: University of Nebraska Press, 1963, pp. 102–03.

6. Peter H. Burnett, *Recollections and Opinions of an Old Pioneer.* New York: Appleton, 1880, p. 155.

7. Charles M. Russell, *Trails Plowed Under.* New York: Doubleday, 1931, pp. 145–46.

8. *Sketches and Eccentricities of Col. David Crockett of West Tennessee.* New York: Harper and Bros., 1833.

9. Thomas B. Thorpe, " The Big Bear of Arkansas." *Spirit of the Times,* Vol. IX, March 27, 1841, pp. 43–44.

10. *Ibid,* Vol. XIV, August 16, 1845, p. 287.

11. Otto E. Rayburn, "Arkansas Folklore, Its Preservation." *Arkansas Historical Quarterly,* Vol. 10, 1951, p. 210.

12. R.D. Holt, "El Rio Pecos." *Cattleman,* Vol. 35, July 1948, p. 21.

13. *Santa Fe Daily New Mexican,* March 28, 1880. Reprinted in Peter Hertzog, *Frontier Humor,* Santa Fe, New Mexico: The Press of the Territorian, 1966, pp. 18–19.

14. William R. Collier and E.V. Westrate, *Reign of Soapy Smith,* New York: Doubleday, 1935; Joseph E. Smith, "Personal Recollections of Early Denver," *Colorado Magazine,* Vol. 20, No. 2, March 1943, p. 60–61; "Soapy Smith, the Robin Hood of the Rockies," *Cattleman,* Vol. 31, June 1944, pp. 34–38.

15. Robert E. Cowen, "Norton I, Emperor of the United States and Protector of Mexico." California Historical Society, *Quarterly,* Vol. II, 1924, pp. 237–45.

16. Levette J. Davidson, "The Pikes Peak Prevaricator." *Colorado Magazine,* Vol. 20, 1943, pp. 216–25.

17. Louise Pound, "The John G. Maher Hoaxes." *Nebraska History,* Vol. 33, 1952, pp. 203–19.

Chapter Six. Having Fun with the Phenomena

1. Nyle H. Miller et al, *Kansas, a Pictorial History.* Topeka: Kansas State Historical Society, 1961, p. 144.

2. G.F. Byers, "Personal Recollections of the Terrible Blizzard of 1886." Kansas State Historical Society, *Transactions,* Vol. 12, 1911–12, p. 109.

3. George A. Root, "Gunnison in the Early Eighties." *Colorado Magazine,* Vol. 9, No. 6, November 1932, p. 212.

4. Reprinted in Mary Dodge Woodward, *The Checkered Years.* Caldwell, Idaho: Caxton Printers, Inc., 1937, pp. 122–23.

5. H. Bailey Carroll, "The Texas Collections." *Southwestern Historical Quarterly,* Vol. XIX, 1946, p. 621.

6. Robert L. DeCoin, *History and Cultivation of Cotton and Tobacco.* London: Chapman and Hall, 1864, p. 129.

7. Charles Kelley, "Gold Seekers on the Hastings Cutoff." *Utah Historical Quarterly,* Vol. 20, 1952, p. 15.

8. *Chloride* (New Mexico) *Black Range,* Dec. 2, 1887, reprinted in Peter Hertzog, *Frontier Humor.* Santa Fe, New Mexico: The Press of the Territorian, 1966, pp. 31–32.

9. Sally Zanjani, "Phantasmagoric Visions Lured Pioneers." *American West,* Vol. 23, No. 4, July–Aug. 1986, p. 58.

10. Edwin Bryant, *What I Saw in California.* New York: Appleton, 1848, pp. 177–78, 219.

11. Sarah Royce, *A Frontier Lady,* edited by Ralph Henry Gabriel. New Haven. Yale University Press, 1932.

Chapter Seven. Violence and Cruelty beneath the Laughter

1. Stories about Black Bart can be found in numerous sources, in particular, the History Room of the Wells Fargo Bank, San Francisco.

2. Frank C. Spencer, "Early Days in Alamosa." *Colorado Magazine,* Vol. 8, No. 2, March 1931, p. 46.

3. Richard Harding Davis, *The West from a Car Window.* New York: Harper and Bros., 1892, p. 296.

4. Wayne Card, "The Role of the Cattle Trails." *Nebraska History,* Vol. 39, 1958, p. 296.

5. Albert D. Richardson, *Beyond the Mississippi.* Hartford: American Publishing Co., 1867, p. 186.

6. John J. Callison, *Bill Jones of Paradise Valley, Oklahoma.* Chicago: M.A. Donahue, 1914, pp. 153–58.

7. Henry W. Lucy, *East by West.* London, 1885, Vol. II, pp. 63–64.

8. Reprinted in Nyle H. Miller and Joseph W. Snell, *Great Gunfighters of the Kansas Cowtowns, 1867–1886.* Lincoln: University of Nebraska Press, 1963, p. 81.

9. John G. Bourke, "Bourke on the Southwest II," edited by Lansing B. Bloom. *New Mexico Historical Review,* Vol. 9, 1934, pp. 73–74.

10. Charles A. Povlovich, Jr., ed., "Will Dewey in Utah." *Utah Historical Quarterly,* Vol. 35, 1965, p. 135.

11. Reprinted in Agnes Wright Spring, *The Cheyenne and Black Hills Stage and Express Routes.* Lincoln: University of Nebraska Press, 1948, p. 29.

12. Reprinted in Dorothy M. Johnson, "Independence Day, 1884!" *Montana, the Magazine of Western History,* Vol. 8, 1958, pp. 2–7.

13. Artemus Ward, *Complete Works.* London: Chatto and Windus, 1899, p. 202.

14. Walter Moffatt, "Out West in Arkansas, 1819–1840." *Arkansas Historical Quarterly,* Vol. 17, 1958, p. 36.

15. George T. Clark, "Diary." *Colorado Magazine,* Vol. 6, 1929, p. 140.

16. John G. Bourke, *On the Border With Crook.* New York: Charles Scribner's Sons, 1891, pp. 404–05.

17. *Army and Navy Journal,* Vol. 8, Oct. 27, 1870, p. 170.

18. John Bratt, *Trails of Yesterday.* Chicago: University Publishing Co., 1921, pp. 126–30.

19. George P. Willison, *Here They Dug the Gold.* New York: Reynal and Hitchcock, 1946, p. 81.

20. Richard Erdoes, *Saloons of the Old West.* New York: Knopf, 1979, p. 130.

21. J.S. McClintock, *Pioneer Days in the Black Hills.* Deadwood, South Dakota, 1939.

22. *New York Times,* Sept. 10, 1872.

Chapter Eight. Lawyers as Entertainers

1. *Dodge City Times,* August 11, 1877, quoted in Nyle H. Miller and Joseph W. Snell, *Great Gunfighters of the Kansas Cowtowns, 1867–1886.* Lincoln: University of Nebraska Press, 1963, pp. 171–72.

2. Jefferson City (Missouri) *Jeffersonian Republican,* July 29, 1842, quoted in Frances McCurdy, "Courtroom Oratory of the Pioneer Period," *Missouri Historical Review,* Vol. LVI, 1961, p. 1.

3. McCurdy, *op. cit.,* p. 5.

4. Elmer E. Ellis, "Recollections of a Bad Lands Rancher." *North Dakota History,* Vol. 1, 1926, pp. 32–34.

5. Evelyn Wells and Harry C. Peterson, *The '49ers.* New York: Doubleday, 1949, p. 206.

6. Edwin L. Sabin, *Building the Pacific Railway.* Philadelphia: Lippincott, 1919, p. 261.

7. Sir Richard Burton, *The Look of the West, 1860.* Lincoln: University of Nebraska Press, 1963, pp. 311–12.

8. *Greeley* (Colorado) *Tribune,* Dec. 1, 1876, quoted in *Colorado Magazine,* Vol. 14, No. 6, November 1937.

9. Joseph Miller, *Arizona, the Last Frontier.* New York: Hastings House, 1956, p. 185.

10. *Santa Fe Weekly Leader,* Dec. 23, 1865.

11. Charles Thomas, "Pioneer Bar of Colorado." *Colorado Magazine,* Vol. 1, No. 5, July 1924, pp. 202–03.

12. *Tombstone Epitaph,* Dec. 18, 1881, reprinted in Jo Ann Schmitt, *Fighting Editors.* San Antonio: The Naylor Company, 1958, pp. 217–19.

13. Albert D. Richardson, *Beyond the Mississippi.* Hartford: American Publishing Company, 1867, p. 384.

14. Jefferson City (Missouri) *Inquirer,* June 12, 1847, reprinted in McCurdy, *op. cit.,* p. 1.

15. Marshall Brown, *Wit and Humor of Bench and Bar.* Chicago, 1899, p. 246.

16. *Spirit of the Times,* Vol. XXI, Aug. 2, 1851, p. 288.

17. Charles B. George, *Forty Years on the Rails.* Chicago: R.R. Donnelly and Sons, 1887, p. 228.

18. McCurdy, *op. cit.,* p. 8.

19. *Santa Fe Republican,* Dec. 25, 1847, reprinted in Peter Hertzog, *Frontier Humor.* Santa Fe: The Press of the Territorian, 1966, p. 7.

20. S. Reynolds Hole, *A Little Tour in America.* London, 1895, p. 3.

21. James Clyman, "California in 1845." *California History,* Vol. 5, 1926, p. 258.

22. *Anaconda* (Montana) *Standard,* Jan. 10, 1897.

23. *Omaha Bee–News,* Nov. 28, 1927.

24. *Dodge City Times,* Nov. 15, 1879, reprinted in Nyle H. Miller, "Some Widely Publicized Western Police Officers." *Nebraska History,* Vol. 39, 1958, p. 311.

25. Reprinted in Schmitt, *op. cit.,* pp. 45 and 91.

26. Leroy R. Hafen, "Early Mail Service." *Colorado Magazine,* Vol. 2, 1925, p. 30.

27. *Batesville* (Arkansas) *News,* Jan. 17, 1839.

28. *Army and Navy Journal,* Vol. 4, 1867, p. 629.

29. John H. Nankivelli, "Fort Garland, Colorado." *Colorado Magazine,* Vol. 16, No. 1, January 1939, p. 26.

Chapter Nine. A Free but Cantankerous Press

1. *Watonga* (Oklahoma) *Republican.* Dec. 20, 1893, quoted in Bobby M. Johnson, "Booster Attitudes of Some Newspapers in Oklahoma Territory." *Chronicles of Oklahoma,* Vol. 43, 1965–66, p. 242.

2. *Fort Scott* (Kansas) *Monitor,* March 17, 1870, reprinted in James C. Malin, "Early Theatre at Fort Scott," *Kansas Historical Quarterly,* Vol. XXIV, 1958, p.33.

3. Walter Colton, *Three Years in California.* New York, 1850.

4. Quoted in John Myers, *Print in a Wild Land.* New York: Doubleday, 1967, p. 113.

5. *Arizona Miner,* Nov. 7, 1874, reprinted in Schmitt, *Fighting Editors.* San Antonio: Naylor Company, 1958, p. 35.

6. *Arizona Sentinel,* Nov. 7, 1874, reprinted in Schmitt, *op. cit.,* p. 96.

7. Quoted in Myers, *op. cit.,* p. 190.

8. *Mesilla Valley Independent,* Sept. 15, 1877, reprinted in Peter Hertzog, *Frontier Humor,* Santa Fe: Press of the Territorian, 1966, p. 16.

9. Reprinted in Porter A. Stratton, *The Territorial Press of New Mexico.* Albuquerque: University of New Mexico Press, 1969, p. 38.

10. *Ibid.*

11. J.L. Waller, "S.H. Newman, Editor of the *Lone Star* of El Paso, Texas." West Texas Historical Association, *Yearbook,* Vol. 14, Oct. 1938, p. 14.

12. Reprinted in Myers, *op. cit.,* p. 114.

13. *Ibid.*

14. *Leavenworth Daily Times,* March 18, 1864.

15. *Watonga* (Oklahoma) *Republican,* Nov. 29, 1893, reprinted in Johnson, *op. cit.,* p. 256.

16. Waller, *op. cit.,* p. 14.

17. Manzano (New Mexico) *Gringo and Greaser,* Jan. 1, 1884, reprinted in Hertzog, *op cit.,* p. 28.

18. *Tombstone Epitaph,* Dec. 26, 1881, reprinted in Schmitt, *op. cit.,* p. 220.

19. Stratton, *op. cit.,* p. 59.

20. Albert D. Richardson, *Beyond the Mississippi.* Hartford: American Publishing Company, 1867, p. 305–06.

21. *Fort Scott* (Kansas) *Daily Monitor,* March 16, 1870, reprinted in Malin, *op. cit.,* p. 33.

22. Quoted in Benjamin Pfeiffer, "The Role of Joseph E. Johnson and His Pioneer Newspapers in the Development of Territorial Nebraska." *Nebraska History,* Vol. 40, 1959, p. 135.

23. Samuel Storey, *To the Golden Land.* London: Walter Scott, 1889, p. 85.

24. *Fort Scott* (Kansas) *Daily Monitor,* Aug. 23, 1872, quoted in Malin, *op. cit.,*

25. Reprinted in Agnes Wright Spring, *The Cheyenne and Black Hills Stage and Express Routes.* Lincoln: University of Nebraska Press, 1948, p. 214.

26. Quoted in Myers, *op. cit.,* p. 109.

27. *Huntsman's Echo,* April 25, 1861, quoted in Pfeiffer, *op. cit.,* p. 135.

28. *Arizona Sentinel,* Oct. 5, 1872, reprinted in Schmitt, *op. cit.,* p.77.

29. *Mesilla* (New Mexico) *News,* June 9, 1874, reprinted in Hertzog, *op. cit.,* p. 13.

30. Bill Nye, *Bill Nye's Sparks.* New York: Hurst and Co., 1901.

31. Mark Twain, *Roughing It.* New York: Harper and Bros., 1908, pp. 198–200.

32. George D. Lyman, *Saga of the Comstock Lode,* New York: Scribner's, 1937, pp. 208–09; C.C. Goodwin, *As I Remember Them,* Salt Lake City, 1913, p. 216; Linda Bosseer, "Sam Clemens and William Wright," *Missouri Historical Review,* 1964–65, p. 434.

33. Lucius Beebe, *Comstock Commotion.* Stanford: Stanford University Press, 1954, p. 83.

34. *Ibid,* p. 80.

Chapter Ten. Masters and Marms

1. Lemuel Clarke McKeeby, "Memoirs." *California History,* Vol. 3, 1924, p. 155.

2. Robert William Mondy, *Pioneers and Preachers; Stories of the Old Frontier.* Chicago: Nelson–Hall, 1980, p. 100.

3. Maxwell P. Gaddis, *Footprints of an Itinerant.* Cincinnati: Methodist Book Concern, 1863, pp. 42–43; Mondy, *op. cit.,* p. 98.

4. George Willison, *Here They Dug the Gold,* New York: Reynal and Hitchcock, 1946, p. 118; W.P.A. Writers Project, *Colorado, A Guide to the Highest State,* New York: Hastings House, 1941, pp. 39–40, 130–32; Joseph E. Smith, "Personal Recollections of Early Denver," *Colorado Magazine,* Vol. 20, No. 1, Jan. 1943, p. 7.

5. Albert Pike, "Letters from Arkansas." *American Monthly Magazine,* Vol. I, January 1836; Fred W. Allsopp, *Albert Pike, a Biography.* Little Rock: Parke–Harper Co., 1928, pp. 50–52.

6. H.M. McIver, "Water Bound in Arkansas." *Arkansas Historical Quarterly,* Vol. 14, 1955, p. 244.

7. Julia L. Lovejoy, "Letters." *Kansas Historical Quarterly,* Vol. XV, 1937, p. 318.

8. Leavenworth (Kansas) *Daily Times,* June 10, 1859.

9. Angie B. Bowden, *Early Schools of Washington Territory.* Seattle, 1935, p. 164.

10. Quoted in Cyril Clemens, *Josh Billings, Yankee Humorist.* Webster Grove, Missouri: International Mark Twain Society, 1932, p. 8.

11. J.L. McConnell, *Western Characters.* New York, 1853, pp. 324–25.

12. Roy Holt, "The Pioneer Teacher." *Sheep and Goat Rancher,* Vol. XXXVI, p. 32.

13. Jacqueline Watie to Stand Watie, April 22, 1871; Stand Watie to Jacqueline Watie, May 10, 1871. Western History Collection, University of Oklahoma.

Chapter Eleven. Servants of the Lord in a Turbulent Land

1. Friedrich Gerstäcker, *Wild Sports in the Far West.* Philadelphia: J.B. Lippincott, 1887, p. 142.

2. Friedrich Gerstäcker, "Friedrich Gerstäcker in Arkansas," translated by Clarence Evans and Liselotte Albrecht. *Arkansas Historical Quarterly,* Vol. 5, 1946, p. 44.

3. *Spirit of the Times,* Oct. 20, 1849.

4. Oran Warder Nolen, "Sheriff When the Nueces was the Deadline." *Cattleman,* Vol. 32, Oct. 1945, p. 134.

5. Ethel Frances Jones, "The Elixir of Youth." *Arkansas Historical Quarterly,* Vol. 23, 1964, p. 236.

6. Thomas Rothrock, "Benjamin Harvey Greathouse." *Arkansas Historical Quarterly,* Vol. 15, 1956, p. 164.

7. *Minneapolis Journal,* Feb. 21, 1890.

8. Muriel Sibell Wolle, "Irwin, a Ghost Town of the Elk Mountain." *Colorado Magazine,* Vol. XXIV, Jan. 1947, p. 13.

9. *Rocky Mountain News,* Jan. 3, 1872.

10. Floyd B. Streeter, *The Kaw.* New York: Farrar and Rinehart, 1941, p. 153.

11. Ed Donnell, "Letters," edited by Charles J. Wilkerson. *Nebraska History,* Vol. 41, 1960, p. 145.

12. *Dodge City Times,* June 8, 1878.

13. W.J. Berger, "A Kansas Revival in 1872." *Kansas Historical Quarterly,* Vol. 23, 1957, p. 369, 372.

14. *Kansas Daily Tribune,* April 14, 1872, quoted in Berger, *op. cit.,* p. 368.

15. *Fort Scott* (Kansas) *Daily Monitor,* April 24, 1872, quoted in Berger, *op. cit.,* p. 380.

16. *Kansas Daily Commonwealth,* March 24, 1872, quoted in Berger, *op. cit.,* p. 377.

17. *Ibid.*

18. *Leavenworth* (Kansas) *Times,* Feb. 13, 1872, quoted in Berger, *op. cit.,* p. 371.

19. Arrell M. Gibson, "Medicine Show." *American West,* Vol. 4, 1967, p. 39.

20. Owen P. White, *Lead and Likker.* New York: Minton, Balch & Co., 1932, p. 87.

21. C.S. Lyman, "The Gold Rush." California Historical Society, *Quarterly,* Vol. 2, 1924, p. 182.

22. *Leadville* (Colorado) *Democrat* and *Leadville* (Colorado) *Chronicle,* quoted in George F. Willison, *Here They Dug the Gold.* New York: Reynal and Hitchcock, 1946, pp. 198–99.

Chapter Twelve. Sawbones and Pill Rollers

1. Edwin Bryant, *What I Saw in California.* New York: Appleton, 1848, p. 90.

2. George D. Lyman, "The Scalpel Under Three Flags." *California History,* Vol. 4, 1925, p. 180.

3. James Thomson, "Colorado Diary," edited by R.J. Fielding. *Colorado Magazine,* Vol. 31, 1954, pp. 207–08.

4. Lyman, *op. cit.*

5. Charles S. Reed, "Life in a Nebraska Soddy." *Nebraska History,* Vol. 39, 1958, p. 65.

6. Edith Thompson Hall, "The Biography of a Pioneer Nebraska Doctor, John Wesley Thompson." *Nebraska History,* Vol. 44, 1963, p. 283.

7. Elizabeth M. Meek, "Two Pioneer Doctors of Southeast Arkansas." *Arkansas Historical Quarterly,* Vol. 5, 1946, p. 121.

8. Lemuel Clarke McKeeby, "Memoirs." *California History,* Vol. 3, 1924, p. 59.

9. Larry Barsness, *Heads, Hides and Horns.* Fort Worth: Texas Christian University Press, 1985, p. 180.

10. E.M. Harmon, "Early Days in Middle Fork." *Colorado Magazine,* Vol. 15, No. 3, Sept. 1938, p. 183.

11. James Holt, "Reminiscences." *Utah Historical Quarterly,* Vol. 23, 1955, p. 167.

12. Francis E. Quebbeman, *Medicine in Territorial Arizona.* Phoenix: Arizona Historical Foundation, 1966, p. 80.

13. Ross Phares, *Texas Tradition.* New York: Holt, 1954, p. 155.

14. San Antonio *Daily Herald,* August 5, 1856, quoted in Phares, *op. cit.,* p. 152.

15. John J. Fox, "The Far West in the '80s," edited by T.A. Larson, *Annals of Wyoming,* Vol. XXI, Jan. 1949, pp. 8–9.

16. Caroline Bancroft, "Pioneer Doctor—F.J. Bancroft." *Colorado Magazine,* Vol. 39, July 1962, p. 202.

17. Mary P. Fletcher, "Some Little Rock Doctors." *Arkansas Historical Quarterly,* Vol. 2, 1943, p. 23.

18. Phares, *op. cit.*

19. Robert W. Glover, ed., "War Letters of a Texas Conscript in Arkansas." *Arkansas Historical Quarterly,* Vol. 20, 1961, p. 368.

20. Arrell M. Gibson, "Medicine Show." *American West,* Vol. 4, 1967, p. 76.

Chapter Thirteen. Greasepaint in the Wilderness

1. Noah M. Ludlow, *Dramatic Life As I Found It.* St. Louis: G.I. Jones and Co., 1880, pp. 47–50.

2. *Fort Scott* (Kansas) *Bulletin,* June 7, 14, 1862.

3. Vance Randolph, "Fabulous Monsters of the Ozarks." *Arkansas Historical Quarterly,* Vol. 9, 1950, p. 68.

4. John J. Fox, "The Far West in the '80s," edited by T.A. Larson. *Annals of Wyoming,* Vol. XXI, 1949, p. 11.

5. New Orleans *Picayune,* Dec. 9, 1849, quoted in John F. McDermott, *Travelers on the Western Frontier.* Urbana: University of Illinois Press, 1970, p. 249.

6. *Fayetteville* (Arkansas) *Democrat,* April 9, 1870.

7. Dardanelle (Arkansas) *Independent,* Dec. 3, 1875.

8. *Fort Smith New Era,* Oct. 6, 1880. (Above three newspapers quoted in Harold C. Tedford, "Circuses in Northwest Arkansas, 1865–1889." *Arkansas Historical Quarterly,* Vol. XXXII, 1973, pp. 166–181.)

9. Julia Cooley Altrocchi, *Spectacular San Franciscans.* New York: Dutton, 1949.

10. Eddie Foy and Alvin F. Harlow, *Clowning Through Life.* New York: Dutton, 1928.

11. Lauren C. Bray, "Hiram Vasquez, Frontiersman." *Colorado Magazine,* Col. 37, 1960.

12. *Leavenworth* (Kansas) *Daily Times,* March 16, 1864, quoted in Robert W. Richmond, "Humorist on Tour: Artemus Ward in Mid-America, 1864." *Kansas Historical Quarterly,* Vol. 33, 1967, p. 477.

13. Edward P. Hingston, *The Genial Showman.* London, 1870, p. 212, quoted in Irving McKee, "Artemus Ward in California and Nevada, 1863–64." *Pacific Historical Review,* Vol. XX, 1951, p. 22.

14. McKee, *op. cit.,* p. 17.

15. *St. Joseph* (Missouri) *Morning Herald,* March 19, 1864, quoted in Richmond, *op. cit.,* p. 474.

16. San Francisco *Golden Era,* Dec. 4, 1864, quoted in Paul Fatout, "Artemus Ward Among the Mormons." *Western Humanities Review,* Vol. 14, 1960, pp. 196–97.

17. Mrs. Frank Leslie, *California, A Pleasure Trip from Gotham to the Golden Gate.* New York, 1877, p. 50.

18. *Ibid,* p. 85.

19. Albert D. Richardson, *Beyond the Mississippi.* Hartford: American Publishing Co., 1867, pp. 358–59.

20. J.H. Beadle, *The Undeveloped West.* Philadelphia: National Publishing Company, 1873, pp. 303–04.

21. Leslie, *op. cit.,* pp. 155–59.

22. Quoted in Richard Erdoes, *Saloons of the Old West.* New York: Knopf, 1979, p. 171.

23. Richardson, *op. cit.,* p. 479.

24. Scott Dial, *Saloons of Denver.* Old Army Press, 1973, p. 50.

25. George F. Willison, *Here They Dug the Gold.* New York: Reynal and Hitchcock, 1946, p. 216.

26. Works Progress Administration, *Colorado, A Guide to the Highest State.* New York: Hastings House, 1941, p. 94.

27. *Muscatine* (Iowa) *Journal,* Feb. 28, 1855, quoted in Pat M. Ryan, Jr., "Mark Twain, Frontier Theater Critic." *Arizona Quarterly,* Vol. 16, 1960, p. 199.

28. Virginia City (Nevada) *Territorial Enterprise,* Sept. 13, 1863, quoted in Ryan, *op. cit.,* pp. 199–200.

29. San Francisco *Golden Era,* Jan. 28, 1866, quoted in Franklin Walker, ed., *The Washoe Giant in San Francisco.* San Francisco: George Fields, 1938, p. 103.

30. Quoted in Ryan, *op. cit.,* p. 203.

31. *Fort Scott* (Kansas) *Daily Monitor,* Jan. 18, 25, 1870; Nov. 14, 1870, quoted in James C. Malin, "Early Theatre at Fort Scott." *Kansas Historical Quarterly,* Vol. XXIV, 1958, pp. 35–36, 50–51.

32. *Atchison* (Kansas) *Globe,* March 2, 1881.

33. Edgar Wilson Nye, *Baled Hay.* Chicago: Homewood Publishing Co., 1883, pp. 230–31.

34. *New York Tribune,* Jan. 3, 1878.

Chapter Fourteen. Cowboys at Play

1. Adapted from W.S. James, *Cowboy Life in Texas.* Chicago: M.A. Donahue, 1893, pp. 55–59.

2. John J. Callison, *Bill Jones of Paradise Valley, Oklahoma.* Chicago: M.A. Donahue, 1914, pp. 112–13.

3. John J. Fox, "The Far West in the '80s," edited by T.A. Larson. *Annals of Wyoming,* Vol. XXI, 1949, pp. 24–26.

4. William M. Breakenridge, *Helldorado.* Boston: Houghton Mifflin, 1928, p. 160.

5. Frank Tanberg, "Cowboy Life on the Open Range of Southeastern Colorado." *Colorado Magazine,* Vol. 12, No. 1, 1935, p. 27.

6. William McLeod Raine and Will C. Barnes, *Cattle.* New York: Doubleday, 1930, p. 115.

7. Hortense W. Ward, "The Old Order Changeth." *Cattleman,* Vol. 32, Sept. 1945, p. 39.

8. J.M. Hendrix, "Salad or Son of a Gun?" *Cattleman,* Vol. 31, Oct. 1944, p. 15.

9. Florence Fenley, "Straight Buffalo Meat." *Cattleman,* Vol. 31, Aug. 1945, p. 15.

10. Ward, *op. cit.,* p. 151.

11. Oren Arnold and John P. Hale, *Hot Irons: Heraldry of the Range.* New York: Macmillan, 1940, p. 52.

12. Las Vegas (New Mexico) *Daily Optic,* Sept. 25, 1884, quoted in Clifford P. Westermeier, "Cowboy Capers." *Annals of Wyoming,* Vol. 22, 1950, p. 19.

13. C. Reginald Enoch, *Farthest West, Life and Travel in the United States.* New York: D. Appleton and Co., 1910, p. 288.

14. *Field and Farm,* Denver, June 30, 1894, quoted in Westermeier, *op. cit.,* p. 20.

15. Joseph Emerson Smith, "Personal Recollections of Early Denver." *Colorado Magazine,* Vol. 20, No. 2, March 1943, p. 69.

16. *Chloride* (New Mexico) *Black Range,* Oct. 22, 1886, quoted in Clifford P. Westermeier, *Trailing the Cowboy.* Caldwell, Idaho: Caxton Printers, Inc., 1955, p. 302.

17. *Raton* (New Mexico) *Weekly Independent,* Jan. 28, 1888, quoted in Westermeier, "Cowboy Capers," p. 21.

18. *Cheyenne Democratic Leader,* April 15 and Sept. 27, 1884, quoted in Westermeier, " Cowboy Capers, " pp. 16–17.

19. N. Howard Thorp, as told to Neil M. Clark, *Pardners of the Wind.* Caldwell: Idaho, Caxton Printers, 1945, p. 210–11.

20. *Carbon County Journal,* Dec. 2, 1882.

21. Charles W. Hurd, "The Fred Harvey System." *Colorado Magazine,* Vol. XXVI, 1949, p. 180.

22. James Clyman, "California in 1845." *California History,* Vol. 5, 1926, p. 257.

23. Rose Pender, *A Lady's Experience in the Far West in 1883.* London, 1888, p. 46.

24. Edward Money, *The Truth About America.* London, 1886, p. 129.

25. Edgar Wilson Nye, *Bill Nye's Western Humor,* selected and with an introduction by T. A. Larson. Lincoln: University of Nebraska Press, 1968, p. 149. Quoted from *Remarks by Bill Nye,* 1886.

26. Philip H. Ault, ed., *The Home Book of Western Humor.* New York: Dodd, Mead and Co., 1967, p. 272.

27. Clarice B. Richards, "The Valley of the Second Sons." *Colorado Magazine,* Vol. 9, No. 4, 1932, pp. 143–44.

Chapter Fifteen. Soldier High Jinks

1. John M. Hollingsworth, "Journal." California Historical Society, *Quarterly,* Vol. 1, No. 3, January 1923, p. 213.

2. John E. Cox, "Soldiering in Dakota Territory in the Seventies; a Communication." *North Dakota History,* Vol. 1, 1926, p. 76.

3. Gordon P. Lester, "A Round Trip to the Montana Mines." *Nebraska History,* Vol. 46, 1965, p. 281.

4. Ellen Williams, *Three Years and a Half in the Army; or History of the Second Colorados.* New York: Fowler and Wells Co., 1885, p. 39.

5. Hollingsworth, *op. cit.,* p. 243.

6. John G. Bourke, "Bourke on the Southwest II" edited by Lansing B. Bloom. *New Mexico Historical Review.* Vol. 9, 1934, p. 52.

7. Walter Lee Brown, "Mexican War Experiences of Albert Pike and the 'Mounted Devils' of Arkansas." *Arkansas Historical Quarterly,* Vol. 12, 1953, p. 305.

8. Henry W. Bigler, "Journal." *Utah State Historical Quarterly,* Vol. 5, No. 2, April 1932, p. 50.

9. *Ibid,* p. 54.

10. Albert Tracy, "Journal." *Utah State Historical Quarterly,* Vol. 13, 1945, pp. 54–55.

11. Luther North, *Man of the Plains,* edited by Donald F. Danker, Lincoln: University of Nebraska Press, 1961, p. 105.

12. Quoted in Peter Hertzog, *Frontier Humor.* Santa Fe: The Press of the Territorian, 1966, p. 25.

13. Williams, *op. cit.,* p. 5.

14. *Army and Navy Journal,* Vol. 4, 1867, p. 458.

15. *Ibid,* Vol. 5, 1868, p. 330.

16. J. Ross Browne, *Adventures in the Apache Country.* New York: Harper and Bros., 1871, pp. 180–86.

Chapter Sixteen. *The Profane Sentimentalists*

1. Dan De Quille, *The Big Bonanza.* Hartford: American Publishing Co., 1876, pp. 51–52.

2. H.T.P. Comstock, Letter to St. Louis *Republican,* quoted in De Quille, *op. cit.,* pp. 49–50.

3. J. Ross Browne, *Adventures in the Apache Country.* New York: Harper and Bros., 1871, pp. 346–48, 362.

4. De Quille, *op. cit.,* pp. 31, 49.

5. *Ibid,* pp. 45–48.

6. George F. Willison, *Here They Dug the Gold.* New York: Reynal and Hitchcock, 1946, p. 158; Iva Evans Morrison, "William H. Stevens." *Colorado Magazine,* Vol. XXI, No. 4, July 1944, p. 127.

7. Federal Writers Project, *Montana, A State Guide Book.* New York: Hastings House, 1939, pp. 360–63.

8. Frank C. Lockwood, *Pioneer Days in Arizona.* New York: Macmillan, 1932, p. 200.

9. *Ibid,* pp. 200–08; Odie B. Faulk, *Tombstone, Myth and Reality.* New York: Oxford University Press, 1972, pp. 47–49, 187.

10. Quoted in Agnes Wright Spring, *The Cheyenne and Black Hills Stage and Express Routes.* Lincoln: University of Nebraska Press, 1948, p. 108.

11. Alexander K. McClure, *Three Thousand Miles Through the Rocky Mountains.* Philadelphia: Lippincott, 1869, pp. 212, 242–43.

12. Mark Twain, *Roughing It.* New York: Harper and Bros., 1908, pp. 64, 107, 110.

Chapter Seventeen. *Sage Hens, Fillies, and Calico Queens*

1. Agnes Wright Spring, *The Cheyenne and Black Hills Stage and Express Routes.* Lincoln: University of Nebraska Press, 1948, p. 297.

2. George W. Featherstonaugh, *Excursion Through the Slave States.* New York: Harper and Bros., 1844, p. 114.

3. W. L. Brown, "Life of an Arkansas Logger." *Arkansas Historical Quarterly,* Vol. 21, 1962, p. 57.

4. *Bingham* (Utah) *Press–Bulletin,* quoted in Helen S. Papanikolas, "Life and Labor Among the Immigrants of Bingham Canyon." *Utah History,* Vol. 33, 1965, p. 293.

5. Minnie Hall Krauser, "The Denver Women's Press Club." *Colorado Magazine,* Vol. 16, No. 2, 1939, pp. 66–67.

6. Louisa A.K.S. Clappe, *The Shirley Letters.* Santa Barbara and Salt Lake City: Peregrine Publishers, Inc., 1970, p. 27.

7. Caroline Leighton, *Life at Puget Sound.* Boston, 1884, p. 106.

8. Illinois State Historical Society, *Journal,* Vol. 42, No. 1, March 1940, p. 89.

9. Benjamin Dore, "Journal." California Historical Society, Vol. 2, No. 2, July 1923, p. 129.

10. Walter Moffatt, "Out West in Arkansas, 1819–1840." *Arkansas Historical Quarterly,* Vol. 17, 1958, pp. 35–36.

11. Joseph Miller, *Arizona, the Last Frontier.* New York: Hastings House, 1956, p. 116.

12. Hiram Whittington, "Letters." Pulaski County Historical Society, *Bulletin,* No. 3, 1956, p. 319.

13. Porter A. Stratton, *The Territorial Press of New Mexico.* Albuquerque: University of New Mexico Press, 1969, p. 42.

14. David F. Spain, "Diary," edited by John D. Morrison. *Colorado Magazine,* Vol. 35, No. 1, 1958, p. 12.

15. *Alta California,* July 14, 1851.

16. Albert D. Richardson, "Letters on the Pike's Peak Gold Region," edited by Louise Barry. *Kansas Historical Quarterly,* Vol. XII, 1948, p. 17.

17. Sir Richard Burton, *The Look of the West, 1860.* Lincoln: University of Nebraska Press, 1963, p. 114.

18. Thomas H. Smith, "An Ohioan's Role in Oregon History." *Oregon Historical Quarterly,* Vol. 66, 1965, p. 230.

19. *Fort Scott* (Kansas) *Daily Monitor,* October 16, 1872.

20. Jim Balch, "The Story of Richwoods Township, Jackson County." *Arkansas Historical Quarterly,* Vol. 16, 1957, p. 375.

21. Nyle H. Miller, "Some Widely Publicized Western Police Officers." *Nebraska History,* Vol. 39, 1958, p. 314.

22. Virginia City *Territorial Enterprise,* January 10, 1863, quoted in William C. Miller, "Mark Twain at the Sanitary Ball—and Elsewhere." California Historical Society, *Quarterly,* Vol. 36, 1957, p. 37.

23. Ray H. Mattison, "The Upper Missouri Fur Trade." *Nebraska History,* Vol. 42, 1961, p. 21.

24. John C. Luttig, Letter from Pork Bayou, Arkansas, April 16, 1815. *Arkansas Historical Quarterly,* Vol. I, 1942, p. 153.

25. John E. Cox, "Soldiering in South Dakota Territory in the Seventiees." *North Dakota History,* Vol. 6, No. 1, 1931, p. 80.

26. Joseph M. Hanson, *The Conquest of the Missouri.* Chicago: A.C. McClurg, 1916, pp. 118–19.

27. William H. Emory, *Notes of a Military Reconnaissance.* Washington, 1848, p. 73.

28. R.H. McKay, *Little Pills.* Pittsburg, Kansas: Pittsburg Headlight, 1918, p. 53.

Chapter Eighteen. The Bawdy Natives

1. Edwin Bryant, *What I Saw in California.* New York: Appleton, 1848, p. 201.

2. George P. Belden, *The White Chief, or Twelve Years Among the Wild Indians of the Plains.* Cincinnati and New York: C. F. Vent, 1870, p. 299.

3. Israel Bennion, "Indian Reminiscences." *Utah State Historical Quarterly,* Vol. 2, No. 2, April 1929, p. 44.

4. Cornelia Adair, *My Diary.* Austin: University of Texas Press, 1965, p. 71.

5. Robert Vaughn, *Then and Now; or Thirty-Six Years in the Rockies.* Minneapolis: Tribune Printing Co., 1900, pp. 193–94.

6. Based on a United Press International report from Crow Agency, Montana, August 12, 1977.

7. Paul Radin, *The Trickster.* New York: Philosophical Library, 1956, pp. 38–39.

8. George A. Dorsey and Alfred L. Kroeber, *Traditions of the Arapaho.* Chicago: Field Columbian Museum, Publication 81, 1913, pp. 64–65.

9. *Ibid.* Adapted from "Split-Feather," pp. 269–72.

10. John H. Swanton, *Haida Texts and Myths.* Washington, U. S. Bureau of American Ethnology, Bulletin 29, 1905, pp. 286–87.

11. George A. Dorsey, *Traditions of the Arikara.* Washington, Carnegie Institution, 1904, pp. 88–90.

12. Adapted from Clark Wissler and D. C. Duvall, *Mythology of the Blackfoot Indians.* New York: American Museum of Natural History, Anthropological Paper, Vol. II, 1908, pp. 152–53.

13. George A. Dorsey, *Traditions of the Caddo.* Washington: Carnegie Foundation, 1905, pp. 104–05.

Index